GOOD EATING
SALADS

D1463952

GOOD EATING

SALADS

YOUR COMPLETE GUIDE TO MAKING PERFECT SALADS EVERY TIME

This edition published in 2012

LOVE FOOD is an imprint of Parragon Books Ltd

Parragon
Queen Street House
4 Queen Street
Bath BA1 1HE, UK

Copyright © Parragon Books Ltd 2010

LOVE FOOD and the accompanying heart device is a registered trademark of Parragon Books Ltd in Australia, the UK, USA, India, and the EU.

www.parragon.com

ISBN 978-1-4454-6613-2

Printed in China

Cover design by Talking Design
Internal design by Simon Levy
New photography by Clive Bozzard-Hill
New home economy by Valerie Barrett
New recipes, introduction and cover text by Angela Drake

Notes for the Reader
This book uses both imperial and metric measurements. Follow the same units of measurement throughout; do not mix imperial and metric. All spoon measurements are level: teaspoons are assumed to be 5 ml, and tablespoons are assumed to be 15 ml. Unless otherwise stated, milk is assumed to be full fat, eggs and individual vegetables are medium, and pepper is freshly ground black pepper.

The times given are an approximate guide only. Preparation times differ according to the techniques used by different people and the cooking times may also vary from those given as a result of the type of oven used. Optional ingredients, variations, or serving suggestions have not been included in the calculations.

Recipes using raw or very lightly cooked eggs should be avoided by infants, the elderly, pregnant women, convalescents, and anyone with a chronic condition. Pregnant and breast-feeding women are advised to avoid eating peanuts and peanut products. People with nut allergies should be aware that some of the prepared ingredients used in the recipes in this book may contain nuts. Always check the package before use.

CONTENTS

INTRODUCTION

FULL OF GOODNESS

Gone are the days when the word 'salad' conjured up the image of a few limp lettuce leaves on the side of your plate. Salads have really come of age with the most vibrant and exciting range of ingredients available to create sensational dishes to suit any occasion.

A quick stroll around even the smallest supermarket or greengrocer will reveal a cornucopia of fantastic salad ingredients, from peppery salad leaves and fragrant herbs to colourful sun-ripened fruit and vegetables – so easy to transform into fresh and appetizing meals with minimum time and effort. Today, salads are the most versatile of dishes incorporating flavours from all around the world. Whether it's a traditional crisp Greek salad, a filling warm chicken and pasta salad or an energy boosting bean salad, you'll find the perfect salad to feed family and friends.

THE HEALTHY OPTION

The health benefits of regularly eating salads cannot be ignored. We all aspire to living a healthier lifestyle and eating salads packed with nutritious leafy greens, vegetables, pulses, herbs, nuts and seeds, will certainly boost your intake of protein and essential vitamins, minerals and fibre. We are frequently reminded that a healthy diet includes eating a minimum of five portions of fruit and vegetables every day – tuck into a hearty salad for lunch or dinner or replace rice or potatoes with a tasty side salad and you will be well on the way to that target.

For those who are constantly having to watch their weight this book will be a revelation. Not long ago anyone on a diet would stick to a simple, but very boring, virtually calorie-free salad of lettuce, tomato, cucumber and celery with no dressing! Well, times have certainly changed. Choose carefully and you can still enjoy a thoroughly satisfying salad without piling on the pounds. Look out for salads that have yogurt-based dressings such as Sweet Potato Salad or ones that are only lightly dressed such as Wild Rice Salad with Cucumber & Orange or Minted Pea & Melon Salad.

However, don't be put off by the quantity of oil in many of the dressings. A healthy balanced diet needs to include a small amount of fat. Nut and vegetable oils (such as sunflower and olive oil) contain unsaturated fat which can help to lower harmful cholesterol in the blood. Also, the fat in some oils and oily fish, such as mackerel, contains the essential omega-3 or omega-6 fatty acids that are important for growth, healthy skin and a strong immune system.

Grains, pulses and beans play an important role in a healthy diet and can release a steady supply of energy throughout the day. On hectic and energetic days pick a fibre-packed salad such as Three Bean or Tabbouleh for lunch and you'll find that hunger pangs are kept well at bay for a good few hours.

A SALAD FOR ALL SEASONS

It's not surprising that many of us only think about eating or cooking salads during the summer – salads are the perfect solution for easy to prepare meals when the days are long and hot. But salads really can be served all year round and in this book you'll find salads to suit all times of year, whatever the weather. We are no longer restricted by seasonal fluctuations for many ingredients and fresh produce can be flown all over the world. Let's face it, nothing can beat the flavour of freshly dug new potatoes in a delicious creamy dressed potato salad – the ideal accompaniment for a sizzling summer barbecue or alfresco supper.

Springtime is one of the best times of the year for serving salads. Shops will be full to the brim with an abundance of crisp young spring vegetables and seasonal salad leaves. With days becoming longer and warmer, light and nutritious salads are the natural choices to boost our energy levels after the winter slump.

In the heat of summer, choose salads that are quick and easy to cook – no one wants to be working away in a hot kitchen when they could be outdoors enjoying the good weather. For alfresco dinner parties, summer buffets and barbecues, pick salads that can be made a few hours in advance or prepare the separate elements of the salads and simply toss together just before serving.

During the colder months of the year, opt for comforting and hearty warm salads or filling pasta or rice salads. Take time to marinate fish, meat and poultry for extra flavour or slow roast vegetables with winter herbs and garlic. If you're entertaining, a salad can be the ideal light starter choice for a winter dinner party.

THE FINEST
INGREDIENTS

Never before has there been such a huge range of salad ingredients to choose from. Here's a quick guide to some of the essentials.

SALAD LEAVES

With an endless variety of shapes, textures, colour and flavour, salad leaves really do make or break a good salad. Leaves with a robust and peppery taste include curly endive (also called frisée), rocket, mizuna and watercress. For a salad with a milder taste, pick delicate lamb's lettuce or a classic round butterhead. For the crispiest salad you can't beat cos or iceberg lettuces. To add extra colour to a leafy salad, look out for chard leaves with ruby red stalks, variegated oak leaf or lollo rosso leaves or firm red chicory leaves.

Many of the recipes in this book suggest using bags of mixed salad leaves and you'll find an ever-changing selection of leafy mixtures in most supermarkets. Quick to buy and very convenient, they are a boon to the busy cook. However, do check them for freshness as the leaves can deteriorate quite quickly. Don't worry if you can't find a specific salad bag for a recipe – simply substitute another one or buy separate leaves and make up your own mix.

HERBS

Fragrant fresh herbs can bring an everyday salad to life. The classic Mediterranean herbs such as basil, oregano and flat-leaf parsley are essentials for many salads and go particularly well with tomatoes, peppers and onions. Coriander and mint add an aromatic touch to Asian and Middle Eastern themed salads, while delicate and feathery herbs such as dill, fennel and chervil with their mild aniseed taste, suit fish and seafood salads. More robust herbs with woody stalks such as thyme and rosemary are great for adding to marinades – simply bruise or break the stalks to release more flavour.

If you have space in the garden it's worth growing your own herbs or planting a few in a window box or hanging basket for handy picking. Alternatively, buy pots of growing herbs and pop them in a shaded spot on the kitchen windowsill and remember to water them regularly.

OILS

The basis of most salad dressings, the choice of good quality oil is vital to a successful salad. Extracted from various nuts, seeds and beans, oils can vary in flavour from bland and virtually tasteless to highly aromatic and intensely rich.

Olive oil is by far the most popular oil to use in most dressings. Produced in hot Mediterranean countries such as France, Greece, Italy and Spain, the prized extra virgin olive oil is considered the finest. It has a dark green colour and strong rich taste and is from the first cold pressing of olives. Use sparingly as it can be overpowering for some delicate salads. Milder and paler olive oils from further pressings may be more suitable for some recipes.

Nut oils can also vary considerably in flavour and intensity. Groundnut oil (also called peanut oil) is a pale oil with a mild and nutty aroma. Walnut and hazelnut oils have wonderfully intense flavours but they can be quite pricey. Buy in small quantities and use within a few months of opening as they can soon go rancid.

Sesame seed oil is frequently used in oriental themed salads. It has a deep amber colour and a heady aroma with a really nutty taste. A few drops are all that's needed for most recipes.

Sunflower and corn oil both have a fairly mild, somewhat bland taste. Use them for dressings and marinades where other stronger flavourings will dominate such as fresh herbs, garlic or chilli. They can also be blended with more expensive oils to dilute the intense flavour.

VINEGARS

The second essential element of a salad dressing is usually vinegar. Those distilled from wine – either white or red – are the most frequently used in salad dressings. Other vinegars such as sherry and cider are popular too and can be used to compliment the ingredients in a salad. Mild and sweet cider vinegar goes particularly well with salads that contain fruit while rich and nutty sherry vinegar is delicious with warm meat and poultry salads.

Balsamic vinegar comes from the Italian region of Modena and is a rich, yet mellow vinegar that has a wonderfully sweet and sour flavour. Just like the finest olive oils it can be very expensive. The vinegar is aged in oak casks between five and twenty years – the longer the ageing process the higher the price. It's delicious used on its own to simply dress sliced ripe tomatoes or roasted vegetable salads or try simmering it with a little sugar to make a divine syrupy balsamic glaze for drizzling over sweet or savoury salads.

SEEDS & NUTS

A sprinkling of crunchy nuts or seeds can add plenty of extra interest to salads as well as boosting your intake of protein, essential vitamins and minerals. Keep small quantities of pumpkin, sunflower and sesame seeds as well as a selection of unsalted nuts in the storecupboard. To bring out more of their flavour, lightly toast nuts and seeds by spreading on a baking sheet and popping under a hot grill for a few minutes.

BEANS, PASTA & RICE

These great energy foods can form the basis of really substantial and filling salads. Although most have a fairly bland flavour on their own, the addition of herbs, spices and dressings can totally transform them. Look out for more unusual grains such as quinoa, bulgar wheat and wild rice. For added fibre opt for wholemeal varieties of pasta or rice.

SALAD SUCCESS

Follow these simple guidelines for the perfect salad every time!

When buying salad leaves pick ones that look fresh and spritely with no wilting or browning leaves. If you buy a ready prepared bag of salad leaves, give the bag a good shake and check for any signs of deterioration. Only buy as much as you need as salad greens don't retain their freshness for long and salad bags once opened will need to be consumed within 24 hours.

Store salad leaves in a plastic box or unsealed bag in the salad drawer of the refrigerator. If you've bought unwashed greens from a farmers' market or greengrocer don't worry about rinsing them until you are ready to use them as they will stay fresher for longer.

Bunches of cut fresh herbs with long stalks such as parsley and mint should be stored in the refrigerator with their stalks in a jug of water. Other herbs with shorter stems and cut basil sprigs are best kept in an open plastic bag or loosely wrapped in damp kitchen paper and stored in the salad drawer of the refrigerator.

To prepare salad leaves, carefully separate them from the stem if necessary. Rinse in a large bowl or sink full of cold water to remove fine grit and dirt. Discard any limp, wilted or browning leaves. Shake the excess water off the leaves then spin until dry in a salad spinner or gently pat dry with a clean tea towel. The leaves should be thoroughly dry before tossing with a dressing otherwise they will dilute the dressing. Salad leaves can be washed and dried a few hours before serving but will need to be stored, without dressing, in the refrigerator.

Most dressings can also be prepared in advance and stored in the refrigerator. Remember they will need a thorough whisking or shaking before adding to the salad and it's also worth checking seasoning at this time as well.

Dress leafy salads just before serving and only use enough of the dressing to lightly coat the leaves otherwise they will quickly wilt. Pour the dressing into a large chilled serving bowl then pile the salad loosely on top. Using salad servers or clean hands, gently toss the leaves in the dressing.

If you're catering for a large number of people and serving a variety of different salads, then prepare the ones with grains, pulses or pasta first as they will keep the longest.

Side salads should complement and enhance the dishes they are served with, not overpower them, so choose carefully and only serve a small bowlful.

Timing is vital when serving warm salads. Prepare everything in advance including the dressing. Allow very hot foods such as chargrilled meats to cool slightly before completing the salad to prevent the heat wilting salad leaves too quickly.

SALAD TECHNIQUES

PEELING TOMATOES

Choose firm and ripe tomatoes for peeling. With the tip of a sharp knife, score a cross through the skin at the base of each tomato. Place in a heatproof bowl, cover with boiling water and leave for 2–3 minutes until the skins begin to wrinkle and split. Drain and plunge the tomatoes into a bowl of ice cold water for 1–2 minutes then drain again and peel the skin away with your fingertips.

BLANCHING VEGETABLES

This technique is used to lightly cook vegetables such as green beans and asparagus, yet still retain their crispness and colour. Plunge the prepared vegetables into a pan of boiling water for about 2 minutes. Quickly drain into a colander then refresh under cold running water to stop the cooking process.

VEGETABLE RIBBONS

These look impressive and are easy to make. Run a swivel-headed vegetable peeler along the length of firm vegetables such as carrot, cucumber or courgette. Use immediately or sprinkle with a little cold water and cover and chill in the refrigerator for no longer than a couple of hours before serving.

INTRODUCTION TO OILS

Edible oil has a rich history shared by many cultures over many centuries. It is used as a cooking medium, a preservative, a medicine and, best of all, food. The Chinese and Japanese developed methods to extract oil from soya plants; Mediterranean people use olives; Mexicans and North Americans are fond of peanuts and sunflower seeds; and in Africa, palms and coconuts provide the basis for oil. Other sources of oil are cotton, safflower seeds, watermelon seeds, grape seeds, rapeseed, corn, nuts, avocados and, of course, animals.

Thanks to the popularity of the Mediterranean diet, olive oil has captured the world's attention with its health-inducing benefits. Other beneficial oils, such as rapeseed, are almost flavourless and present the perfect backdrop for flavourful additions.

There are just a few guidelines to follow before getting started. The most important to remember is this: oil improperly stored can encourage the growth of bacteria. When herbs or vegetables with a high water content (like garlic) are mixed with oil and stored in a non-refrigerated place, an oxygen-free environment is created that can lead to botulism.

GARLIC, CHILLI & OREGANO OIL

5 garlic cloves
2 tbsp red hot chilli
1 tsp dried oregano
250 ml/9 fl oz rapeseed oil

Preheat the oven to 150°C/300°F/Gas Mark 2.

Cut the garlic cloves in half lengthways. Using gloves, remove the seeds from the chilli and chop the flesh into small pieces equalling 2 tablespoons.

Combine the garlic, chilli and oregano with the oil in an ovenproof glass dish. Place in the centre of the oven and heat for 1½–2 hours. The temperature of the oil should reach 120°C/250°F if you are using a digital thermometer.

Remove from the oven, leave to cool and then strain through muslin into a clean jar. Store covered in the refrigerator. You can also leave the garlic and chilli pieces in the oil and strain before using.

PARSLEY & CORIANDER OIL

10 g/¼ oz fresh parsley leaves
10 g/¼ oz fresh coriander leaves
250 ml/9 fl oz rapeseed oil

Wash and drain the leaves. Prepare a pot of water, bring to the boil and submerge the leaves. Blanch for 5 seconds. Drain the leaves and dry well.

Heat the oil in a saucepan, bring almost to the boil and allow to simmer for 1–2 minutes.

Combine the warmed oil and leaves in a blender bowl or food processor. Process until well combined. Pour through muslin and strain into a clean jar. Cover and refrigerate.

INTRODUCTION TO VINEGARS

Our ancestors were very wise about vinegar. The ancient Babylonians used it as a preservative, the Romans drank it, Helen of Troy bathed in it and Cleopatra dissolved a pearl in it to prove that she could consume a fortune in a single meal. It is mentioned numerous times in the Bible, and Hippocrates recommended its therapeutic properties.

As with oils, there are many types of vinegars: balsamic (produced from selected grapes and fermented for a long time), red and white wine vinegar, rice vinegar and cider vinegar. There are also speciality vinegars like raspberry, sherry and champagne vinegar.

Good vinegar can be utilized in so many ways. It is used to prepare and preserve food. It also has health-giving properties: a tablespoon a day of cider vinegar is said to be most beneficial. Even its hygienic properties are well known; your grandmother was right when she told you that there is nothing like a spray of vinegar for cleaning.

Best of all, vinegar plays an important role in dressings, sauces and mustards. It adds just the right kick to a barbecue sauce; it brings tanginess to a vinaigrette; it sweetens a wine reduction sauce. Infusing vinegar with other flavours is a great way to add yet another layer of aroma and flavour.

LEMON, BASIL & CHIVE VINEGAR

zest of ¹/₂ lemon

5 basil leaves

10 stalks chives

250 ml/9 fl oz white wine vinegar

When peeling the lemon for the zest (using only half the lemon), be sure to avoid the white pith. Wash and dry the basil leaves and the chives, then crush them or chop roughly. Place the zest, basil and chives in a clean jar.

In a saucepan over a medium heat, heat the white wine vinegar until it starts to bubble around the edges of the pan. Wait until it cools just a little, then add it to the jar with the other ingredients. When it is completely cool, cover the jar and store in a cool, dark and dry place.

ROSEMARY & GARLIC BALSAMIC VINEGAR

ten 5-cm/2-inch sprigs rosemary

4 garlic cloves

250 ml/9 fl oz balsamic vinegar

Wash the rosemary sprigs, dry and tear off the leaves from the stems. Cut the garlic cloves in half lengthways. Combine the leaves and garlic halves in a clean jar.

In a saucepan over a medium heat, heat the balsamic vinegar until it just starts to bubble around the edges of the pan. Wait until it cools a little, then pour into the jar with the rosemary and garlic. When it is completely cool, cover the jar and store in a cool, dark place. Check occasionally to see whether the vinegar has reached the desired strength.

Before using, strain the vinegar through a fine sieve or muslin into clean jars. Add a fresh sprig of rosemary for decoration and again cover and store in a cool, dark place.

MEAT

WARM BEEF SALAD NIÇOISE

Place the steaks in a shallow dish. Blend the vinegar with 1 tablespoon of orange juice and 1 teaspoon of mustard. Pour over the steaks, cover and leave in the refrigerator for at least 30 minutes. Turn over halfway through the marinating time. Place the eggs in a pan and cover with cold water. Bring to the boil, then reduce the heat to a simmer and cook for 10 minutes. Remove and plunge the eggs into cold water. Once cold, shell and reserve.

Meanwhile, place the potatoes in a saucepan and cover with cold water. Bring to the boil, cover and simmer for 15 minutes, or until tender when pierced with a fork. Drain and reserve.

Bring a saucepan of water to the boil, add the beans and cook for 5 minutes, or until just tender. Drain, plunge into cold water and drain again. Arrange the potatoes and beans on top of the salad leaves together with the yellow pepper, cherry tomatoes and olives, if using. Blend the remaining orange juice and mustard with the olive oil and reserve.

Heat a griddle pan until smoking. Drain the steaks and cook for 3–5 minutes on each side or according to personal preference. Slice the steaks and arrange on top of the salad, then pour over the dressing and serve.

SERVES 4

4 fillet steaks, about 115 g/4 oz each, trimmed of any visible fat

2 tbsp red wine vinegar

2 tbsp orange juice

2 tsp ready-made English mustard

2 eggs

175 g/6 oz new potatoes

115 g/4 oz French beans, trimmed

175 g/6 oz mixed salad leaves, such as baby spinach, rocket and mizuna

1 yellow pepper, peeled, skinned and cut into strips

175 g/6 oz cherry tomatoes, halved

black olives, stoned (optional)

2 tsp extra virgin olive oil

ROAST BEEF SALAD

Preheat the oven to 220°C/425°F/Gas Mark 7. Rub the beef with pepper to taste and Worcestershire sauce. Heat 2 tablespoons of the oil in a small roasting tin over a high heat, add the beef and sear on all sides. Transfer the dish to the preheated oven and roast for 30 minutes. Remove and leave to cool.

Bring a saucepan of water to the boil, add the beans and cook for 5 minutes, or until just tender. Remove with a slotted spoon and refresh the beans under cold running water. Drain and put into a large bowl.

Return the bean cooking water to the boil, add the pasta and cook for 11 minutes, or until tender. Drain, return to the saucepan and toss with the remaining oil.

Add the pasta to the beans with the onions, radicchio leaves, olives and hazelnuts, mix gently and transfer to a serving bowl or dish. Arrange some thinly sliced beef on top.

To make the dressing, put all the ingredients into a small screw-top jar and shake until well blended. Pour over the salad and serve immediately with extra sliced beef. Season with extra pepper, if liked.

SERVES 4

750 g/1 lb 10 oz beef fillet, trimmed of any visible fat

2 tsp Worcestershire sauce

3 tbsp olive oil

400 g/14 oz French beans

100 g/3½ oz dried orecchiette pasta

2 red onions, finely sliced

1 large head radicchio

50 g/1¾ oz green olives, stoned

50 g/1¾ oz shelled hazelnuts, whole

pepper

dressing

1 tsp Dijon mustard

2 tbsp white wine vinegar

5 tbsp olive oil

BEEF SATAY SALAD

SERVES 4

2 sirloin steaks, about 225 g/8 oz each, trimmed of any visible fat

2 tbsp soy sauce

1 tbsp lime juice

1 garlic clove, crushed

1 tsp dried chilli flakes

350 g/12 oz Chinese leaves, shredded

¼ cucumber, thinly sliced

4 spring onions, sliced

fresh coriander leaves and sliced red chilli pepper, to garnish

lime wedges, to serve

satay dressing

2 tbsp crunchy peanut butter

3 tbsp coconut milk

1 tbsp soy sauce

1 tbsp lime juice

2 tsp soft brown sugar

Place the steaks in a shallow dish. Mix together the soy sauce, lime juice, garlic and chilli flakes and pour over the steaks. Cover and leave to marinate at room temperature for 1 hour.

Heat a cast-iron griddle pan until very hot. Add the steaks and cook for 3–5 minutes on each side, depending on how well done you like your steak. Transfer the steaks to a plate and cover and leave to rest for 5 minutes.

To make the satay dressing, place all the ingredients in a small saucepan and heat gently, stirring all the time, until the peanut butter has melted. Simmer for 1 minute. If the dressing becomes too thick add a little water and stir well to make a pouring consistency.

Mix together the Chinese leaves, cucumber and spring onions and place on a serving platter. Thinly slice the steaks and arrange on top of the salad. Drizzle over the satay dressing and garnish with coriander leaves and chilli pepper. Serve with lime wedges.

SICHUAN NUMBING BEEF SALAD

Slice the beef into neat strips measuring about 1 x 4 cm/
½ x 1½ inches. Combine the marinade ingredients and pour over
the beef. Leave at room temperature for 30 minutes or in the
refrigerator for up to 2 days.

Cook the noodles in a saucepan of boiling water for 4 minutes,
or according to the instructions on the packet, until soft. Allow
to cool. Snip into shorter lengths. Whisk the dressing ingredients
until well blended. Combine the noodles, onion, radishes and
salad leaves in a large bowl. Whisk the dressing again and pour
two thirds of it over the salad. Toss to distribute the noodles,
then divide between individual serving plates.

Heat a wok over a medium–high heat, then add the groundnut
oil and the Sichuan pepper. Stir for a few seconds to flavour
the oil. Add the beef and marinade, and stir-fry for 4–5 minutes
until caramelized. To make the dressing, whisk the ingredients
together in a bowl until well blended. Pour over the remaining
dressing.

SERVES 4

350 g/12 oz sirloin steak, trimmed
    of any visible fat

90 g/3½ oz egg noodles

1 small red onion, halved and
    thinly sliced into crescents

6 radishes, sliced

4 good handfuls of peppery leaves
    such as tatsoi, mustard greens
    and rocket

1½ tbsp groundnut oil

1 tsp Sichuan pepper, crushed

marinade

4 tsp Chinese rice wine or dry
    sherry

½ tbsp soy sauce

4 tsp sugar

2 tbsp hoisin sauce

2.5-cm/1-inch piece fresh ginger,
    squeezed in a garlic press

dressing

2 tsp Sichuan pepper, crushed

1½ tbsp light soy sauce

1½ tbsp rice vinegar

2 tbsp cold-pressed sesame oil

WARM BACON
& EGG SALAD

SERVES 4

2 cos lettuce hearts,
   roughly torn

4 eggs

2 tbsp sunflower oil

2 thick slices of white bread,
   crusts removed, cut into cubes

225 g/8 oz smoked bacon lardons

12 cherry tomatoes, halved

dressing

2 tbsp extra virgin olive oil

1 tbsp red wine vinegar

1 tsp Dijon mustard

pepper

To make the dressing, put all the ingredients into a small
screw-top jar and shake until well blended. Put the lettuce leaves
in a salad bowl.

Place the eggs in a saucepan and cover with cold water. Bring
to the boil and boil for 4 minutes. Drain and plunge the eggs into
cold water for 2 minutes. Peel off the shells and cut into quarters.

Heat the sunflower oil in a large frying pan and fry the bread
cubes for 3–4 minutes, turning frequently until golden brown.
Remove with a slotted spoon and set aside.

Add the bacon lardons to the pan and fry over a medium–high
heat until crisp and golden. Add the tomatoes and dressing to
the pan and cook for a further minute.

Gently toss the bacon, tomatoes and dressing into the salad
leaves. Add the quartered eggs and scatter over the croûtons.
Serve immediately.

BLT SALAD

Preheat the grill to high. Place the bacon rashers on the grill pan and grill for 3–4 minutes, turning once, until crisp.

To make the dressing, place the mayonnaise, soured cream, milk and mustard in a bowl and whisk together until smooth. Season with salt and pepper.

Divide the lettuce wedges between 4 serving plates with the tomatoes and cucumber. Toss the avocado slices in the lemon juice and add to the salads.

Drizzle the dressing over the salads. Halve the bacon rashers and stack on top of the salads. Sprinkle over the grated cheese, if using. Serve immediately.

SERVES 4

8 thick rashers back bacon

1 iceberg lettuce, cut into 12 wedges

2 beef tomatoes, sliced into wedges

¼ cucumber, thickly sliced

½ ripe avocado, sliced

1 tbsp lemon juice

85 g/3 oz Cheddar cheese, roughly grated (optional)

dressing

4 tbsp mayonnaise

2 tbsp soured cream

1 tbsp milk

2 tsp wholegrain mustard

salt and pepper

CRISPY SPINACH & BACON SALAD

Heat 2 tablespoons of the olive oil over a high heat in a large frying pan. Add the diced bacon to the pan and cook for 3–4 minutes, or until crisp. Remove with a slotted spoon, draining carefully, and set aside.

Toss the cubes of bread in the fat remaining in the pan over a high heat for about 4 minutes, or until crisp and golden. Remove the croûtons with a slotted spoon, draining carefully, and set them aside.

Add the remaining oil to the frying pan and heat. Toss the spinach in the oil over a high heat for about 3 minutes, or until it has just wilted. Turn into a serving bowl and sprinkle with the bacon and croûtons. Serve immediately.

SERVES 4

4 tbsp olive oil

4 rashers of streaky bacon, diced

1 thick slice of white bread, crusts removed, cut into cubes

450 g/1 lb fresh spinach, torn or shredded

WALNUT, PEAR & CRISPY BACON SALAD

SERVES 4

4 lean bacon rashers

85 g/3 oz walnut halves

2 Red William pears, cored and sliced lengthways

1 tbsp lemon juice

175 g/6 oz watercress, tough stalks removed

dressing

3 tbsp extra virgin olive oil

2 tbsp lemon juice

½ tsp clear honey

salt and pepper

Preheat the grill to high. Place the bacon rashers on the grill pan and grill for 3–4 minutes, turning once, until crisp. Set aside to cool, then cut into 1-cm/½-inch pieces.

Meanwhile, heat a dry frying pan over a medium heat and lightly toast the walnuts, shaking the pan frequently, for 3 minutes, or until lightly browned. Set aside to cool.

Toss the pears in the lemon juice to prevent discoloration. Put the watercress, walnuts, pears and bacon into a salad bowl.

To make the dressing, place the oil, lemon juice and honey in a bowl and whisk together until smooth. Season to taste with salt and pepper, then pour over the salad. Toss well to combine and serve.

MEAT

37

ROAST PORK & PUMPKIN SALAD

Preheat the oven to 200°C/400°F/Gas Mark 6. Cut the pumpkin halves into wedges about 4 cm/1½ inches wide. Very lightly brush the pumpkin and onion wedges with the olive oil, place in a roasting pan and roast for 25–30 minutes until the pumpkin and onions are tender but holding their shape.

Bring a saucepan of water to the boil, add the beans and cook for 5 minutes, or until just tender. Remove with a slotted spoon and refresh the beans under cold running water. Drain and put into a large bowl.

Remove the pumpkin and onion wedges from the oven as soon as they are tender-crisp and leave to cool completely. When the pumpkin is cool, peel and cut into bite-sized pieces.

To make the dressing, put all the ingredients into a small screw-top jar and shake until well blended.

Put the pumpkins, onions, beans, pork, rocket, feta, pine kernels and parsley in a large bowl, pour over the dressing and gently toss until coated. Divide between individual bowls and serve.

SERVES 4–6

1 small pumpkin, about 1.6 kg/ 3½ lb, cut in half and deseeded

2 red onions, cut into wedges

olive oil, for brushing

100 g/3½ oz French beans, topped and tailed and cut in half

600 g/1 lb 5 oz roast pork, trimmed of any visible fat and cut into bite-sized chunks

large handful of rocket leaves

100 g/3½ oz feta cheese, drained and crumbled

2 tbsp toasted pine kernels

2 tbsp chopped fresh flat-leaf parsley

salt and pepper

dressing

6 tbsp extra virgin olive oil

3 tbsp balsamic vinegar

½ tsp sugar

½ tsp Dijon or wholegrain mustard

HOISIN PORK WITH RIBBON SALAD

Slice the pork fillet into 2 pieces and place in a shallow dish. Pour over the hoi sin sauce, cover and leave to marinate at room temperature for 1 hour.

Preheat the oven to 190°C/375°F/ Gas Mark 5.

Place the pork fillet on a wire rack set over a roasting tin half filled with water (this helps to keep the pork moist during cooking). Roast for 35–40 minutes until the pork is cooked through and lightly charred in places. Cool for 10 minutes.

Use a potato peeler to peel the carrots and cucumber into thin ribbons. Place in a bowl and toss together with the spring onions and radishes.

Heat a non-stick frying pan and add the sesame seeds. Cook over a medium heat for 3–4 minutes until lightly toasted. Add to the salad. To make the dressing, put the sesame oil and vinegar into a small screw-top jar and shake until well blended. Pour half over the salad and toss well to mix.

Slice the pork fillet and arrange on individual serving plates with the ribbon salad on the side. Drizzle the rest of the dressing over the pork and serve immediately.

SERVES 4

450 g/1 lb pork fillet

3 tbsp hoi sin sauce

175 g/6 oz carrots

½ cucumber

4 spring onions, finely shredded

4 radishes, very thinly sliced

2 tbsp sesame seeds

dressing

2 tbsp toasted sesame oil

2 tbsp rice vinegar

PORK & CUCUMBER SALAD

MEAT

43

SERVES 4

450 g/1 lb pork fillet, trimmed of any visible fat

6 spring onions, halved lengthways and sliced into 3

1 ridge cucumber

4 handfuls shredded crisp lettuce

20 g/³⁄₄ oz coriander leaves

10 g/¹⁄₄ oz mint leaves

4 tbsp dry-roasted peanuts, lightly crushed

finely grated zest of 1 lime

1 tsp salt

1 tsp sugar

2 tsp sesame oil

1 tbsp groundnut oil

marinade

2 small red chillies, deseeded and very finely chopped

4 tbsp sugar

3 tbsp Thai fish sauce

4 tbsp lime juice

4 tbsp rice vinegar

Thinly slice the pork diagonally. Cut each slice in half lengthways. Put in a bowl with the spring onions.

Peel the cucumber, halve lengthways and scoop out the seeds. Thinly slice diagonally and put in a bowl.

To make the marinade, use a large mortar and pestle and pound the chopped chillies and the sugar to a watery red paste. Add the fish sauce, lime juice and rice vinegar, stirring to dissolve the sugar. Pour into a measuring jug. Pour one half over the pork and onions, and one half over the cucumber. Leave to marinate for 1 hour, then drain, reserving the cucumber marinade.

Put the shredded lettuce, coriander and mint in a bowl, and toss to mix. Divide between individual serving plates. Arrange the cucumber slices on top and dress with the reserved marinade.

Mix the nuts with the lime zest, salt and sugar.

Drain the pork and discard the marinade. Heat a wok over a high heat, then add the oils. Stir-fry the pork for 5 minutes until cooked through and slightly caramelized. Arrange the pork slices on top of the cucumber and sprinkle with the nut mixture. Serve immediately.

SPINACH & PANCETTA SALAD

To make the dressing, put all the ingredients into a small screw-top jar and shake until well blended. Rinse the baby spinach under cold running water, then drain and place in a large salad bowl.

Heat the oil in a large frying pan. Add the pancetta and fry for 3 minutes. Add the mushrooms and cook for 3–4 minutes, or until tender.

Pour the dressing into the frying pan and immediately turn the fried mixture and dressing into the bowl with the spinach. Toss until coated with the dressing and serve immediately.

SERVES 4

275 g/9¾ oz baby spinach leaves

2 tbsp olive oil

150 g/5½ oz pancetta

280 g/10 oz mixed wild mushrooms, sliced

dressing

5 tbsp olive oil

1 tbsp balsamic vinegar

1 tsp Dijon mustard

pinch of sugar

salt and pepper

PASTRAMI & PEPPER ANTIPASTI SALAD

Tear the lettuce into small chunks and place in a serving bowl. Drain the pepper antipasti and sunblush tomatoes reserving 4 tbsp of the oil. Roughly chop the peppers and tomatoes and toss into the lettuce with the olives.

To make the dressing, put the reserved oil and the rest of the dressing ingredients into a small screw-top jar and shake until well blended. Pour half the dressing over the salad and toss well to mix. Arrange the pastrami in ruffles on top of the salad. Serve drizzled with the rest of the dressing and garnished with basil leaves.

SERVES 4

1 iceberg lettuce

1 x 285 g jar chargrilled pepper antipasti in oil

115 g/4 oz sunblush tomatoes

115 g/4 oz green olives, stoned

115 g/4 oz wafer thin pastrami

fresh basil leaves, to garnish

dressing

2 tbsp balsamic vinegar

1 tsp Dijon mustard

pinch of sugar

salt and pepper

ARTICHOKE & PROSCIUTTO SALAD

SERVES 4

275 g/9¾ oz canned artichoke hearts in oil, drained

4 small tomatoes

25 g/1 oz sun-dried tomatoes in oil, drained

40 g/1½ oz prosciutto

25 g/1 oz black olives, stoned and halved

handful of fresh basil sprigs

fresh crusty bread, to serve

dressing

3 tbsp olive oil

1 tbsp white wine vinegar

1 garlic clove, crushed

½ tsp mild mustard

1 tsp clear honey

salt and pepper

Make sure the artichoke hearts are thoroughly drained, then cut them into quarters and put into a serving bowl. Cut each fresh tomato into wedges. Slice the sun-dried tomatoes into thin strips. Cut the prosciutto into thin strips and add to the bowl with the tomatoes and olive halves.

Keeping a few basil sprigs whole for garnishing, tear the remainder of the leaves into small pieces and add to the bowl containing the other salad ingredients.

To make the dressing, put all the ingredients into a small screw-top jar and shake until well blended.

Pour the dressing over the salad and toss together. Garnish the salad with a few basil sprigs and serve with crusty bread.

HAM & SALAMI SALAD WITH FIGS

Trim the stems of the figs to leave just a short length, then cut the figs into quarters.

Arrange the ham and salami on a large serving platter.

Wash and dry the herbs and rocket and put in a bowl with the prepared figs.

To make the dressing, whisk all the ingredients together in a small bowl. Pour over the herbs and salad leaves and carefully turn the figs and leaves in the dressing until they are well coated.

Spoon the figs and salad onto the meat and arrange around the platter.

SERVES 6

9–12 ripe figs, depending on size

6 thin slices dry-cured Italian ham

12 thin slices salami

1 small bunch fresh basil sprigs

few fresh mint sprigs

1 small bunch rocket leaves

dressing

2 tbsp freshly squeezed lemon juice

4 tbsp extra virgin olive oil

salt and pepper

SALAMI PASTA SALAD

Bring a large saucepan of lightly salted water to the boil. Add the pasta and return to the boil. Cook for 10–12 minutes until just tender.

Drain the pasta well and transfer to a bowl. Mix together the pesto sauce and olive oil and stir into the hot pasta. Leave to cool, stirring occasionally.

Add the peppers, onion, olives, tomatoes, salami and mozzarella cheese to the pasta and toss well to mix. Season to taste with salt and pepper. Serve garnished with the basil sprigs.

SERVES 4–6

350 g/12 oz dried penne pasta

2 tbsp pesto sauce

3 tbsp olive oil

1 orange pepper, deseeded and diced

1 yellow pepper, deseeded and diced

1 red onion, finely diced

85 g/3 oz black olives, stoned

115 g/4 oz cherry tomatoes, halved

175 g/6 oz piece Milano salami, cut into small chunks

125 g/4½ oz mozzarella cheese, torn into small pieces

salt and pepper

fresh basil sprigs, to garnish

ONION & HERB SALAD WITH CHORIZO

SERVES 2

1 tbsp sunflower oil

1 small onion, finely sliced

250 g/9 oz canned butter beans, drained and rinsed

1 tsp balsamic vinegar

2 chorizo sausages, sliced diagonally

1 small tomato, diced

2 tbsp harissa paste

85 g/3 oz mixed herb salad

Heat the oil in a non-stick frying pan over a medium heat, add the onion and cook, stirring frequently, until softened but not browned. Add the beans and cook for a further 1 minute, then add the vinegar, stirring well. Keep warm.

Meanwhile, heat a separate dry frying pan over a medium heat, add the chorizo slices and cook, turning occasionally, until lightly browned. Remove with a slotted spoon and drain on kitchen paper.

Mix the tomato and harissa paste together in a small bowl. Divide the herb salad between 2 plates, spoon over the bean mixture and scatter over the warm chorizo slices. Top with a spoonful of the tomato and harissa mixture and serve immediately.

SPICY SAUSAGE PASTA SALAD

Bring a large saucepan of lightly salted water to the boil. Add the pasta and return to the boil. Cook for 10–12 minutes until just tender. Drain the pasta and reserve.

Heat the oil in a pan over a medium heat. Add the onion and fry until translucent. Stir in the garlic, yellow pepper and sliced sausage and cook for about 3–4 minutes, stirring once or twice.

Add the wine, vinegar and reserved pasta to the pan, stir to blend well and bring the mixture just to the boil over a medium heat.

Arrange the salad leaves on 4 large serving plates, spoon over the warm sausage and pasta mixture and serve immediately.

SERVES 4

125 g/4½ oz dried conchiglie pasta

2 tbsp olive oil

1 medium onion, chopped

2 garlic cloves, crushed

1 small yellow pepper, deseeded and cut into matchsticks

175 g/6 oz spicy pork sausage, such as chorizo, Italian pepperoni or salami, skinned and sliced

2 tbsp red wine

1 tbsp red wine vinegar

125 g/4½ oz mixed salad leaves

salt

HOT SAUSAGE & POTATO SALAD

Place the potatoes in a saucepan and cover with cold water. Bring to the boil, cover and simmer for 15 minutes, or until tender when pierced with a fork.

Meanwhile, heat the sunflower oil in a large frying pan and fry the sausages for 5 minutes. Add the onions to the pan and continue cooking for a further 8–10 minutes, turning frequently, until the sausages are cooked through and the onions are golden and tender. Remove the onions and sausages from the pan and drain on kitchen paper. Slice each sausage diagonally into 4 pieces.

Drain the potatoes and place in a large bowl with the onions and sausages.

To make the dressing, put all the ingredients in a small screw-top jar and shake until well blended. Pour over the hot salad and toss well to coat. Serve immediately, garnished with chopped parsley, if using.

SERVES 4

700 g/1 lb 9 oz new potatoes, halved

1 tbsp sunflower oil

6 thick pork sausages

2 onions, sliced into thin wedges

chopped fresh flat-leaf parsley, to garnish (optional)

dressing

4 tbsp olive oil

1 tbsp white wine vinegar

2 tsp wholegrain mustard

2 tsp clear honey

salt and pepper

ARTICHOKE & CHORIZO SALAD

SERVES 8

12 small globe artichokes

juice of ½ lemon

2 tbsp olive oil

1 small orange-fleshed melon,
   such as cantaloupe

200 g/7 oz chorizo sausage,
   outer casing removed

fresh tarragon or flat-leaf parsley
   sprigs, to garnish

dressing

3 tbsp extra virgin olive oil

1 tbsp red wine vinegar

1 tsp prepared mustard

1 tbsp chopped fresh tarragon

salt and pepper

Cut the artichokes into quarters and brush with lemon juice to prevent discoloration.

Heat the olive oil in a large, heavy-based frying pan. Add the prepared artichokes and fry, stirring frequently, for 5 minutes, or until the artichoke leaves are golden brown. Remove from the frying pan, transfer to a large serving bowl and leave to cool.

To prepare the melon, cut in half and scoop out the seeds with a spoon. Cut the flesh into bite-sized cubes. Add to the cooled artichokes. Cut the chorizo into bite-sized chunks and add to the melon and artichokes.

To make the dressing, put all the ingredients into a small screw-top jar and shake until well blended. Just before serving, pour the dressing over the prepared salad ingredients and toss together. Serve the salad garnished with tarragon.

MEAT

61

GRILLED LAMB WITH YOGURT DRESSING

Mix the 2 tablespoons of oil, tomato purée, cumin, lemon juice, garlic, cayenne and salt and pepper to taste together in a non-metallic bowl. Add the lamb fillets and rub all over with the marinade. Cover the bowl and marinate in the fridge for at least 2 hours, but ideally overnight.

To make the dressing, whisk the lemon juice and honey together until the honey dissolves. Whisk in the yogurt until well blended. Stir in the herbs and add salt and pepper to taste. Cover and chill until required. Preheat the grill to high.

Remove the lamb from the fridge 15 minutes before you are ready to cook. Brush the grill rack with oil. Grill the lamb fillet, turning it once, for 10 minutes for medium and 12 minutes for well done. Leave the lamb to cool completely, then cover and chill until required.

Thinly slice the lamb fillets, then divide between 4 plates. Pour the dressing over the lamb slices, sprinkle with toasted sesame seeds and parsley and serve.

SERVES 4

2 tbsp sunflower oil, plus extra for grilling

1 tbsp tomato purée

½ tbsp ground cumin

1 tsp lemon juice

1 garlic clove, crushed

pinch of cayenne pepper

500 g/1 lb 2 oz lamb neck fillets, trimmed of any visible fat

oil, for brushing

salt and pepper

toasted sesame seeds and sprigs of fresh flat-leaf parsley, to garnish

dressing

2 tbsp fresh lemon juice

1 tsp clear honey

85 g/3 oz Greek yogurt

2 tbsp finely shredded fresh mint

2 tbsp chopped fresh flat-leaf parsley

1 tbsp finely snipped fresh chives

LAMB KOFTE & HERB SALAD

Place 8 wooden skewers in a shallow bowl of cold water and leave to soak for 30 minutes. Place the lamb, onion, spices and coriander and mint in a food processor with plenty of salt and pepper. Process for 1–2 minutes until finely minced. Transfer to a bowl and cover and chill in the refrigerator for 30 minutes. Preheat the grill to medium–high.

Divide the mixture into 8. Wrap the mixture around the soaked wooden skewers to form oval shapes. Brush with a little of the oil and grill for 15–20 minutes, turning frequently until cooked through.

Meanwhile, mix the yogurt, cucumber and mint sauce together in a small bowl and season with salt and pepper.

Place the salad leaves in a large bowl. Whisk together the rest of the oil with the lemon juice and season to taste. Pour the dressing over the salad leaves and toss to coat. Serve the hot koftes, on or off the skewers, with the salad and cucumber and mint yogurt.

SERVES 4

400 g/14 oz lean minced lamb

1 small onion, finely chopped

2 tsp each ground coriander, ground cumin and paprika

1 tbsp chopped fresh coriander

2 tbsp chopped fresh mint

3 tbsp olive oil

6 tbsp natural yogurt

85 g/3 oz cucumber, grated

2 tsp mint sauce

115 g/4 oz mixed baby leaf and herb salad

1 tbsp lemon juice

salt and pepper

POULTRY

LAYERED
CHICKEN SALAD

Place the potatoes in a saucepan and cover with cold water.
Bring to the boil, cover and simmer for 15 minutes, or until tender
when pierced with a fork. Preheat the grill to high. Place the
pepper halves, skin side up, and grill until the skins blacken and
begin to char.

Remove the peppers with tongs, place in a bowl and cover with
clingfilm. Set aside until cool enough to handle, then peel off the
skins and slice the flesh.

Bring a small pan of lightly salted water to the boil. Add the
courgettes, bring back to the boil and simmer for 3 minutes.
Drain, rinse under cold running water to prevent any further
cooking and drain again. Set aside.

To make the dressing, whisk the yogurt, mayonnaise and
snipped chives together in a small bowl until well blended.
Season to taste with salt and pepper.

When the potatoes are tender, drain, cool and slice them.
Add them to the dressing and mix gently to coat evenly. Spoon
the potatoes on to 4 serving plates, dividing them equally.

Top each plate with one quarter of the pepper slices and
courgettes. Layer one quarter of the onion and tomato slices,
then the sliced chicken, on top of each serving. Garnish with
snipped chives and serve immediately.

SERVES 4

750 g/1 lb 10 oz new potatoes

1 red pepper, halved and
    deseeded

1 green pepper, halved and
    deseeded

2 small courgettes, sliced

1 small onion, thinly sliced

3 tomatoes, sliced

350 g/12 oz cooked chicken,
    sliced

snipped fresh chives, to garnish

dressing

150 ml/5 fl oz natural yogurt

3 tbsp mayonnaise

1 tbsp snipped fresh chives

salt and pepper

CORONATION
CHICKEN SALAD

Heat the oil in a frying pan. Add the cashew nuts and almonds and fry for 2–3 minutes until golden. Remove with a slotted spoon and drain on kitchen paper.

Add the onion to the pan and fry gently for 6–7 minutes until soft and golden. Stir in the curry paste and cook for a further minute. Transfer to a bowl and cool.

Stir the mayonnaise, yogurt and mango chutney into the onion and mix well. Add the chicken strips to the dressing. Toss well to coat. Season with salt and pepper.

Place the salad leaves in a shallow serving bowl. Add the curried chicken and mango slices to the bowl and toss gently into the salad leaves. Scatter over the fried nuts and serve garnished with the coriander leaves.

SERVES 4

1 tbsp sunflower oil

1 tbsp cashew nuts

1 tbsp whole blanched almonds

1 onion, chopped

1 tbsp mild curry paste

4 tbsp mayonnaise

4 tbsp natural yogurt

1 tbsp mango chutney

450 g/1 lb boneless cooked chicken, torn into large strips

140 g/5 oz watercress, spinach and rocket salad

1 small mango, peeled, stoned and sliced

salt and pepper

fresh coriander leaves, to garnish

CHICKEN & CHEESE SALAD

SERVES 4

150 g/5½ oz rocket leaves

2 celery sticks, trimmed and sliced

½ cucumber, sliced

2 spring onions, trimmed and sliced

2 tbsp chopped fresh flat-leaf parsley

25 g/1 oz walnut pieces

350 g/12 oz boneless roast chicken, sliced

125 g/4½ oz Stilton cheese, cubed

handful of seedless red grapes, halved (optional)

salt and pepper

dressing

2 tbsp olive oil

1 tbsp sherry vinegar

1 tsp Dijon mustard

1 tbsp chopped mixed herbs

Wash the rocket leaves, pat dry with kitchen paper and put them into a large salad bowl. Add the celery, cucumber, spring onions, parsley and walnuts and mix together well. Transfer onto a large serving platter. Arrange the chicken slices over the salad, then scatter over the cheese. Add the red grapes, if using. Season well with salt and pepper.

To make the dressing, put all the ingredients into a small screw-top jar and shake until well blended. Drizzle the dressing over the salad and serve.

SMOKED
CHICKEN SALAD

To make the dressing, put the avocado, lemon juice and vinegar in a food processor or blender and process until smooth, scraping down the side with a rubber spatula. Add the yogurt, garlic and tarragon leaves and process again. Season with salt and pepper to taste, then transfer to a bowl. Cover with clingfilm and chill for 2 hours.

To assemble the salad, divide the tomato slices between 4–6 individual plates. Toss the smoked chicken, watercress, beansprouts and parsley leaves together. Divide the salad ingredients between the plates.

Adjust the seasoning in the dressing, if necessary. Spoon dressing over each salad and serve.

SERVES 4–6

2 large, juicy beefsteak tomatoes, sliced

600 g/1 lb 5 oz smoked chicken, skinned and cut into slices

250 g/9 oz fresh watercress, any thick stems or yellow leaves removed, then rinsed and patted dry

85 g/3 oz beansprouts, soaked for 20 minutes in cold water, then drained well and patted dry

leaves from several sprigs fresh flat-leaf parsley or coriander

dressing

1 ripe, soft avocado

2 tbsp lemon juice

1 tbsp tarragon vinegar

85 g/3 oz Greek yogurt

1 small garlic clove, crushed

1 tbsp chopped fresh tarragon leaves

salt and pepper

CHICKEN AVOCADO SALAD

To make the dressing, put all the ingredients into a small screw-top jar and shake until well blended.

Put the salad leaves into a bowl, add about one third of the dressing and lightly toss. Add the chicken, satsumas, celery, onion, chives and the remaining dressing and toss again.

Cut the avocados in half and remove the stone, then peel away the skin. Cut the flesh into thin slices, add to the other ingredients and gently toss together, making sure the avocado slices are completely coated with dressing so they don't discolor.

Arrange on individual plates, sprinkle with sunflower seeds and serve with pitta crisps on the side.

SERVES 4

125 g/4½ oz mixed salad leaves, such as beetroot greens, escarole, endive and radicchio, rinsed and dried

400 g/14 oz boneless cooked chicken, shredded

2 satsumas, separated into segments

2 celery sticks, thinly sliced

½ red onion, halved and thinly sliced

2 tbsp snipped fresh chives

2 avocados

toasted sunflower seeds, to garnish

pitta crisps, to serve

dressing

125 ml/4 fl oz extra virgin olive oil

3 tbsp Chinese rice wine vinegar

½ tsp Dijon mustard

salt and pepper

ROAST CHICKEN WITH PESTO CREAM SALAD

SERVES 4–6

600 g/1 lb 5 oz boneless cooked
  chicken, any skin removed and
  cut into bite-sized pieces

3 celery sticks, chopped

2 large skinned red peppers from
  a jar, well drained and sliced

salt and pepper

iceberg lettuce leaves, to serve

pesto cream
150 ml/5 fl oz crème fraîche or
  soured cream

about 4 tbsp bottled pesto sauce

To make the pesto cream, put the crème fraîche into a large bowl,
then beat in the pesto sauce. Taste and add more pesto if you
want a stronger flavour.

Add the chicken, celery and red peppers to the bowl and gently
toss together. Add salt and pepper to taste and toss again. Cover
and chill until required.

Remove the salad from the fridge 10 minutes before serving
to return to room temperature. Give the salad ingredients a
good stir, then divide between individual plates lined with
lettuce leaves.

CHICKEN & PANCETTA CAESAR SALAD

To make the dressing, place all the ingredients in a food processor or hand blender and process until smooth.

Heat a large non-stick frying pan and add the pancetta slices. Cook over a high heat for about 2 minutes until crisp and frazzled. Remove with a slotted spoon and drain on kitchen paper. Add the chicken to the pan and fry over a medium–high heat for 5–6 minutes until golden and cooked through. Remove and drain with the pancetta.

Add the garlic and oil to the pan and stir in the bread cubes. Fry over a high heat, turning frequently, for 2–3 minutes until crisp and golden.

Place the lettuce and dressing in a serving bowl and toss together thoroughly. Add the pancetta and chicken and toss in gently. Scatter over the garlic croûtons and Parmesan cheese shavings and serve immediately.

SERVES 2

12 thin smoked pancetta slices

225 g/8 oz skinless, boneless chicken breasts, cubed

1 garlic clove, crushed

3 tbsp olive oil

1 small rustic or ciabatta roll, cut into chunky cubes

1 small cos lettuce, chopped into large pieces

fresh Parmesan cheese shavings, to serve

dressing

3 tbsp mayonnaise

2 tbsp soured cream

1 tbsp milk

1 garlic clove, crushed

½ tsp Dijon mustard

2 tbsp finely grated Parmesan cheese

2 anchovy fillets in oil, drained and finely chopped

pepper

WARM CHICKEN LIVER SALAD

Arrange the salad leaves on serving plates.

Heat the oil in a non-stick frying pan, add the onion and cook for 5 minutes, or until softened. Add the chicken livers, tarragon and mustard and cook for 3–5 minutes, stirring, until tender. Place on top of the salad leaves.

Add the vinegar, salt and pepper to the pan and heat, stirring all the time, until all the sediment has been lifted from the pan. Pour over the chicken livers and serve warm.

SERVES 4

225 g/8 oz mixed salad leaves

1 tbsp olive oil

1 small onion, finely chopped

450 g/1 lb frozen chicken livers, thawed

1 tsp chopped fresh tarragon

1 tsp wholegrain mustard

2 tbsp balsamic vinegar

salt and pepper

CHINESE
CHICKEN SALAD

SERVES 4

3 boneless, skinless chicken
  breasts, weighing 450 g/1 lb in
  total, cut into bite-sized pieces

2 tsp soy sauce

¼ tsp freshly ground white pepper

2 tbsp groundnut oil, plus extra
  for deep-frying

50 g/1¾ oz thin rice noodles

½ head Chinese leaves, thinly
  sliced diagonally

3 spring onions, green parts
  included, sliced diagonally

40 g/1½ oz almonds with skin,
  sliced lengthways

sesame seeds, to garnish
  (optional)

dressing

5 tbsp olive oil

3 tbsp rice vinegar

3 tbsp soy sauce

a few drops sesame oil

salt and pepper

Sprinkle the chicken with the soy sauce and white pepper.
To make the dressing, whisk the ingredients together in a bowl
until well blended.

Heat a wok over a high heat, then add the groundnut oil.
Stir-fry the chicken for 4–5 minutes until brown and crisp. Drain
on kitchen paper and allow to cool. Wipe out the wok.

Pour enough groundnut oil for deep-frying into the wok. Heat
to 180°C/350°F or until a cube of bread browns in 30 seconds,
then fry a few noodles at a time until puffed up and crisp. Drain
on kitchen paper.

Arrange the Chinese leaves in a shallow serving dish. Place the
noodles in a pile on top of the leaves on one side of the dish.
Arrange the chicken, spring onion and almonds in the remaining
space. Whisk the dressing again and pour over the salad. Dress
with the sesame seeds, if using. Serve.

BANG BANG
CHICKEN SALAD

To make the dressing, place the peanut butter in a heatproof bowl. Set the bowl over a saucepan of simmering water and stir until the peanut butter has melted. Stir in the chilli sauce, soy sauce and rice vinegar. Remove from the heat and gradually stir in the sunflower and peanut oil to make a dressing with a smooth pouring consistency.

Arrange the Chinese leaves on a serving platter and top with the carrots, cucumber and beansprouts. Top with the shredded chicken and spoon over the warm dressing. Sprinkle with the sesame seeds and peanuts and serve immediately.

SERVES 4

225 g/8 oz Chinese leaves, roughly torn

2 carrots, cut into thin sticks

½ cucumber, deseeded and cut into thin sticks

55 g/2 oz beansprouts

400 g/14 oz cooked boneless chicken breast, shredded

1 tbsp toasted sesame seeds

1 tbsp salted peanuts, chopped

dressing
4 tbsp smooth peanut butter

2 tbsp sweet chilli sauce

1 tbsp soy sauce

1 tbsp rice vinegar

1 tbsp sunflower oil

1 tbsp roasted peanut oil

GINGERED CHICKEN SALAD

Mix together the spring onions, ginger, crushed garlic and 2 tablespoons of the oil in a shallow dish and add the chicken. Cover and marinate for at least 3 hours. Lift the meat out of the marinade and set aside.

Heat a wok over a high heat, then add the remaining oil. Cook the onion for 1–2 minutes. Add the chopped garlic, baby corn, mangetout and pepper and cook for 2–3 minutes, until just tender. Add the cucumber, half the soy sauce, the sugar and the basil and mix gently.

Soak the noodles for 2–3 minutes or until tender, and drain well. Sprinkle the remaining soy sauce over them and arrange on plates. Top with the cooked vegetables.

Add a little more oil to the wok if necessary and cook the chicken over a fairly high heat until browned on all sides and cooked through. Arrange the chicken cubes on top of the salad and serve hot or warm.

SERVES 4

4 spring onions, chopped

2.5-cm/1-inch piece fresh ginger, finely chopped

4 garlic cloves, 2 crushed and 2 chopped

3 tbsp vegetable or groundnut oil

4 skinless, boneless chicken breasts, cut into cubes

1 onion, sliced

115 g/4 oz baby corn, halved

115 g/4 oz mangetout, halved lengthways

1 red pepper, deseeded and sliced

7.5-cm/3-inch piece cucumber, peeled, deseeded and sliced

4 tbsp soy sauce

1 tbsp soft light brown sugar

few Thai basil leaves

175 g/6 oz fine egg noodles

NOODLE BASKETS WITH CHICKEN SALAD

SERVES 4

groundnut or corn oil,
for deep-frying

250 g/9 oz fresh fine or medium
egg noodles

chicken salad

6 tbsp soured cream

6 tbsp mayonnaise

2.5-cm/1-inch piece fresh ginger,
grated

grated rind and juice of 1 lime

4 skinless, boneless chicken
thighs, poached and cooled,
then cut into thin strips

1 carrot, grated

1 cucumber, cut in half
lengthways, deseeded and
sliced

1 tbsp finely chopped fresh
coriander

1 tbsp finely chopped fresh mint

1 tbsp finely chopped fresh
parsley

salt and pepper

To shape the noodle baskets, you will need a special set of
2 long-handled wire baskets that clip inside each other, available
from specialist kitchen stores. Dip the larger wire basket in
oil, then line it completely and evenly with one quarter of the
noodles. Dip the smaller wire basket in oil, then position it inside
the larger basket and clip it into position.

Heat the oil in a wok to 180°C/350°F, or until a cube of bread
browns in 30 seconds. Lower the baskets into the oil and
deep-fry for 2–3 minutes, or until the noodles are golden brown.
Remove the baskets from the oil and drain on kitchen paper.
Unclip the 2 wire baskets and carefully remove the small one.
Use a palette knife, if necessary, to prise the noodle basket from
the wire frame. Repeat to make 3 more baskets. Set aside
to cool.

To make the chicken salad, combine the soured cream,
mayonnaise, ginger and lime rind. Gradually add the lime juice
until you get the flavour you like. Stir in the chicken, carrot
and cucumber and season to taste with salt and pepper.
Cover and chill.

To serve, stir in the herbs and spoon the salad into the
noodle baskets.

CAJUN CHICKEN SALAD

Make 3 diagonal slashes across each chicken breast. Put the chicken into a shallow dish and sprinkle all over with the Cajun seasoning. Cover and refrigerate for at least 30 minutes.

When ready to cook, brush a griddle pan with the sunflower oil, if using. Heat over a high heat until very hot and a few drops of water sprinkled into the pan sizzle immediately. Add the chicken and cook for 7–8 minutes on each side, or until thoroughly cooked. If still slightly pink in the centre, cook a little longer. Remove the chicken and reserve.

Add the mango slices to the pan and cook for 2 minutes on each side. Remove and reserve.

Meanwhile, arrange the salad leaves in a salad bowl and scatter over the onion, beetroot, radishes and walnut halves.

To make the dressing, put all the ingredients into a small screw-top jar and shake until well blended. Pour over the salad.

Add the mango, top with the chicken breast and sprinkle with sesame seeds. Serve.

SERVES 4

- 4 skinless, boneless chicken breasts, about 140 g/5 oz each
- 4 tsp Cajun seasoning
- 2 tsp sunflower oil (optional)
- 1 ripe mango, peeled, stoned and cut into thick slices
- 200 g/7 oz mixed salad leaves
- 1 red onion, thinly sliced and cut in half
- 175 g/6 oz cooked beetroot, diced
- 85 g/3 oz radishes, sliced
- 55 g/2 oz walnut halves
- sesame seeds, to garnish

dressing
- 4 tbsp walnut oil
- 1–2 tsp Dijon mustard
- 1 tbsp lemon juice
- salt and pepper

BBQ CHICKEN SALAD

Place the oil, tomato sauce, honey, Worcestershire sauce and mustard powder in a shallow bowl and mix together well. Season with salt and pepper. Add the chicken and turn to coat in the marinade. Cover and leave to marinate in the refrigerator for 3–4 hours or overnight.

Preheat the oven to 200°C/400°F/ Gas Mark 6. Place the chicken on a rack set over a roasting tin. Spoon over any remaining marinade and roast in the oven for 40–45 minutes until cooked through and lightly charred in places. Cool for 5 minutes.

Arrange the lettuce leaves, carrots, sweetcorn and pepper on 4 serving plates. To make the dressing, mix the soured cream and chives in a small bowl and season with salt and pepper.

Thickly slice each chicken breast and arrange on the salads. Serve with fresh chives, if using.

SERVES 4

1 tbsp olive oil

4 tbsp tomato sauce

1 tbsp clear honey

1 tbsp Worcestershire sauce

1 tsp mustard powder

4 boneless chicken breasts (with skin), about 140 g/5 oz each

4 Little Gem lettuces, separated into leaves

4 carrots, roughly grated

6 tbsp canned sweetcorn, drained

½ red pepper, thinly sliced

salt and pepper

fresh chives, to garnish (optional)

dressing

6 tbsp soured cream

2 tbsp snipped fresh chives

CHICKEN FAJITA SALAD

SERVES 4

450 g/1 lb skinless, boneless chicken breasts, sliced

2 tbsp lime juice

2 tbsp olive oil

1 tsp each pepper, dried oregano and mild chilli powder

1 onion, sliced into thin wedges

1 red pepper, deseeded and thickly sliced

200 g/7 oz mixed salad leaves

lime slices and soured cream, to serve

avocado salsa

1 ripe avocado, finely diced

2 ripe tomatoes, finely chopped

1 tbsp fresh chopped coriander

1 tbsp lime juice

salt and pepper

To make the avocado salsa, place the avocado in a small bowl and stir in the tomatoes, coriander and lime juice. Season with salt and pepper. Cover the surface closely with clingfilm and chill in the refrigerator.

Place the chicken in a bowl. Add the lime juice, oil, pepper, oregano and chilli powder. Toss to coat. Cover and leave to marinate at room temperature for 1 hour.

Heat a cast iron griddle pan until very hot and add the chicken slices. Cook for 5–6 minutes, turning occasionally, until the chicken is cooked through and charred in places. Remove from the pan and keep warm. Add the onion and pepper to the pan and cook for 3–4 minutes, turning once until just tender.

Divide the salad leaves between 4 serving plates and top with the chicken, onion and pepper. Serve immediately with the avocado salsa, lime slices and soured cream.

HONEY & CHICKEN PASTA SALAD

To make the dressing, place all the ingredients in a small bowl and whisk together.

Bring a large saucepan of lightly salted water to the boil. Add the pasta and return to the boil. Cook for 10–12 minutes until just tender.

Meanwhile, heat the oil in a large frying pan. Add the onion and garlic and fry for 5 minutes. Add the chicken and cook, stirring frequently, for 3–4 minutes until just cooked through. Stir the mustard and honey into the pan and cook for a further 2–3 minutes until the chicken and onion are golden brown and sticky.

Drain the pasta and transfer to a serving bowl. Pour over the dressing and toss well. Stir in the chicken and onion and leave to cool.

Gently stir the tomatoes and mizuna into the pasta. Serve garnished with the thyme leaves.

SERVES 4

250 g/9 oz dried fusilli pasta

2 tbsp olive oil

1 onion, thinly sliced

1 garlic clove, crushed

400 g/14 oz skinless, boneless chicken breast, thinly sliced

2 tbsp wholegrain mustard

2 tbsp clear honey

175 g/6 oz cherry tomatoes, halved

handful of mizuna or rocket leaves

fresh thyme leaves, to garnish

dressing

3 tbsp olive oil

1 tbsp sherry vinegar

2 tsp clear honey

1 tbsp fresh thyme leaves

salt and pepper

BRAISED CHICKEN SALAD

Preheat the oven to 180°C/350°F/Gas Mark 4. Heat the olive oil in an ovenproof casserole over medium–high heat. Add the chicken and fry for 15 minutes, turning, until golden all over. Pour in the wine and simmer for 2 minutes, then add the onion, carrot, celery and bay leaf. Season with salt and pepper. Cover tightly and transfer to the oven. Bake for 45–50 minutes, turning every 20 minutes, until the juices from the thickest part of the thigh run clear when pierced with a skewer. Discard the liquid and solids. When cool enough to handle, remove and discard the skin. Strip the meat from the bone, slicing any large chunks into bite-sized pieces.

Arrange the chicken in a dish. Sprinkle with salt, a few peppercorns and the bay leaves. Pour in enough oil to generously coat. Cover tightly with clingfilm and marinate in the refrigerator for 1–2 days.

Remove the chicken from the fridge 2 hours before serving. Place in a colander set over a bowl to drain, and leave to stand until the oil has liquefied.

To make the salad, combine the spinach, celery and chicory in a large serving dish. Toss with salt, enough oil from the chicken to just coat the leaves, and the wine vinegar. Arrange the chicken on top, discarding the peppercorns and bay leaves. Sprinkle with the balsamic vinegar before serving.

SERVES 4

3 tbsp olive oil

1 chicken, weighing about 1.3 kg/3 lb

200 ml/7 fl oz dry white wine

1 onion, chopped

1 carrot, chopped

1 celery stalk, chopped

1 fresh bay leaf

salt and pepper

marinade

1 tsp black peppercorns

4 fresh bay leaves

125 ml/4 fl oz olive oil

salad

150 g/5½ oz baby spinach leaves, chopped

5 tender celery stalks

1 head chicory

1 tsp wine vinegar

1 tsp balsamic vinegar

CHICKEN, RAISIN & PINE KERNEL SALAD

SERVES 6–8

4 large skinless, boneless chicken breasts, about 600 g/1 lb 5 oz in total

5 tbsp olive oil

1 garlic clove, finely chopped

150 g/5½ oz pine kernels

100 ml/3½ fl oz extra virgin olive oil

1 small bunch of fresh flat-leaf parsley, finely chopped

salt and pepper

dressing

50 ml/2 fl oz red wine vinegar

25 g/1 oz caster sugar

1 bay leaf

pared rind of 1 lemon

150 g/5½ oz seedless raisins

To make the dressing, put the vinegar, sugar, bay leaf and lemon rind in a saucepan and bring to the boil, then remove from the heat. Stir in the raisins and leave to cool.

When the dressing is cool, slice the chicken breasts widthways into very thin slices. Heat the olive oil in a large frying pan, add the chicken slices and cook over a medium heat, stirring occasionally, for 8–10 minutes until lightly browned and tender.

Add the garlic and pine kernels and cook, stirring constantly and shaking the pan, for 1 minute, or until the pine kernels are golden brown. Season to taste with salt and pepper.

Pour the cooled dressing into a large bowl, discarding the bay leaf and lemon rind. Add the extra virgin olive oil and whisk together. Season to taste with salt and pepper. Add the chicken mixture and parsley and toss together. Turn the salad into a serving dish and serve warm or, if serving cold, cover and chill in the refrigerator for 2–3 hours before serving.

TURKEY COUSCOUS SALAD

Place the couscous in a large heatproof bowl. Pour over enough boiling water to cover. Stir well, cover and leave to soak for about 15 minutes until all the liquid has been absorbed. Use a fork to break up any clumps and stir in 3 tbsp of the olive oil and the vinegar. Season with plenty of salt and pepper.

Heat the rest of the oil in a large frying pan and add the turkey and harissa paste. Fry for 3 minutes, turning frequently, until the turkey is no longer pink. Add the courgettes and onion to the pan and fry for a further 10–12 minutes, stirring occasionally, until the turkey and vegetables are golden brown and tender.

Stir the turkey and vegetables into the couscous with the apricots and pine kernels. Cool for 10 minutes then stir in the chopped coriander and adjust the seasoning to taste. Serve piled into bowls garnished with coriander sprigs.

SERVES 4

225 g/ 8 oz couscous

5 tbsp olive oil

3 tbsp red wine vinegar

350 g/12 oz turkey breast fillet, cubed

1 tsp harissa paste

175 g/6 oz courgettes, diced

1 onion, chopped

115 g/4 oz no-need-to-soak dried apricots, chopped

2 tbsp toasted pine kernels

2 tbsp chopped fresh coriander

salt and pepper

fresh coriander sprigs, to garnish

TURKEY & RICE SALAD

Reserve 3 tablespoons of the chicken stock and bring the remainder to the boil in a large saucepan. Add the rice and cook for 30 minutes, or until tender. Drain and leave to cool slightly.

Meanwhile, heat 1 tablespoon of the oil in a preheated wok or frying pan. Stir-fry the turkey over a medium heat for 3–4 minutes, or until cooked through. Using a slotted spoon, transfer the turkey to a dish. Add the mangetout and mushrooms to the wok and stir-fry for 1 minute. Add the reserved stock, bring to the boil, then reduce the heat, cover and simmer for 3–4 minutes. Transfer the vegetables to the dish and leave to cool slightly.

Thoroughly mix the rice, turkey, mangetout, mushrooms, nuts, coriander and garlic chives together, then season to taste with salt and pepper. Drizzle with the remaining sunflower oil and the vinegar and garnish with fresh garlic chives. Serve warm.

SERVES 4

1 litre/1¾ pints chicken stock

175 g/6 oz mixed long-grain and wild rice

2 tbsp sunflower or corn oil

225 g/8 oz skinless, boneless turkey breast, trimmed of all visible fat and cut into thin strips

225 g/8 oz mangetout

115 g/4 oz oyster mushrooms, torn into pieces

55 g/2 oz shelled pistachio nuts, finely chopped

2 tbsp chopped fresh coriander

1 tbsp snipped fresh garlic chives

1 tbsp balsamic vinegar

salt and pepper

fresh garlic chives, to garnish

ROAST DUCK SALAD

SERVES 4

2 duck breasts

2 Little Gem lettuces, shredded

115 g/4 oz beansprouts

1 yellow pepper, deseeded and cut into thin strips

½ cucumber, deseeded and cut into matchsticks

shredded lime zest and shredded coconut, to garnish

dressing

juice of 2 limes

3 tbsp Thai fish sauce

1 tbsp soft brown sugar

2 tsp sweet chilli sauce

2.5 cm/1 inch fresh ginger, grated

3 tbsp chopped fresh mint

3 tbsp chopped fresh basil

Preheat the oven to 200°C/400°F/Gas Mark 6. Place the duck breasts on a rack set over a roasting tin and roast in the oven for 20–30 minutes, or until cooked as desired and the skin is crisp. Remove from the oven and set aside to cool.

In a large bowl, combine the lettuces, beansprouts, pepper and cucumber. Cut the cooled duck into slices and add to the salad. Mix well.

To make the dressing, whisk together the lime juice, Thai fish sauce, sugar, chilli sauce, ginger, mint and basil in a bowl. Add the dressing to the salad and toss well.

Turn the salad out onto a serving platter and garnish with the lime zest and shredded coconut before serving.

WARM DUCK, SHALLOT & ORANGE SALAD

Halve and squeeze the juice from 1 of the oranges. Using a serrated knife remove all the peel and white pith from the other orange and halve and thinly slice.

Preheat the oven to 200°C/400°F/Gas Mark 6. Season the duck fillets with salt and pepper. Heat a large heavy-based frying pan and add the duck fillets, skin side down. Cook over a medium–high heat for 5–6 minutes until the skin is golden brown. Turn over and cook for a further minute. Place the duck fillets in a shallow roasting tin and roast in the preheated oven for 10 minutes. Cook for a little longer if you prefer the duck well done.

Add the shallots to the pan and turn to coat in the duck fat. Fry gently for 7–8 minutes until golden and tender. Remove with a slotted spoon and keep warm. Pour the orange juice into the pan and bring to the boil. Whisk in the sugar, oil and vinegar and simmer for 2–3 minutes until just syrupy. Season to taste with salt and pepper.

Arrange the spinach, chard leaves and orange slices on 4 serving plates. Slice each duck fillet and place on top of the salad with the shallots. Spoon over the warm dressing and serve immediately.

SERVES 4

2 large oranges

4 duck breast fillets, about 175 g/6 oz each

12 small shallots, halved

1 tbsp sugar

2 tbsp olive oil

1 tbsp red wine vinegar

55 g/2 oz baby spinach leaves

55 g/2 oz baby red chard leaves

salt and pepper

DUCKLING & RADISH SALAD

Put each duckling breast between sheets of greaseproof paper or clingfilm. Use a meat mallet or rolling pin to beat them out and flatten them slightly.

Sprinkle the flour onto a large plate and season with salt and pepper. Beat the egg and water together in a shallow bowl, then sprinkle the sesame seeds on to a separate plate.

Dip the duckling breasts first into the seasoned flour, then into the egg mixture and finally into the sesame seeds, to coat the duckling evenly. Heat the sesame oil in a preheated wok or large frying pan.

Fry the duckling breasts over a medium heat for about 8 minutes, turning once. To test whether they are cooked, insert a sharp knife into the thickest part – the juices should run clear. Lift them out and drain on kitchen paper.

To make the dressing for the salad, whisk together the lime rind and juice, olive oil, soy sauce and chopped basil. Season with a little salt and pepper.

Arrange the Chinese leaves, celery and radishes on a serving plate. Slice the duckling breasts thinly and place on top of the salad.

Drizzle with the dressing and garnish with fresh basil leaves. Serve immediately.

SERVES 4

350 g/12 oz boneless duckling breasts

2 tbsp plain flour

1 egg

2 tbsp water

2 tbsp sesame seeds

3 tbsp sesame oil

½ head Chinese leaves, shredded

3 celery sticks, sliced finely

8 radishes, trimmed and halved

fresh basil leaves, to garnish

salt and pepper

dressing

finely grated rind of 1 lime

2 tbsp lime juice

2 tbsp olive oil

1 tbsp light soy sauce

1 tbsp chopped fresh basil

DUCK SALAD WITH SWEET CHILLI DRESSING

SERVES 4

2 duck leg portions, about
175 g/6 oz each

300 ml/½ pt boiling water

1 tsp Chinese five-spice powder

175 g/6 oz mangetout

1 small iceberg lettuce, finely
shredded

2 celery sticks, very thinly sliced

6 spring onions, finely shredded

dressing

1 tbsp sunflower oil

3 tbsp sweet chilli sauce

1 tbsp rice vinegar

salt and pepper

Preheat the oven to 200°C/400°F/Gas Mark 6. Place the duck
legs in a roasting tin and pour the boiling water over the skin.
Drain off the water and pat the skins dry with kitchen paper.

Rub the Chinese five-spice powder into the duck skin. Roast the
duck legs in the preheated oven for 1¼ – 1½ hours until cooked
through with golden crispy skin. Cool for 10 minutes.

To make the dressing, place all the ingredients in a small bowl
and whisk together.

Bring a small saucepan of water to the boil and add the
mangetout. Cook for 2 minutes then drain and refresh under cold
running water. Thinly slice the mangetout lengthways and place
in a bowl with the lettuce, celery and nearly all the spring onions.
Toss well to mix.

Peel off the crispy skin from the roast duck and cut into
thin strips. Using 2 forks pull and shred all the duck flesh from
the bones.

Arrange the salad on a platter and top with the shredded duck
and crispy skin. Drizzle over the dressing and garnish with the
rest of the spring onions. Serve immediately.

DUCK & NOODLE SALAD WITH PEANUT SAUCE

Preheat the grill to high. Cut the carrots, celery and cucumber into thin strips and set aside.

Grill the duck breasts for about 5 minutes on each side until cooked through. Leave to cool.

Meanwhile, heat all the ingredients for the peanut sauce in a small saucepan until combined and the sugar has dissolved completely. Stir until smooth.

Slice the duck breasts. Divide the noodles among 3 serving bowls. Place the reserved carrots, celery and cucumber on top of the noodles, arrange the duck slices on top and drizzle with the sauce. Serve immediately.

SERVES 3

2 carrots, peeled

2 celery sticks

1 cucumber

three 140-g/5-oz duck breasts

350 g/12 oz rice noodles, cooked according to the instructions on the packet, rinsed and drained

peanut sauce

2 garlic cloves, crushed

2 tbsp dark brown sugar

2 tbsp peanut butter

2 tbsp coconut cream

2 tbsp soy sauce

2 tbsp rice vinegar

2 tbsp sesame oil

½ tsp pepper

½ tsp Chinese five-spice powder

½ tsp ground ginger

FISH & SEAFOOD

SALAD NIÇOISE

Heat a ridged cast-iron griddle pan over a high heat until you can feel the heat rising from the surface. Brush the tuna steaks with oil, place oiled side down on the hot pan, and chargrill for 2 minutes. Lightly brush the top side of the tuna steaks with more oil. Use a pair of tongs to turn the tuna steaks over, then season to taste with salt and pepper. Continue chargrilling for a further 2 minutes for rare or up to 4 minutes for well done. Leave to cool.

Meanwhile, bring a saucepan of salted water to the boil. Add the beans to the pan and return to the boil, then boil for 3 minutes, or until tender-crisp. Drain the beans and immediately transfer them to a large bowl. Pour over the vinaigrette and stir together, then leave the beans to cool in the dressing.

Bring a saucepan of water to the boil, add the beans and cook for 5 minutes, or until just tender. Remove with a slotted spoon and refresh the beans under cold running water. Drain and put into a large bowl. Arrange the hard-boiled eggs and tomatoes around the side. Place the anchovy fillets over the salad, then scatter with the olives. Pour over the vinaigrette and stir together.

SERVES 4

2 fresh tuna steaks, about 2 cm/ ³⁄₄ inch thick

olive oil, for brushing

250 g/9 oz French beans, topped and tailed

125 ml/4 fl oz vinaigrette or garlic vinaigrette dressing

2 hearts of lettuce, leaves separated

3 large hard-boiled eggs, quartered

2 juicy vine-ripened tomatoes, cut into wedges

50 g/1³⁄₄ oz anchovy fillets in oil, drained

55 g/2 oz Niçoise olives, stoned

salt and pepper

CARAMELIZED TUNA SALAD

To make the dressing, heat a small wok over high heat. Add the oil and fry the ginger and chilli for a few seconds. Add the soy sauce, Thai fish sauce and tamarind paste. Stir for 30 seconds, then add the sugar and stir until dissolved. Remove the wok from the heat and set aside.

Rinse the beansprouts in boiling water and drain. Blot dry with kitchen paper. Peel the cucumber, halve lengthways and scoop out the seeds. Thinly slice the flesh diagonally.

Put the beansprouts, cucumber, coriander and mint leaves in a bowl. Season with a pinch of salt and a few drops of toasted sesame oil. Toss to combine, then divide between individual serving plates.

Heat a wok over a high heat, then add the groundnut and sesame oils. Quickly stir-fry the tuna, turning with tongs, until coloured on the outside but still slightly red in the middle. Arrange the tuna chunks on top of the salad.

Reheat the dressing, thinning with a spoonful of water if necessary, and pour over the tuna. Sprinkle with the crushed peanuts and serve immediately.

SERVES 4

175 g/6 oz beansprouts

10-cm/4-inch piece of cucumber

20 g/¾ oz coriander leaves

20 g/¾ oz mint leaves

1 tsp sesame oil, plus a few drops for drizzling

1 tbsp groundnut oil

450 g/1 lb fresh tuna, cut into 2.5-cm/1-inch chunks

salt

salted roasted peanuts, crushed, to garnish

dressing

2 tsp rapeseed oil

1 tsp finely chopped fresh ginger

½–1 small red chilli, deseeded and finely chopped

4 tbsp light soy sauce

1 tbsp Thai fish sauce

1 tbsp tamarind paste

6 tbsp soft brown sugar

TUNA, LENTIL & POTATO SALAD

SERVES 4

200 g/7 oz Puy or brown lentils

2 tbsp olive oil, plus extra for brushing

300 g/10½ oz baby new potatoes

1 Little Gem lettuce

4 fresh tuna steaks, about 100 g/3½ oz each

12 small cherry tomatoes, halved

40 g/1½ oz rocket leaves

salt and pepper

dressing

5 tbsp fruity olive oil

1 tbsp balsamic vinegar

2 tsp red wine vinegar

1 tsp smooth Dijon mustard

1 tsp soft light brown sugar

Cook the lentils in a saucepan of boiling water for 25 minutes, or until tender. Drain, tip into a bowl and stir in the oil.

Meanwhile, place the potatoes in a saucepan and cover with cold water. Bring to the boil, cover and simmer for 15 minutes, or until tender when pierced with a fork.

Break off the outer lettuce leaves and cut the heart into 8 evenly sized pieces. Arrange on 4 individual serving plates.

To make the dressing, put all the ingredients into a small screw-top jar and shake until well blended.

When the potatoes are nearly cooked, lightly brush a ridged griddle pan with oil and heat over a high heat. When very hot, add the tuna steaks and cook for 1½ minutes on each side to sear. Remove to a chopping board and cut each steak into 6 chunks.

Drain the potatoes and roughly chop any larger ones. Arrange with the lentils, tuna and tomatoes on the serving plates, sprinkle over the rocket leaves and spoon over the dressing. Serve immediately.

TUNA & TWO-BEAN SALAD

To make the dressing, put all the ingredients into a small screw-top jar and shake until well blended.

Bring a saucepan of lightly salted water to the boil. Add the French beans and cook for 3 minutes. Add the white beans and cook for a further 4 minutes until the French beans are tender-crisp and the white beans are heated through. Drain well and add to the bowl with the dressing and spring onions. Toss together.

To cook the tuna, heat a ridged griddle pan over a high heat. Lightly brush the tuna steaks with oil, then season to taste with salt and pepper. Cook the steaks for 2 minutes, then turn over and cook on the other side for a further 2 minutes for rare or up to 4 minutes for well done.

Remove the tuna from the griddle pan and leave to rest for 2 minutes, or alternatively leave until completely cool. When ready to serve, add the tomatoes to the bean mixture and toss lightly. Line a serving platter with lettuce leaves and pile on the bean salad. Place the tuna over the top. Serve warm or at room temperature, garnished with the herbs.

SERVES 4

200 g/7 oz French beans

400 g/14 oz canned small white beans, such as haricot, rinsed and drained

4 spring onions, finely chopped

2 fresh tuna steaks, about 225 g/ 8 oz each and 2 cm/¾ inch thick

olive oil, for brushing

250 g/9 oz cherry tomatoes, halved

handful lettuce leaves

salt and pepper

fresh mint and flat-leaf parsley sprigs, to garnish

dressing

handful of fresh mint leaves, shredded

handful of fresh flat-leaf parsley leaves, chopped

1 garlic clove, crushed

4 tbsp extra virgin olive oil

1 tbsp red wine vinegar

salt and pepper

TUNA & HERBED PASTA SALAD

Bring a large saucepan of lightly salted water to the boil. Add the pasta and return to the boil. Cook for 10–12 minutes until just tender. Meanwhile, preheat the grill to high.

Put the pepper quarters under the grill and cook for 10–12 minutes until the skins begin to blacken. Transfer to a plastic bag, seal and set aside.

Bring a separate pan of water to the boil, add the asparagus, and blanch for 4 minutes.

Drain and plunge into cold water, then drain again. Remove the pasta from the heat, drain, and set aside to cool. Remove the pepper quarters from the bag and peel off the skins.

Slice the pepper into strips. To make the dressing, put all the dressing ingredients in a large bowl and stir together well. Add the pasta, pepper strips, asparagus, onion, tomatoes and tuna.

Toss together gently, then divide among serving bowls. Garnish with basil sprigs and serve.

SERVES 4

200 g/7 oz dried fusilli pasta

1 red pepper, deseeded and cut into quarters

150 g/5½ oz asparagus spears

1 red onion, sliced

4 tomatoes, sliced

200 g/7 oz canned tuna in brine, drained and flaked

dressing

6 tbsp basil-flavoured oil or extra virgin olive oil

3 tbsp white wine vinegar

1 tbsp lime juice

1 tsp mustard

1 tsp honey

4 tbsp chopped fresh basil, plus extra sprigs to garnish

TOMATO, SALMON & PRAWN SALAD

SERVES 4

115 g/4 oz cherry or baby plum
   tomatoes

handful lettuce leaves

4 ripe tomatoes, roughly chopped

100 g/3½ oz smoked salmon

200 g/7 oz large cooked prawns,
   thawed if frozen

pepper

dressing

1 tbsp Dijon mustard

2 tsp caster sugar

2 tsp red wine vinegar

2 tbsp medium olive oil

few fresh dill sprigs, plus extra
   to garnish

Halve most of the cherry tomatoes. Place the lettuce leaves around the edge of a bowl and add all the tomatoes and cherry tomatoes. Using scissors, snip the smoked salmon into strips and scatter over the tomatoes, then add the prawns.

To make the dressing, mix the mustard, sugar, vinegar and oil together in a small bowl, then tear most of the dill sprigs into it. Mix well and pour over the salad. Toss well to coat the salad with the dressing. Snip the remaining dill over the top and season to taste with pepper.

SMOKED SALMON & ROCKET SALAD

Shred the rocket and arrange in 4 individual bowls. Scatter over the chopped parsley and spring onions.

Halve, peel and stone the avocados and cut into thin slices or small chunks. Brush with the lemon juice to prevent discoloration, then divide between the salad bowls. Mix together gently. Cut the smoked salmon into strips and scatter over the top.

To make the dressing, put the mayonnaise in a bowl, then add the lime juice, lime rind and chopped parsley. Mix together well. Spoon some of the dressing on top of each salad and garnish with parsley sprigs.

SERVES 4

50 g/1¾ oz rocket leaves

1 tbsp chopped fresh flat-leaf parsley

2 spring onions, finely diced

2 large avocados

1 tbsp lemon juice

250 g/9 oz smoked salmon

dressing

150 ml/5 fl oz mayonnaise

2 tbsp lime juice

finely grated rind of 1 lime

1 tbsp chopped fresh flat-leaf parsley, plus extra sprigs to garnish

TERIYAKI
SALMON SALAD

Place half the shredded spring onions in a small bowl of cold water with a couple of ice cubes. Leave in the refrigerator for at least 1 hour until the spring onions are curly.

Put the salmon fillets in a shallow dish and pour over the teriyaki sauce. Cover and leave to marinate at room temperature for 30 minutes.

Cook the noodles in a saucepan of boiling water for 4 minutes, or according to the instructions on the packet, until soft. Drain well and refresh under cold running water. Transfer to a bowl.

Heat the oil in a wok and add the ginger, pepper, carrot and remaining spring onions. Stir-fry for 1 minute. Add the sesame seeds and stir-fry for a further minute. Cool for 10 minutes then add to the noodles with the vinegar and toss well to mix. Season with salt and pepper.

Heat a non-stick frying pan and add the salmon fillets, skin side down. Cook for 1 minute on each side until browned. Pour in the teriyaki marinade. Reduce the heat and cook for a further 3–4 minutes on each side until just cooked through.

Divide the noodle salad between 4 serving plates and top each with a salmon fillet. Drain the spring onion curls and pat dry on kitchen paper. Arrange on top of the salmon fillets and serve with lime wedges.

SERVES 4

6 spring onions, finely shredded

4 salmon fillets (with skin), about 115 g/4 oz each

4 tbsp teriyaki sauce

225 g/8 oz thread egg noodles

2 tsp toasted sesame oil

1 tsp grated fresh ginger

1 green pepper, finely shredded

2 carrots, finely shredded

2 tbsp sesame seeds

2 tbsp rice vinegar

salt and pepper

lime wedges, to serve

WARM SALMON & MANGO SALAD

SERVES 4

115 g/4 oz yellow or red cherry tomatoes

85 g/3 oz salmon fillets, skinned and cut into small cubes

1 large ripe mango (about 150 g/ 5½ oz peeled fruit), peeled and cut into small chunks

2 tbsp orange juice

1 tbsp soy sauce

115 g/4 oz mixed salad leaves

½ cucumber, trimmed and sliced into batons

6 spring onions, trimmed and chopped

dressing

4 tbsp low fat natural yogurt

1 tsp soy sauce

1 tbsp finely grated orange rind

Cut half the tomatoes in half and set aside.

Thread the salmon with the whole tomatoes and half the mango chunks onto 4 kebab sticks. Mix the orange juice and soy sauce together in a small bowl and brush over the kebabs. Leave to marinate for 15 minutes, brushing with the remaining orange juice mixture at least once more.

Arrange the salad leaves on a serving platter with the reserved halved tomatoes, mango chunks, the cucumber batons and the spring onions.

Preheat the grill to high and line the grill rack with foil. To make the dressing, mix the yogurt, soy sauce and grated orange rind together in a small bowl and reserve.

Place the salmon kebabs on the grill rack, brush again with the marinade and grill for 5–7 minutes, or until the salmon is cooked. Turn the kebabs over halfway through cooking and brush with any remaining marinade.

Divide the prepared salad between 4 plates, top each with a kebab, and then drizzle with the dressing.

SMOKED TROUT, CHICORY & PEAR SALAD

Toss the sliced pears in the lemon juice to prevent discoloration. Place in a serving dish with the chicory leaves and watercress.

Flake the smoked trout, removing any skin and fine bones. Scatter over the salad with the grapes.

To make the dressing, place the crème fraîche, milk, horseradish and lemon juice in a small bowl and whisk until smooth. Season to taste with salt and pepper. Drizzle the dressing over the salad just before serving. Season with a little more pepper.

138

SERVES 4

2 ripe red William pears, cored and sliced

1 tbsp lemon juice

3 heads chicory, trimmed and leaves separated

55 g/2 oz watercress, tough stalks removed

225 g/8 oz smoked trout fillets

85 g/3 oz seedless green grapes, halved

dressing

4 tbsp crème fraîche

1 tbsp milk

1 tsp creamed horseradish

2 tsp lemon juice

salt and pepper

CAESAR
SALAD

Bring a small, heavy-based saucepan of water to the boil.

Meanwhile, make the garlic croûtons. Heat the olive oil in a heavy-based frying pan. Add the garlic and diced bread and cook, stirring and tossing frequently, for 4–5 minutes, or until the bread is crispy and golden all over. Remove from the frying pan with a slotted spoon and drain on kitchen paper.

While the bread is frying, add the egg to the boiling water and cook for 1 minute, then remove from the saucepan and reserve.

Arrange the lettuce leaves in a salad bowl. Mix the olive oil and lemon juice together, then season to taste with salt and pepper. Crack the egg into the dressing and whisk to blend. Pour the dressing over the lettuce leaves, toss well, then add the croûtons and chopped anchovies and toss the salad again. Sprinkle with Parmesan cheese shavings and serve.

SERVES 4

4 tbsp olive oil

2 garlic cloves

5 slices white bread, crusts removed, cut into 1-cm/½-inch cubes

1 egg

2 cos lettuces or 3 Little Gem lettuces

6 tbsp olive oil

2 tbsp lemon juice

8 canned anchovy fillets, drained and roughly chopped

salt and pepper

fresh Parmesan cheese shavings, to serve

ANCHOVY & OLIVE SALAD

SERVES 4

125 g /4½ oz mixed lettuce leaves

12 cherry tomatoes, halved

20 black olives, stoned and halved

6 canned anchovy fillets, drained and thinly sliced

1 tbsp chopped fresh oregano

lemon wedges, to garnish

fresh crusty bread rolls, to serve

dressing

4 tbsp extra virgin olive oil

1 tbsp white wine vinegar

1 tbsp lemon juice

1 tbsp chopped fresh flat-leaf parsley

salt and pepper

To make the dressing, put all the ingredients into a small bowl and stir together well.

To assemble the salad, arrange the lettuce leaves in a serving dish. Scatter the cherry tomatoes on top, followed by the olives, anchovies and oregano. Drizzle the dressing over the top.

Transfer to individual plates, garnish with lemon wedges and serve with crusty bread rolls.

FISH & SEAFOOD

143

WARM MACKEREL & POTATO SALAD

Make 3–4 diagonal slashes in the skin of each mackerel fillet. Mix together the coarsely ground pepper, lemon rind and juice and oil and pour over the fillets. Cover and leave to marinate at room temperature for 20 minutes. Preheat the grill to high.

Cook the mackerel fillets under the grill for 7–8 minutes, turning once, until just cooked through. Meanwhile, place the potatoes in a saucepan and cover with cold water. Bring to the boil, cover and simmer for 12–15 minutes, or until tender when pierced with a fork.

To make the dressing, whisk the olive oil, vinegar, mustard and sugar together in a bowl until well blended. Stir in the dill and season to taste with salt and pepper.

Drain the potatoes and mix gently with the spring onions and half the dressing. Arrange on 4 serving plates and scatter over the rocket leaves. Top each salad with a hot mackerel fillet and drizzle over the rest of the dressing. Garnish with fresh dill sprigs and serve.

SERVES 4

4 mackerel fillets, about 140 g/ 5 oz each

1 tsp coarsely ground black pepper

1 small lemon, finely pared rind and juice

1 tbsp virgin olive oil

450 g/1 lb new potatoes, sliced

4 spring onions, thinly sliced

25 g/1 oz rocket leaves

fresh dill sprigs, to garnish

dressing

5 tbsp virgin olive oil

2 tbsp white wine vinegar

1 tsp Dijon mustard

pinch of sugar

1 tbsp chopped fresh dill

salt and pepper

SEARED SWORDFISH WITH SALSA

To make the tomato and olive salsa, whisk the olive oil and vinegar together in a bowl large enough to hold all the ingredients. Gently stir in the tomatoes, olives, shallot and capers with salt and pepper to taste. Cover and chill until required.

Season the swordfish steaks on both sides with salt. Melt the butter with the oil in a frying pan large enough to hold the swordfish steaks in a single layer. (If you don't have a large enough pan, cook the steaks in 2 batches.)

Add the swordfish steaks to the pan in a single layer and fry for 5 minutes, or until golden brown, then carefully turn the fish over and continue frying about 3 minutes longer until the fish is cooked through and flakes easily. Remove the fish from the pan and set aside to cool completely. Cover and chill for at least 2 hours.

When ready to serve, remove the fish from the fridge at least 15 minutes in advance. Stir the basil into the salsa, then adjust the seasoning if necessary. Break the swordfish into large flakes and gently stir into the salsa – take care not to break up the fish too much. Arrange the fish salad in 4 bowls, spooning over any of the leftover juices and serve with slices of crusty bread.

SERVES 4

4 boneless swordfish steaks, about 140 g/5 oz each

knob of butter

1 tbsp olive oil

fresh crusty bread, to serve

tomato & olive salsa

4 tbsp extra virgin olive oil

1 tbsp red wine vinegar

600 g/1 lb 5 oz ripe, juicy beef tomatoes, cored, deseeded and finely chopped

140 g/5 oz large black olives, stoned and cut in half

1 shallot, finely chopped or thinly sliced

1 tbsp capers in brine, rinsed and dried

3 tbsp finely shredded fresh basil leaves

salt and pepper

SWEET & SOUR FISH SALAD

SERVES 4

225 g/8 oz trout fillets

225 g/8 oz white fish fillets
(such as haddock or cod)

300 ml/½ pint water

1 stalk lemon grass

2 lime leaves

1 large red chilli

1 bunch spring onions, trimmed
and shredded

115 g/4 oz fresh pineapple flesh,
diced

1 small red pepper, deseeded and
diced

1 bunch watercress, washed and
trimmed

fresh snipped chives, to garnish

dressing

1 tbsp sunflower oil

1 tbsp rice wine vinegar

pinch of chilli powder

1 tsp clear honey

salt and pepper

Rinse the fish, place in a frying pan and pour over the water.
Bend the lemon grass in half to bruise it and add to the pan with
the lime leaves. Prick the chilli with a fork and add to the pan.
Bring to the boil and simmer for 7–8 minutes. Let cool.

Drain the fish fillet thoroughly, flake the flesh away from
the skin and place in a bowl. Gently stir in the spring onions,
pineapple and pepper.

Arrange the washed watercress on 4 serving plates and spoon
the cooked fish mixture on top.

To make the dressing, put all the ingredients into a small
bowl and mix well. Spoon over the fish and serve garnished
with chives.

SPICED FISH SKEWERS & TOMATO SALAD

Place the fish cubes in a shallow bowl. Mix together 2 tablespoons of the lime juice and 2 tablespoons of the oil with the chilli powder and oregano. Season with salt and pepper and pour over the fish. Cover and leave to marinate at room temperature for 1 hour.

Preheat the grill to medium. Thread the fish and lemon wedges onto 8 metal skewers and cook the fish skewers for 8–10 minutes, turning occasionally, until just cooked.

Meanwhile, mix together the tomatoes, onion and coriander in a bowl. Whisk the remaining lime juice and oil together with the sugar and mustard. Pour the dressing over the tomatoes and toss well to mix. Season with salt and pepper.

Divide the tomato salad between 4 serving dishes and top each with two fish skewers. Serve immediately.

SERVES 4

- 450 g/1 lb cod loin or monkfish, cut into 2.5-cm/1-inch cubes
- 3 tbsp lime juice
- 4 tbsp sunflower oil
- 2 tsp mild chilli powder
- 1 tsp dried oregano
- 1 lemon, cut into 8 wedges
- 225 g/8 oz cherry tomatoes, halved
- 225 g/8 oz yellow cherry tomatoes, halved
- ½ small onion, thinly sliced
- 2 tbsp roughly chopped fresh coriander
- ½ tsp sugar
- 1 tsp mild mustard
- salt and pepper

PRAWN & WHITE BEAN SALAD

Place the beans, onion, celery, prawns and garlic in a large shallow bowl. Add the lemon juice, 2 tablespoons of the oil and the chopped parsley. Season lightly with salt and pepper. Stir well then cover and set aside.

Brush the slices of bread with some of the remaining olive oil. Cook on a hot griddle for 2–3 minutes on each side until golden or toast under a hot grill. Place on 4 serving plates.

Gently stir the tomatoes and parsley leaves into the salad. Pile the salad onto the hot toasts. Drizzle over the rest of the olive oil, season with a little more pepper and serve.

SERVES 4

400 g/14 oz can haricot beans, drained and rinsed

½ red onion, finely chopped

1 celery stick, finely diced

300 g/10½ oz cooked, large peeled prawns with tails intact

1 garlic clove, finely chopped

juice of 1 lemon

5 tbsp extra virgin olive oil

2 tbsp chopped fresh flat-leaf parsley

4 thick slices country bread (pain de campagne)

85 g/3 oz baby plum tomatoes, halved

handful of fresh flat-leaf parsley leaves

salt and pepper

COCONUT & PRAWN SALAD

SERVES 4

200 g/7 oz brown basmati rice

½ tsp coriander seeds

2 egg whites, lightly beaten

100 g/3½ oz unsweetened desiccated coconut

24 raw tiger prawns, peeled

½ cucumber

4 spring onions, thinly sliced lengthways

1 tsp sesame oil

1 tbsp finely chopped fresh coriander

Bring a large saucepan of water to the boil, add the rice and cook for 25 minutes, or until tender. Drain and keep in a colander covered with a clean tea towel to absorb the steam.

Meanwhile, soak 8 wooden skewers in cold water for 30 minutes, then drain. Crush the coriander seeds in a mortar with a pestle. Heat a non-stick frying pan over a medium heat, add the crushed coriander seeds and cook, turning, until they begin to colour. Tip onto a plate and set aside.

Put the egg whites into a shallow bowl and the coconut into a separate bowl. Roll each prawn first in the egg whites, then in the coconut. Thread onto a skewer. Repeat so that each skewer is threaded with 3 coated prawns.

Preheat the grill to high. Using a potato peeler, peel long strips from the cucumber to create ribbons, put into a colander to drain, then toss with the spring onions and oil in a bowl and set aside.

Cook the prawns under the preheated grill for 3–4 minutes on each side, or until slightly browned.

Meanwhile, mix the rice with the toasted coriander seeds and fresh coriander and divide this and the cucumber salad between bowls. Serve with the hot prawn skewers.

LAYERED
CRAYFISH
SALAD

To make the dressing, put all the ingredients into a small bowl and mix well.

Divide the grated carrot, lettuce, corn and cucumber between four bowls.

Spoon over the dressing and pile the crayfish tails on top. Sprinkle with the cayenne pepper. Garnish with lemon wedges, if using. Serve.

SERVES 4

115 g/4 oz carrots, peeled and grated

1 Little Gem lettuce, shredded

85 g/3 oz canned sweetcorn kernels, drained

¼ cucumber, diced

175 g/6 oz cooked crayfish tails in brine, thoroughly drained

½ tsp cayenne pepper

lemon wedges, to garnish (optional)

dressing

8 tbsp mayonnaise

1 tbsp tomato ketchup

dash of Worcestershire sauce

1 tbsp lemon juice

salt and pepper

THAI CRAB PATTY SALAD

Place the crab, prawns, lime juice and curry paste in a food processor and process for a few seconds until finely minced. Add the egg white and chopped coriander and season well with salt and pepper. Process for a further few seconds until well mixed.

Transfer the mixture to a bowl and using lightly floured hands, shape into 12 small cakes. Coat lightly in the flour. Cover and chill in the refrigerator for 1 hour.

Heat the oil in a large frying pan and fry the crab cakes, in 2 batches, for 3–4 minutes until golden brown, turning once. Drain on kitchen paper.

Place the cucumber, beansprouts, salad cress and coriander stalks in a bowl and toss together with the rice vinegar. Divide between 4 serving plates. Top with the hot crabcakes and spoon over the chilli sauce. Serve garnished with coriander leaves and lime wedges.

SERVES 4

2 x 170 g/5¾ oz cans white crabmeat, drained

140 g/ 5 oz cooked peeled prawns

1 tsp lime juice

2 tsp Thai red curry paste

1 tbsp beaten egg white

1 tbsp chopped fresh coriander

flour, for dusting

sunflower oil, for shallow frying

½ cucumber, peeled, deseeded and thinly sliced

225 g/8 oz beansprouts

25 g/1 oz salad cress

2 tbsp chopped fresh coriander stalks

1 tbsp rice vinegar

4 tbsp sweet chilli sauce

salt and pepper

fresh coriander leaves and lime wedges, to garnish

LOBSTER & SUMMER HERB SALAD

SERVES 4–6

750–800 g/1 lb 10 oz–1 lb 12 oz
freshly cooked lobster meat,
cut into bite-sized chunks

1 large avocado, peeled, stoned
and cut into chunky dice

4 ripe but firm tomatoes

250 g/9 oz mixed herb salad
leaves

1–2 tbsp fruity olive oil

squeeze of lemon juice

salt and pepper

saffron mayonnaise

pinch of saffron threads

1 egg

1 tsp Dijon mustard

1 tbsp white wine vinegar

pinch of salt

300 ml/10 fl oz sunflower oil

To make the saffron mayonnaise, soak the saffron threads in a little warm water. Meanwhile, put the egg, mustard, vinegar and salt in a blender and whiz to combine. With the motor running, slowly trickle in about one third of the sunflower oil. Once the mixture starts to thicken, add the remaining oil more quickly. When all the oil has been incorporated, add the saffron and its soaking water and whiz to combine. Add more salt, and pepper, to taste, cover and refrigerate until required.

Put the lobster meat and avocado in a bowl. Quarter the tomatoes and remove the seeds. Cut the flesh into fairly chunky dice and add to the bowl. Season the lobster mixture to taste with salt and pepper and gently stir in enough of the mayonnaise to give everything a light coating.

Toss the salad leaves with the olive oil and lemon juice. Divide between four to six plates and top with the lobster mixture. Serve immediately.

SEAFOOD
SALAD

Clean the mussels by scrubbing or scraping the shells and pulling out any beards that are attached to them. Discard any with broken shells or any that refuse to close when tapped. Put the mussels in a colander and rinse well under cold running water. Put them in a large saucepan with a little water and cook, covered, over a high heat, shaking the saucepan occasionally, for 3–4 minutes, or until the mussels have opened. Discard any mussels that remain closed. Strain the mussels, reserving the cooking liquid. Refresh the mussels under cold running water, drain and set aside.

Return the reserved cooking liquid to the saucepan and bring to the boil, add the scallops and squid and cook for 3 minutes. Remove from the heat and drain. Refresh under cold running water and drain again. Remove the mussels from their shells. Put them in a bowl with the scallops and squid and leave to cool. Cover with clingfilm and chill in the refrigerator for 45 minutes.

Divide the seafood between 4 serving plates and top with the onion. To make the dressing, combine the ingredients together in a bowl until well blended. Garnish with chopped parsley and serve with lemon wedges.

SERVES 4

250 g/9 oz live mussels

350 g/12 oz live scallops, shucked and cleaned

250 g/9 oz prepared squid, cut into rings and tentacles

1 red onion, halved and finely sliced

chopped fresh flat-leaf parsley, to garnish

lemon wedges, to serve

dressing

4 tbsp extra virgin olive oil

2 tbsp white wine vinegar

1 tbsp lemon juice

1 garlic clove, finely chopped

1 tbsp chopped fresh flat-leaf parsley

salt and pepper

SEAFOOD & SPINACH SALAD

Put the mussels into a large pan with a little water, bring to the boil and cook over a high heat for 4 minutes. Drain and reserve the liquid. Discard any mussels that remain closed. Return the reserved liquid to the pan and bring to the boil. Add the prawns and scallops and cook for 3 minutes. Drain. Remove the mussels from their shells. Rinse the mussels, prawns and scallops in cold water, drain and put them in a large bowl. Cool, cover with clingfilm and chill for 45 minutes.

Meanwhile, rinse the baby spinach leaves and transfer them to a pan with the water. Cook over a high heat for 1 minute, transfer to a colander, refresh under cold running water and drain.

To make the dressing, put all the ingredients into a small bowl and mix well. Arrange the spinach on serving dishes, then scatter over half of the spring onions. Top with the mussels, prawns and scallops, then scatter over the remaining spring onions. Drizzle over the dressing and serve.

SERVES 4

500 g/1 lb 2 oz live mussels, soaked and cleaned

100 g/3½ oz prawns, peeled and deveined

350 g/12 oz scallops

500 g/1 lb 2 oz baby spinach leaves

4 tbsp water

3 spring onions, trimmed and diced

dressing

4 tbsp extra virgin olive oil

2 tbsp white wine vinegar

1 tbsp lemon juice

1 tsp finely grated lemon rind

1 garlic clove, chopped

1 tbsp grated fresh ginger

1 small red chilli, deseeded and diced

1 tbsp chopped fresh coriander

salt and pepper

NEAPOLITAN
SEAFOOD
SALAD

SERVES 4

450 g/1 lb prepared squid,
    cut into strips

750 g/1 lb 10 oz cooked mussels

450 g/1 lb cooked cockles in brine

150 ml/5 fl oz white wine

300 ml/10 fl oz olive oil

225 g/8 oz dried campanelle
    pasta

juice of 1 lemon

1 bunch chives, snipped

1 bunch fresh flat-leaf parsley,
    finely chopped

125 g/4½ oz mixed salad leaves

salt and pepper

4 large tomatoes, to garnish

Put all of the seafood into a large bowl, pour over the wine and
half of the olive oil, and set aside for 6 hours.

Put the seafood mixture into a saucepan and simmer over a low
heat for 10 minutes. Set aside to cool.

Bring a large saucepan of lightly salted water to the boil. Add
the pasta and 1 tablespoon of the remaining olive oil and cook for
10–12 minutes until just tender. Drain and refresh in cold water.

Strain off about half of the cooking liquid from the seafood and
discard the rest. Mix in the lemon juice, chives, parsley and the
remaining olive oil. Season to taste with salt and pepper. Drain
the pasta and add to the seafood.

Shred the leaves and arrange them at the base of a salad bowl.
Cut the tomatoes into quarters. Spoon the seafood salad into the
bowl, garnish with the tomatoes and serve.

VEGETARIAN

TRADITIONAL GREEK SALAD

To make the dressing, put all the ingredients into a small screw-top jar and shake until well blended. Set aside. Cut the feta cheese into cubes about 2.5 cm/1 inch square. Put the lettuce, tomatoes and cucumber in a salad bowl. Scatter over the cheese and toss together.

Just before serving, whisk the dressing, pour over the salad leaves and toss together. Scatter over the olives and chopped herbs and serve.

SERVES 4

200 g/7 oz Greek feta cheese

½ head of iceberg lettuce or
 1 lettuce such as cos or escarole,
 shredded or sliced

4 tomatoes, quartered

½ cucumber, sliced

12 Greek black olives, stoned

2 tbsp chopped fresh herbs such
 as oregano, flat-leaf parsley,
 mint or basil

dressing

6 tbsp extra virgin olive oil

2 tbsp fresh lemon juice

1 garlic clove, crushed

pinch of sugar

salt and pepper

ROASTED VEGETABLE SALAD

Preheat the oven to 200°C/400°F/Gas Mark 6. Cut all the vegetables into even-sized wedges, put into a roasting tin and scatter over the garlic.

Pour over 2 tablespoons of the olive oil and turn the vegetables in the oil until well coated. Add a little salt and pepper. Roast in the preheated oven for 40 minutes, or until tender, adding the extra olive oil if becoming too dry.

To make the dressing, put all the ingredients into a small screw-top jar and shake until well blended.

Once the vegetables are cooked, remove from the oven, arrange on a serving dish and pour over the dressing. Garnish with the basil and serve with Parmesan cheese and crusty bread.

SERVES 4

1 onion

1 aubergine, about 225 g/8 oz in weight

1 red pepper, deseeded

1 orange pepper, deseeded

1 large courgette, about 175 g/6 oz

2–4 garlic cloves

2–4 tbsp olive oil

salt and pepper

fresh basil leaves, to garnish

fresh Parmesan shavings and fresh crusty bread, to serve

dressing

1 tbsp balsamic vinegar

2 tbsp extra virgin olive oil

TUSCAN BREAD SALAD

SERVES 4

1 small stale ciabatta loaf

2–3 tbsp cold water

6 large ripe plum tomatoes

¼ cucumber, peeled and roughly chopped

1 small red onion, very thinly sliced

handful fresh basil leaves

dressing

4 tbsp extra virgin olive oil, plus extra to drizzle

1 tbsp red wine vinegar

pinch of sugar

2 tsp capers, drained and rinsed

salt and pepper

Tear the bread into bite-sized chunks and place in a large shallow dish. Sprinkle with the water. Roughly chop 3 of the tomatoes and add to the dish with the cucumber and onion. Stir to mix. Tear half the basil leaves and scatter over the top.

Halve the remaining tomatoes and squeeze each half to extract as much of the juice and seeds as possible into a small bowl. Discard any remaining skin and flesh.

To make the dressing, add the olive oil, vinegar, sugar and capers to the tomato juice and seeds and whisk together. Season with salt and pepper. Pour the tomato dressing over the bread slices and toss until coated. Chill in the refrigerator for at least 30 minutes. Serve garnished with the remaining basil leaves and drizzled with a little more olive oil.

TOMATO &
MOZZARELLA
SALAD

Using a sharp knife, cut the tomatoes into thick wedges and place in a large serving dish. Drain the mozzarella and roughly tear into pieces. Cut the avocados in half and remove the stones. Cut the flesh into slices, then arrange the mozzarella cheese and avocado with the tomatoes.

To make the dressing, mix the oil, vinegar and mustard together in a small bowl, add salt and pepper to taste, then drizzle over the salad.

Scatter the basil and olives over the top and serve immediately with fresh crusty bread.

SERVES 4

2 ripe beef tomatoes

150 g/5½ oz fresh mozzarella

2 avocados

few fresh basil leaves, torn into pieces

20 black olives

fresh crusty bread, to serve

dressing

4 tbsp olive oil

1½ tbsp white wine vinegar

1 tsp coarse-grain mustard

salt and pepper

SUN-DRIED TOMATO SALAD

To make the dressing, put the sun-dried tomatoes, basil, parsley, capers, vinegar and garlic in a food processor or blender. Measure the oil from the sun-dried tomatoes jar and make it up to 150 ml/5 fl oz with more olive oil if necessary. Add it to the food processor or blender and process until smooth. Season with pepper.

Divide the salad leaves between 4 individual serving plates. Top with the slices of mozzarella and spoon the dressing over them. Serve immediately.

178

SERVES 4

100 g/3½ oz mixed salad leaves, such as oakleaf lettuce, baby spinach and rocket

500 g/1 lb 2 oz smoked mozzarella, sliced

dressing

140 g/5 oz sun-dried tomatoes in olive oil (drained weight), reserving the oil from the bottle

15 g/½ oz fresh basil, roughly shredded

15 g/½ oz fresh flat-leaf parsley, roughly chopped

1 tbsp capers, rinsed

1 tbsp balsamic vinegar

1 garlic clove, roughly chopped

extra olive oil, if necessary

pepper

ASPARAGUS & TOMATO SALAD

SERVES 4

225 g/8 oz asparagus spears

1 lamb's lettuce, washed and torn

25 g/1 oz rocket or mizuna leaves

450 g/1 lb ripe tomatoes, sliced

12 black olives, stoned and chopped

1 tbsp toasted pine kernels

dressing

1 tsp lemon oil

1 tbsp olive oil

1 tsp wholegrain mustard

2 tbsp balsamic vinegar

salt and pepper

Steam the asparagus spears for about 8 minutes or until tender. Rinse under cold running water to prevent them cooking any further, then cut into 5-cm/2-inch pieces.

Arrange the lettuce and rocket leaves around a salad platter to form the base of the salad. Place the sliced tomatoes in a circle on top and the asparagus in the centre. Add the olives and the pine kernels.

To make the dressing, put all the ingredients into a small screw-top jar and shake until well blended. Drizzle over the salad and serve.

CAULIFLOWER, BROCCOLI & CASHEW NUT SALAD

Heat the oil in a preheated wok, add the onions and stir-fry over a medium–high heat for 3–4 minutes, until starting to brown. Add the cauliflower and broccoli and stir-fry for 1–2 minutes. Stir in the curry paste and stir-fry for 30 seconds, then add the coconut milk, soy sauce, palm sugar and salt. Bring gently to the boil, stirring occasionally, then reduce the heat and simmer gently for 3–4 minutes, until the vegetables are almost tender.

Meanwhile, heat a separate dry frying pan until hot, add the cashew nuts and cook, shaking the pan frequently, for 2–3 minutes, until lightly browned. Add to the stir-fry with the coriander, stir well and serve immediately, garnished with the torn coriander sprigs.

SERVES 4

2 tbsp groundnut or vegetable oil

2 red onions, cut into wedges

1 small head cauliflower, cut into florets

1 small head broccoli, cut into florets

2 tbsp ready-made yellow curry paste or red curry paste

400 ml/14 fl oz canned coconut milk

1 tsp soy sauce

1 tsp palm sugar

1 tsp salt

85 g/3 oz unsalted cashew nuts

handful of fresh coriander, chopped, plus extra sprigs, torn, to garnish

NEW POTATO & RADISH SALAD

Place the potatoes in a saucepan and cover with cold water. Bring to the boil, cover and simmer for 15 minutes, or until tender when pierced with a fork. Drain well and leave to cool. Transfer to a serving bowl and stir in the radishes.

To make the dressing, place the soured cream and milk in a bowl and whisk until smooth. Stir in the gherkins and dill and season with salt and pepper.

Pour the dressing over the potatoes and radishes and toss to coat. Add the red onion and rocket leaves and mix gently. Serve.

SERVES 4

500 g/1 lb 2 oz new potatoes, halved

8 radishes, thinly sliced

1 small red onion, thinly sliced

25 g/1 oz rocket leaves

dressing

150 ml carton soured cream

2 tbsp milk

3 gherkins, drained and finely chopped

2 tbsp chopped fresh dill

salt and pepper

WARM NEW POTATO & LENTIL SALAD

85 g/3 oz puy lentils

450 g/1 lb new potatoes

6 spring onions

1 tbsp olive oil

2 tbsp balsamic vinegar

salt and pepper

Bring a large pan of water to the boil. Rinse the lentils then cook for about 20 minutes or until tender. Drain, rinse and leave to one side.

Meanwhile, place the potatoes in a saucepan and cover with cold water. Bring to the boil, cover and simmer for 15 minutes, or until tender when pierced with a fork. Drain and halve.

Trim the base from the spring onions and cut in long strips.

Put the lentils, potatoes and spring onions into a serving dish and toss with the olive oil and vinegar. Season with plenty of pepper and a little salt if required.

VEGETARIAN

187

SWEET POTATO SALAD

Bring a saucepan of water to the boil over a medium heat. Add the sweet potato and cook for 10 minutes, or until tender. Drain, transfer to a bowl and reserve until required.

Cook the carrots in a separate saucepan of boiling water for 1 minute. Drain thoroughly and add to the sweet potato. Cut the tops off the tomatoes and scoop out the seeds. Chop the flesh and add to the bowl with the celery and beans. Mix well.

Line a large serving bowl with the mixed salad leaves. Spoon the sweet potato and bean mixture on top, then sprinkle with the sultanas and spring onions.

To make the dressing, put all the ingredients into a small screw-top jar and shake until well blended. Pour over the salad and serve.

SERVES 4

1 sweet potato, peeled and diced

4 baby carrots, halved

4 tomatoes

4 celery sticks, chopped

225 g/8 oz canned borlotti beans, drained and rinsed

115 g/4 oz mixed salad leaves, such as curly endive, rocket, radicchio and oakleaf lettuce

1 tbsp sultanas

4 spring onions, sliced diagonally

dressing

2 tbsp lemon juice

1 garlic clove, crushed

150 ml/5 fl oz natural yogurt

2 tbsp olive oil

salt and pepper

SWEET POTATO
& BEAN SALAD

Peel and dice the sweet potato. Bring a saucepan of water to the boil over a medium heat. Add the sweet potato and cook for 10 minutes, or until tender. Drain, transfer to a bowl and reserve until required.

Cook the carrots in a separate pan of boiling water for 1 minute. Drain thoroughly and add to the sweet potato. Cut the tops off the tomatoes and scoop out the seeds. Chop the flesh and add to the bowl with the celery and beans. Mix well.

Line a large serving bowl with the mixed salad leaves. Spoon the sweet potato and bean mixture on top, then sprinkle with the sultanas and spring onions.

To make the dressing, place all the ingredients in a screw-top jar and shake vigorously until they are well blended. Pour over the salad and serve.

SERVES 4

1 sweet potato, peeled and diced

4 baby carrots, halved

4 tomatoes

4 celery stalks, chopped

225 g/8 oz canned cranberry beans, drained and rinsed

125 g/4½ oz mixed salad leaves, such as curly endive, rocket, radicchio, and oak leaf lettuce

1 tbsp sultanas

4 spring onions, sliced diagonally

dressing

2 tbsp lemon juice

1 garlic clove, crushed

150 ml/5 fl oz natural yogurt

2 tbsp olive oil

salt and pepper

BEAN SALAD
WITH FETA

SERVES 4

350 g/12 oz French beans,
  trimmed

1 red onion, chopped

3–4 tbsp chopped fresh coriander

2 radishes, thinly sliced

75 g/2¾ oz feta cheese, crumbled

1 tsp chopped fresh oregano or
  ½ tsp dried oregano

2 tbsp red wine or fruit vinegar

5 tbsp extra virgin olive oil

3 ripe tomatoes, cut into wedges

pepper

Place the beans in a saucepan and cover with cold water. Bring to
the boil, cover and simmer for 15 minutes, or until tender when
pierced with a fork. Drain and halve.

Transfer the beans to a bowl and add the onion, coriander,
radishes and cheese.

Sprinkle the oregano over the salad, then grind pepper over to
taste. Whisk the vinegar and olive oil together and pour over the
salad. Toss gently to mix well.

Transfer to a serving platter, add the tomato wedges and serve
at once or chill until ready to serve.

VEGETARIAN

BEAN & WALNUT SALAD

Bring a large saucepan of water to the boil, add the beans and cook for 5 minutes, or until just tender. Remove with a slotted spoon and refresh the beans under cold running water. Drain and put into a mixing bowl and add the onion, garlic and cheese.

To make the dressing, put all the ingredients in a small screw-top jar and shake until well blended. Cover with clingfilm and chill for at least 30 minutes. Remove the salad from the refrigerator 10 minutes before serving. Give it a quick stir and transfer to serving dishes.

Toast the nuts in a dry frying pan over a medium heat for 2 minutes, or until they begin to brown. Sprinkle the toasted nuts over the salad and serve.

SERVES 2

450 g/1 lb French beans

1 small onion, finely chopped

1 garlic clove, chopped

4 tbsp freshly grated Parmesan cheese

2 tbsp chopped walnuts or almonds, to garnish

dressing

2 tbsp white wine vinegar

6 tbsp olive oil

2 tsp chopped fresh tarragon

salt and pepper

HERBED MIXED BEAN SALAD

To make the dressing, put all the ingredients into a small screw-top jar and shake until well blended. Set aside.

Prepare a bowl of iced water. Bring a saucepan of lightly salted water to the boil. Add the French beans and the broad beans and blanch for 3 minutes, or until just tender. Use a slotted spoon to remove the beans from the water and immediately transfer them to the iced water.

Return the water to the boil and blanch the peas for 3 minutes, or until tender. Remove from the water and add to the iced water to cool.

Drain the beans and peas and pat dry with kitchen paper. Transfer to a large bowl, add the dressing, haricot beans, onion and herbs and toss. Cover and chill.

To make the fried halloumi cheese, just before you are ready to serve, heat a thin layer of oil in a large frying pan over a medium–high heat. Lightly dust each slice of cheese with flour, shaking off the excess. Place as many pieces as will fit in the pan and fry for 30–60 seconds until golden brown. Flip the cheese over and continue frying until lightly browned on the other side, then remove from the pan and keep warm while you fry the remaining pieces.

Toss the salad again, add the rocket and then add extra seasoning, if necessary. Divide the salad between individual plates and arrange the hot cheese alongside. Drizzle the cheese with olive oil, grind over some pepper and serve.

SERVES 4–6

115 g/4 oz French beans, topped and tailed and cut into bite-sized pieces

115 g/4 oz shelled broad beans, grey outer skins removed if not young

115 g/4 oz fresh or frozen shelled peas

400 g/14 oz canned haricot beans, drained and rinsed

1 small red onion, thinly sliced

2 tbsp chopped fresh parsley

1 tbsp snipped fresh chives

85 g/3 oz rocket or watercress leaves

salt and pepper

dressing
5 tbsp extra virgin olive oil

2 tbsp tarragon vinegar

½ tsp mixed grain mustard

pinch of sugar

fried halloumi cheese
olive oil, to drizzle

350 g/12 oz halloumi cheese, drained, patted dry and cut into 12 slices

PASTA SALAD
WITH PEPPERS

SERVES 4

1 red pepper

1 orange pepper

280 g/10 oz dried conchiglie pasta

5 tbsp extra virgin olive oil

2 tbsp lemon juice

2 tbsp bottled pesto sauce

1 garlic clove, finely chopped

3 tbsp shredded fresh basil leaves

salt and pepper

Preheat the grill to high. Put the whole peppers on a baking sheet and place under the hot grill, turning frequently, for 15 minutes, or until charred all over. Remove with tongs and place in a bowl. Cover with crumpled kitchen paper and reserve.

Bring a large saucepan of lightly salted water to the boil. Add the pasta and return to the boil. Cook for 10–12 minutes until just tender.

Combine the olive oil, lemon juice, pesto sauce and garlic in a bowl, whisking well to mix. Drain the pasta, add it to the pesto mixture while still hot and toss well. Reserve until required.

When the peppers are cool enough to handle, peel off the skins, then cut open and remove the seeds. Chop the flesh roughly and add to the pasta with the basil. Season to taste with salt and pepper and toss well. Serve.

VEGETARIAN

199

MARINATED
PEPPER SALAD

Preheat the oven to 190°C/375°F/Gas Mark 5. Halve the peppers, keeping the stalks on. Remove the white seeds and pith. Place the peppers, cut side up, in a shallow roasting tin. Scatter over the onion and garlic, season with salt and pepper and drizzle over half the olive oil. Roast for 40 minutes until the peppers are tender. Leave to cool.

Arrange the cold peppers on a serving plate and pour over any juices left in the roasting tin. Scatter over the olives, mozzarella pearls and basil.

Whisk together the remaining olive oil with the balsamic vinegar and pour over the peppers. Cover and leave to marinate in the refrigerator for at least 2 hours (or overnight) before serving.

SERVES 4

2 red peppers

2 yellow peppers

1 red onion, roughly chopped

2 garlic cloves, chopped

6 tbsp olive oil

115 g/4 oz marinated black olives, drained

100 g/3½ oz mini mozzarella pearls, drained

2 tbsp roughly torn fresh basil leaves

2 tbsp balsamic vinegar

salt and pepper

WILD RICE
SALAD

Put the wild rice and water into a large pan and bring to the boil. Stir, cover and simmer for about 40 minutes or until the rice is al dente (firm to the bite). Uncover the rice for the last few minutes of cooking to allow any excess water to evaporate.

To make the dressing, put all the ingredients into a small screw-top jar and shake until well blended. Add extra vinegar, oil or seasoning as required.

Drain the rice and turn into a large bowl. Pour over the dressing and mix in. Then mix in the chopped peppers, cucumber, orange, tomatoes, red onion and parsley. Serve.

SERVES 4

225 g/8 oz wild rice

850 ml/1½ pints water

1 each red, yellow and orange peppers, skinned, deseeded and thinly sliced

½ cucumber, halved lengthways and sliced

1 orange, peeled, pith removed and cubed

3 ripe tomatoes, cut into chunks

1 red onion, finely chopped

generous handful of chopped flat-leaf parsley

dressing

1 clove garlic, crushed

1 tbsp balsamic vinegar

2 tbsp extra virgin olive oil

salt and pepper

SPICED ORANGE & CARROT SALAD

SERVES 4

500 g/1lb 2 oz carrots, roughly grated

4 spring onions, finely shredded

2 oranges

55 g/2 oz raisins

3 tbsp chopped fresh coriander

fresh coriander sprigs, to garnish (optional)

dressing

3 tbsp olive oil

3 tbsp orange juice

2 tsp lemon juice

½ tsp ground cumin

½ tsp ground coriander

salt and pepper

Place the carrot and spring onions in a large bowl and toss gently to mix. Using a serrated knife remove all the peel and pith from the oranges then cut into segments between the membranes. Gently toss the orange segments into the bowl with the raisins and chopped coriander.

To make the dressing, place the olive oil, orange and lemon juice, ground cumin and coriander in a bowl and whisk together. Season to taste with salt and pepper.

Pour the dressing over the carrot salad and toss thoroughly. Cover with clingfilm and chill in the refrigerator for 30 minutes. Adjust the seasoning to taste. Serve garnished with coriander sprigs, if using.

WARM RED LENTIL SALAD

Heat half the olive oil in a large saucepan over a medium heat, add the cumin seeds, garlic and ginger and cook for 2 minutes, stirring constantly.

Stir in the lentils, then add the stock, a ladleful at a time, until it is all absorbed, stirring constantly – this will take about 20 minutes. Remove from the heat and stir in the herbs.

Meanwhile, heat the remaining olive oil in a frying pan over a medium heat, add the onions and cook, stirring frequently, for 10 minutes, or until soft and lightly browned.

Toss the spinach in the hazelnut oil in a bowl, then divide between 4 serving plates.

Mash the goat's cheese with the yogurt in a small bowl and season to taste with pepper.

Divide the lentils between the serving plates and top with the onions and goat's cheese mixture.

SERVES 4

2 tbsp olive oil

2 tsp cumin seeds

2 garlic cloves, crushed

2 tsp fresh ginger, grated

300 g/10½ oz split red lentils

700 ml/1¼ pints vegetable stock

2 tbsp chopped fresh mint

2 tbsp chopped fresh coriander

2 red onions, thinly sliced

200 g/7 oz baby spinach leaves

1 tsp hazelnut oil

150 g/5½ oz soft goat's cheese

4 tbsp Greek yogurt

pepper

GOAT'S CHEESE CROÛTON & SPINACH SALAD

To make the dressing, put all the ingredients into a small screw-top jar and shake until well blended.

Preheat the grill to medium. Lightly brush the slices of French bread with olive oil. Toast the rounds for 1–2 minutes on each side until just golden. Top each with a slice of goat's cheese, season with pepper and grill for a further 1–2 minutes until the cheese has melted.

Meanwhile, place the spinach in a large bowl. Add nearly all the dressing and toss gently to coat the leaves. Divide between 2 serving plates. Add the sun blush tomatoes and top with the cheese croûtons. Drizzle over the rest of the dressing and serve immediately.

SERVES 2

6 thin slices French bread

1 tbsp olive oil

115 g/4 oz round goat's cheese (with rind)

85 g/3 oz baby spinach leaves

55 g/2 oz sun blush tomatoes, drained

dressing

3 tbsp extra virgin olive oil

1 tbsp sherry vinegar

1 tsp wholegrain mustard

pinch of sugar

salt and pepper

CHILLI-SPICED PANEER SALAD

SERVES 2

6 tbsp sunflower oil

225 g/8 oz paneer, cubed

1 tsp mustard seeds

1 tsp ground cumin

1 garlic clove, crushed

1 small green chilli pepper, deseeded and finely chopped

4 spring onions, finely chopped

85 g/3 oz baby salad leaves

tomato chutney

2 ripe tomatoes, skinned, deseeded and diced

1 shallot, finely chopped

2 tbsp sunflower oil

2 tsp lemon juice

1 tbsp chopped fresh coriander

salt and pepper

To make the tomato chutney, place all the ingredients in a small bowl and mix together well. Chill in the refrigerator for 30 minutes.

Heat the oil in a large frying pan. Add the paneer cubes and fry over a medium–high heat for 4–5 minutes, turning frequently, until golden brown all over (take care as the oil may spit). Remove the paneer with a slotted spoon and drain on kitchen paper.

Carefully pour off half the hot oil from the pan. Add the mustard seeds and ground cumin to the remaining oil and fry for a few seconds. Stir in the garlic, chilli pepper and spring onions and fry for 1–2 minutes. Return the paneer to the pan and toss to coat well in the spicy mixture.

Divide the salad leaves between 2 serving plates. Top with the hot paneer. Spoon over the tomato chutney and serve immediately.

BUCKWHEAT
NOODLE SALAD

Cook the noodles in a saucepan of boiling water for 4 minutes, or according to the instructions on the packet, until soft.

To make the dressing, blend the ginger, garlic, silken tofu, tamari, oil and water together in a small bowl until smooth and creamy. Season to taste with salt.

Place the smoked tofu in a steamer. Steam for 5 minutes, then cut into thin slices.

Meanwhile, put the cabbage, carrots, spring onions and chilli into a bowl and toss to mix. To serve, arrange the noodles on serving plates and top with the carrot salad and slices of tofu. Spoon over the dressing and sprinkle with sesame seeds.

SERVES 2

200 g/7 oz buckwheat noodles

250 g/9 oz firm smoked tofu (drained weight)

200 g/7 oz white cabbage, finely shredded

250 g/9 oz carrots, finely shredded

3 spring onions, diagonally sliced

1 fresh red chilli, deseeded and finely sliced into rounds

2 tbsp sesame seeds, lightly toasted

dressing

1 tsp fresh ginger, grated

1 garlic clove, crushed

175 g/6 oz silken tofu (drained weight)

4 tsp tamari (wheat-free soy sauce)

2 tbsp sesame oil

4 tbsp hot water

salt

RED CABBAGE
& BEETROOT
SLAW

Place the cabbage, beetroot and apple slices in a large bowl. Add the lemon juice and mix well.

To make the dressing, place the mayonnaise, yogurt and red wine vinegar in a bowl and mix together until smooth. Pour over the salad and stir well. Season with salt and pepper and cover and chill in the refrigerator for at least 1 hour.

Stir the salad thoroughly and adjust the seasoning to taste. Sprinkle with the sunflower and pumpkin seeds just before serving.

SERVES 4

350 g/12 oz red cabbage, finely shredded

175 g/6 oz cooked beetroot, sliced into thin matchsticks

1 apple, cored and thinly sliced

1 tbsp lemon juice

1 tbsp sunflower seeds

1 tbsp pumpkin seeds

salt and pepper

dressing

3 tbsp mayonnaise

2 tbsp Greek yogurt

1 tbsp red wine vinegar

HEALTH-BOOSTING

GREEK FETA
SALAD

To make the dressing, put all the ingredients into a small screw-top jar and shake until well blended.

Arrange the vine leaves on a serving dish and then the tomatoes, cucumber and onion. Scatter the cheese and olives on top. Pour the dressing over the salad, season and serve.

SERVES 4

handful vine leaves
4 tomatoes, sliced
½ cucumber, peeled and sliced
1 small red onion, sliced thinly
115 g/4 oz feta cheese, cubed
8 black olives

dressing
3 tbsp extra virgin olive oil
1 tbsp lemon juice
½ tsp dried oregano
salt and pepper

SALAD WITH GARLIC DRESSING

Gently mix the cucumber batons, spring onions, tomato wedges, yellow pepper strips, celery, radishes and rocket in a large serving bowl.

To make the dressing, stir the lemon juice, garlic, natural yogurt and olive oil together in a small bowl until thoroughly combined. Season with salt and pepper to taste.

Spoon the dressing over the salad and toss to mix. Sprinkle the salad with chopped mint, if using. Serve.

SERVES 4

85 g/3 oz cucumber, cut into batons

6 spring onions, halved

2 tomatoes, deseeded and cut into 8 wedges

1 yellow pepper, deseeded and cut into strips

2 celery sticks, cut into strips

4 radishes, quartered

85 g/3 oz rocket

chopped fresh mint, to garnish (optional)

dressing

2 tbsp lemon juice

1 garlic clove, crushed

150 ml/5 fl oz natural yogurt

2 tbsp olive oil

salt and pepper

NUTTY BEETROOT SALAD

SERVES 4

3 tbsp red wine vinegar or fruit vinegar

3 cooked beetroot, grated

2 tart apples, such as Granny Smith

2 tbsp lemon juice

4 large handfuls mixed salad leaves, to serve

4 tbsp pecans, to garnish

dressing

50 ml/2 fl oz plain yogurt

50 ml/2 fl oz mayonnaise

1 garlic clove, chopped

1 tbsp chopped fresh dill

salt and pepper

Sprinkle vinegar over the beetroot, cover with clingfilm and chill for at least 4 hours.

Core and slice the apples, place the slices in a dish and sprinkle with the lemon juice to prevent discoloration.

Combine the dressing ingredients in a small bowl. Remove the beetroot from the refrigerator and dress. Add the apples to the beetroot and mix gently to coat with the salad dressing.

To serve, arrange a handful of salad leaves on each plate and top with a large spoonful of the apple and beetroot mixture.

Toast the pecans in a dry frying pan over a medium heat for 2 minutes, or until they begin to brown. Sprinkle over the beetroot and apple to garnish.

BULGAR WHEAT
SALAD

Preheat the oven to 200°C/400°F/Gas Mark 6. Place the halved tomatoes in a roasting tin, cut side up. Scatter over the garlic, sugar and sea salt and drizzle with 2 tablespoons of the olive oil. Roast in the preheated oven for 20 minutes until soft. Cool.

Place the bulgar wheat in a heatproof bowl and pour over enough boiling water to cover the grains. Cover the bowl and leave for 30 minutes until all the liquid has been absorbed. Pour over the vinegar and the rest of the olive oil and stir thoroughly with a fork. Season well with salt and pepper.

Stir the cucumber, chopped herbs, and pine kernels into the bulgar wheat. Gently stir in the roasted tomatoes and any juices from the roasting tin. Chill in the refrigerator for 30 minutes. Adjust the seasoning to taste and serve garnished with the parsley sprigs.

SERVES 4

350 g/12 oz small vine-ripened tomatoes, halved

2 garlic cloves, finely chopped

1 tsp sugar

1 tsp sea salt flakes

4 tbsp extra virgin olive oil

200 g/7 oz bulgar wheat

2 tbsp white wine vinegar

85 g/3 oz cucumber, peeled and diced

2 tbsp chopped fresh flat-leaf parsley

2 tbsp chopped fresh mint

2 tbsp pine kernels, lightly toasted

salt and pepper

fresh flat-leaf parsley sprigs, to garnish

TABBOULEH

Put the quinoa into a medium-sized saucepan and cover with the water. Bring to the boil, then reduce the heat, cover and simmer over a low heat for 15 minutes. Drain if necessary.

Leave the quinoa to cool slightly before combining with the remaining ingredients in a salad bowl. Adjust the seasoning to taste before serving.

SERVES 4

175 g/6 oz quinoa

600 ml/1 pint water

10 vine-ripened cherry tomatoes, deseeded and halved

7.5-cm/3-inch piece cucumber, diced

3 spring onions, finely chopped

juice of ½ lemon

2 tbsp extra virgin olive oil

4 tbsp chopped fresh mint

4 tbsp chopped fresh coriander

4 tbsp chopped fresh flat-leaf parsley

salt and pepper

QUINOA SALAD WITH SUN-DRIED TOMATOES

SERVES 4

235 g/8½ oz quinoa

500 ml/18 fl oz water

10 sun-dried tomatoes
(in oil, drained)

50 g/1¾ oz feta cheese, crumbled

2 spring onions, white parts,
chopped

20 g/¾ oz mixed fresh herbs
(basil, flat-leaf parsley,
coriander), chopped

50 g/1¾ oz stoned black olives,
chopped

dressing

5 tbsp roasted tomato oil

3 tbsp fresh lemon juice

1 garlic clove, crushed

salt and pepper

Put the quinoa into a medium-sized saucepan and cover with the water. Bring to the boil, then reduce the heat, cover and simmer over a low heat for 15 minutes. Drain if necessary. Rinse the grains thoroughly in a fine-mesh sieve and drain.

In a medium saucepan, bring the water to the boil over a high heat, stir in the quinoa and return to the boil. Lower the heat, cover, and simmer for about 15 minutes or until all the liquid has been absorbed. Remove from the heat, fluff up the quinoa with a fork and transfer to a bowl. Leave to cool a little.

Leave the quinoa to cool slightly before combining with the remaining ingredients in a salad bowl. Whisk the dressing ingredients together, pour over the quinoa, toss and serve.

SUCCATASH
SALAD

Beat the vinegar, mustard and sugar together. Gradually whisk in the olive and sunflower oils to form an emulsion.

Stir in the sweetcorn kernels, runner beans, red peppers and spring onions. Add salt and pepper to taste and stir together again. Cover and chill for up to one day until required.

When ready to serve, adjust the seasoning, if necessary, and garnish with the parsley.

SERVES 4–6

1 tbsp cider vinegar

1 tsp wholegrain mustard

1 tsp sugar

3 tbsp garlic-flavoured olive oil

1 tbsp sunflower oil

400 g/14 oz canned sweetcorn kernels, rinsed and drained

400 g/14 oz runner beans, finely chopped

2 peeled red peppers from a jar, drained and finely chopped

2 spring onions, finely chopped

salt and pepper

chopped fresh flat-leaf parsley, to garnish

RED PEPPER & RADICCHIO SALAD

Core and deseed the peppers and cut into rounds.

Arrange the radicchio leaves in a salad bowl. Add the pepper, beetroot, radishes and spring onions. Drizzle with the dressing and serve with crusty bread.

SERVES 4

2 red peppers

1 head radicchio, separated into leaves

4 cooked whole beetroot, cut into matchsticks

12 radishes, sliced

4 spring onions, finely chopped

4 tbsp basic salad dressing

fresh crusty bread, to serve

WATERCRESS, COURGETTE & MINT SALAD

SERVES 4

2 courgettes, cut into
   batons

100 g/3½ oz French beans,
   cut into thirds

1 green pepper, deseeded
   and cut into strips

2 celery sticks, sliced

1 bunch watercress

dressing
200 ml/7 fl oz natural
   yogurt

1 garlic clove, crushed

2 tbsp chopped fresh mint

pepper

Bring a large saucepan of water to the boil, add the courgette batons and beans and cook for 5 minutes, or until just tender. Remove with a slotted spoon and refresh the beans under cold running water. Set aside to cool completely.

Mix the courgettes and beans with the pepper strips, celery and watercress in a large serving bowl.

To make the dressing, combine the yogurt, garlic and mint in a small bowl. Season with pepper to taste.

Spoon the dressing on to the salad and serve immediately.

CHICKPEA & TOMATO SALAD

If using dried chickpeas, soak overnight then boil for at least 30 minutes until soft. Leave to cool.

To make the dressing, put all the ingredients into a small screw-top jar and shake until well blended. Taste and add more lemon juice or oil if necessary.

Add the tomatoes, onion and basil to the chickpeas and mix gently. Pour over the dressing and mix again. Arrange on a bed of lettuce and serve with crusty bread.

SERVES 4

175 g/6 oz dried chickpeas or 400 g/14 oz canned chickpeas, drained and rinsed

225 g/8 oz ripe tomatoes, roughly chopped

1 red onion, thinly sliced

handful fresh basil leaves, torn

1 cos or romaine lettuce, torn

fresh crusty bread, to serve

dressing

1 green chilli, deseeded and finely chopped

1 clove garlic, crushed

juice and zest of 2 lemons

2 tbsp olive oil

1 tbsp water

pepper

MINTED PEA & RUNNER BEAN RICE SALAD

To make the dressing, put all the ingredients in a bowl and whisk together well.

Cook the rice in a saucepan of lightly salted boiling water for 10–12 minutes or until just tender. Drain well and transfer to a large serving bowl. Stir in the dressing and leave to cool.

Cook the runner beans, mangetout and peas in a saucepan of boiling water for 2 minutes. Drain well and refresh under cold running water. Stir into the rice. Adjust the seasoning to taste and serve garnished with the mint leaves.

SERVES 6

175 g/6 oz easy-cook long grain rice

140 g/5 oz runner beans, trimmed and diagonally sliced

85 g/3 oz mangetout, thinly sliced

115 g/4 oz frozen peas

few fresh mint leaves, to garnish

dressing

4 spring onions, finely chopped

4 tbsp sunflower oil

2 tbsp white wine vinegar

½ tsp Dijon mustard

2 tbsp finely chopped fresh mint

salt and pepper

THREE BEAN SALAD

SERVES 4–6

175 g/6 oz mixed salad leaves, such as spinach, rocket and curly endive

1 red onion

85 g/3 oz radishes

175 g/6 oz cherry tomatoes

115 g/4 oz cooked beetroot

280 g/10 oz canned cannellini beans, drained and rinsed

200 g/7 oz canned red kidney beans, drained and rinsed

300 g/10½ oz canned flageolet beans, drained and rinsed

40 g/1½ oz dried cranberries

55 g/2 oz roasted cashew nuts

225 g/8 oz feta cheese (drained weight), crumbled

dressing

4 tbsp extra virgin olive oil

1 tsp Dijon mustard

2 tbsp lemon juice

1 tbsp chopped fresh coriander

salt and pepper

Arrange the salad leaves in a salad bowl and reserve.

Thinly slice the onion, then cut in half to form half moons and put into a bowl.

Thinly slice the radishes, cut the tomatoes in half and peel the beetroot, if necessary, and dice. Add to the onion with the remaining ingredients, except the nuts and cheese. To make the dressing, put all the ingredients into a screw-top jar and shake until well blended. Pour over the bean mixture, toss lightly, then spoon on top of the salad leaves.

Scatter over the nuts and cheese and serve immediately.

SOYA BEAN & MUSHROOM SALAD

Steam the soya beans in a steamer or metal colander set over a pan of simmering water for 5–6 minutes until just tender. Rinse with cold water, drain well and transfer to a serving bowl. Add the mushrooms, spinach and rocket leaves and gently toss together.

To make the dressing, place all the ingredients in a bowl and whisk together. Pour the dressing over the salad and toss well to mix. Serve immediately with extra pepper.

SERVES 2

200 g/7 oz fresh soya (edamame) beans

55 g/2 oz closed-cup mushrooms, sliced

55 g/2 oz baby spinach leaves

handful of rocket leaves

dressing

3 tbsp light olive oil

1½ tbsp lemon juice

½ tsp Dijon mustard

1 tbsp snipped fresh chives

1 tbsp chopped fresh flat-leaf parsley

salt and pepper

FRUITY COTTAGE CHEESE SALAD

Place the cottage cheese in a bowl and stir in the chopped herbs. Cover lightly and reserve.

Cut the peeled peppers into thin strips and reserve. Cut the melon in half, discard the seeds and cut into small wedges.

Arrange the salad leaves on a large serving platter with the melon wedges.

Spoon the herb-flavoured cottage cheese on the platter and arrange the reserved peppers, grapes and red onion slices around the cheese.

To make the dressing, mix the lime juice, chilli, honey and soy sauce together in a small bowl. Drizzle over the salad and serve.

SERVES 4

85 g/3 oz cottage cheese

1 tsp chopped fresh flat-leaf parsley

1 tbsp snipped fresh chives

1 tsp chopped fresh chervil or basil

2 assorted coloured peppers, deseeded and peeled

1 small melon, such as Ogen (about 300 g/10½ oz after peeling and deseeding)

175 g/6 oz mixed salad leaves

55 g/2 oz seedless red grapes

1 red onion, thinly sliced

dressing

3 tbsp freshly squeezed lime juice

1 small fresh red chilli, deseeded and finely chopped

1 tsp clear honey

1 tbsp soy sauce

INDONESIAN WARM SALAD

SERVES 4

8 outer leaves of cos lettuce or
   similar dark, crisp lettuce leaves

100 g/3½ oz French beans, lightly
   cooked

100 g/3½ oz baby carrots, lightly
   cooked

250 g/9 oz new potatoes, cooked
   until just tender

1 tbsp groundnut oil

125 g/4½ oz fresh beansprouts

8-cm/3¼-inch piece cucumber,
   deseeded and cut into 4-cm/
   1½-inch batons

4 eggs, hard-boiled

1 small onion, sliced into rings

sauce

4 tbsp canned reduced-fat coconut
   milk

3 tbsp sugar-free smooth peanut
   butter

juice of ½ lime

2 tsp light soy sauce

dash of Tabasco sauce or any chilli
   sauce

Roughly tear the lettuce leaves, if large, and arrange on
4 individual serving plates. Halve the beans and cut the carrots,
as necessary, into batons. Arrange these with the potatoes (cut
into chunks if large) on the plates.

Heat the oil in a non-stick frying pan or wok over a high heat,
add the beansprouts and stir-fry for 2 minutes until lightly
cooked but still crisp. Remove with a slotted spoon and sprinkle
over the cooked vegetables with the cucumber. Peel and quarter
the eggs, then arrange on top of the salad.

Add the onion rings to the oil remaining in the frying pan or
wok and stir-fry over a high heat for 5 minutes, or until golden
and crisp. To make the sauce, combine all the ingredients in a
bowl and pour over the salad. Top with the onion rings and
serve immediately.

VEGETABLE & RICE NOODLE SALAD

To make the dressing, whisk all the ingredients together in a small bowl. Place the noodles in a shallow bowl, pour over boiling water and leave to soak for 5 minutes. Drain well and refresh under cold running water. Transfer to a salad bowl, pour over half the salad dressing and toss well.

Heat the sesame oil in a wok and stir-fry the garlic and ginger for 1 minute. Add the sweetcorn, broccoli, mangetout and pepper and stir-fry over a high heat for 2–3 minutes.

Add the hot vegetables to the noodles with the rest of the salad dressing and toss together. Cool, then stir in the beansprouts. Serve garnished with coriander leaves and chilli pepper.

248

SERVES 2

125 g/4½ oz rice noodles

2 tsp toasted sesame oil

1 garlic clove, crushed

1 tsp fresh ginger, grated

55 g/2 oz baby sweetcorn, thinly sliced

55 g/2 oz tiny broccoli florets

55 g/2 oz mangetout, thinly sliced

½ red pepper, deseeded and thinly sliced

85 g/3 oz beansprouts

fresh coriander leaves and chopped red chilli pepper, to garnish

dressing

2 tbsp peanut oil

1½ tbsp lime juice

2 tbsp sweet chilli sauce

salt and pepper

WARM ORIENTAL-STYLE SALAD

Cut the broccoli into tiny florets then bring a small saucepan of water to the boil and add the halved carrots. Cook for 3 minutes then add the broccoli and cook for a further 2 minutes. Drain and plunge into cold water then drain again and reserve.

Arrange 25 g/1 oz of pak choi on a large serving platter. Shred the remainder and set aside.

Heat a wok and when hot, add the oil and heat for 30 seconds. Add the sliced onion, chillies, ginger and star anise and stir-fry for 1 minute. Add the pepper strips, courgettes and baby sweetcorn and stir-fry for a further 2 minutes.

Pour in the orange juice and soy sauce and continue to stir-fry for a further 1 minute before adding the reserved shredded pak choi, broccoli and carrots. Stir-fry for 2 minutes, or until the vegetables are tender but still firm to the bite. Arrange the warm salad on the pak choi-lined serving platter, scatter the cashew nuts over the top and serve.

SERVES 4

- 115 g/4 oz broccoli florets
- 115 g/4 oz baby carrots, scraped and cut in half lengthways
- 140 g/5 oz pak choi
- 2 sprays sunflower oil
- 1 red onion, sliced
- 1–2 fresh bird's eye chillies, deseeded and sliced
- 2.5-cm/1-inch fresh ginger, grated
- 2 whole star anise
- 1 red pepper, deseeded and cut into strips
- 1 orange pepper, deseeded and cut into strips
- 115 g/4 oz baby courgettes, trimmed and sliced diagonally
- 115 g/4 oz baby sweetcorn, sliced in half lengthways
- 2 tbsp orange juice
- 1 tbsp soy sauce
- 1 tbsp cashew nuts

CHICKEN & SPINACH SALAD

SERVES 4

3 celery sticks, thinly sliced

½ cucumber, thinly sliced

2 spring onions, thinly sliced

250 g/9 oz young spinach leaves

3 tbsp chopped fresh flat-leaf parsley

350 g/12 oz boneless, roast chicken, sliced thinly

smoked almonds, to garnish

dressing

2.5-cm/1-inch piece of fresh ginger, grated finely

3 tbsp olive oil

1 tbsp white wine vinegar

1 tbsp clear honey

½ tsp ground cinnamon

salt and pepper

Toss the celery, cucumber and spring onions in a large bowl with the spinach leaves and parsley.

Transfer the salad to serving plates and arrange the chicken on top.

To make the dressing, put all the ingredients into a small screw-top jar and shake until well blended. Pour the dressing over the salad. Garnish with a few smoked almonds.

THAI-STYLE CHICKEN SALAD

Bring two saucepans of water to the boil. Put the potatoes in one saucepan and cover with cold water. Bring to the boil, cover and simmer for 15 minutes, or until tender when pierced with a fork. Put the baby sweetcorn into the other saucepan and cook for 5 minutes until tender. Drain the potatoes and baby sweetcorn well and leave to cool.

When the vegetables are cool, transfer them into a large serving dish. Add the beansprouts, spring onions, chicken, lemon grass and coriander and season with salt and pepper.

To make the dressing, put all the ingredients into a screw-top jar and shake well. Drizzle the dressing over the salad and garnish with lime wedges and coriander leaves. Serve immediately.

SERVES 4

400 g/14 oz new potatoes, halved lengthways

200 g/7 oz baby sweetcorn

150 g/5½ oz beansprouts

3 spring onions, trimmed and sliced

4 cooked, skinless chicken breasts, sliced

1 tbsp chopped lemon grass

2 tbsp chopped fresh coriander

salt and pepper

wedges of lime and fresh coriander leaves, to garnish

dressing

6 tbsp chilli oil or sesame oil

2 tbsp lime juice

1 tbsp light soy sauce

1 tbsp chopped fresh coriander

1 small red chilli, deseeded and finely sliced

TURKEY SALAD PITTAS

Preheat the grill to high.

Put the spinach leaves, red pepper, carrot and hummus into a large bowl and stir together, so all the salad ingredients are coated with the hummus. Stir in the turkey and sunflower seeds and season with salt and pepper to taste.

Put the pitta bread under the grill for about 1 minute on each side to warm through, but do not brown. Cut it in half to make 2 'pockets' of bread.

Divide the salad between the bread pockets and serve.

MAKES 2

small handful baby leaf spinach, rinsed, patted dry and shredded

½ red pepper, deseeded and thinly sliced

½ carrot, peeled and roughly grated

4 tbsp hummus

85 g/3 oz boneless, skinless cooked turkey meat, thinly sliced

½ tbsp toasted sunflower seeds

1 wholemeal pitta bread

salt and pepper

TUNA &
AVOCADO
SALAD

SERVES 4

2 avocados, stoned, peeled and
  cubed

250 g/9 oz cherry tomatoes,
  halved

2 red peppers, deseeded and
  chopped

handful fresh flat-leaf parsley

2 garlic cloves, crushed

1 fresh red chilli, deseeded and
  finely chopped

juice of ½ lemon

6 tbsp olive oil

3 tbsp sesame seeds

4 fresh tuna steaks,
  about 150 g/5½ oz each

8 cooked new potatoes, cubed

fresh rocket leaves and fresh
  crusty bread, to serve

pepper

Toss the avocados, tomatoes, red peppers, parsley, garlic, chilli,
lemon juice and 2 tablespoons of the oil together in a large bowl.
Season to taste with pepper, cover and chill in the refrigerator for
30 minutes.

Lightly crush the sesame seeds in a mortar with a pestle. Tip
the crushed seeds on to a plate and spread out. Press each tuna
steak in turn into the crushed seeds to coat on both sides.

Heat 2 tablespoons of the remaining oil in a frying pan, add
the potatoes and cook, stirring frequently, for 5–8 minutes, or
until crisp and brown. Remove from the pan and drain on
kitchen paper.

Wipe out the pan, add the remaining oil and heat over a high
heat until very hot. Add the tuna steaks and cook for 3–4 minutes
on each side.

To serve, divide the avocado salad between 4 serving plates.
Top each with a tuna steak, scatter over the potatoes and rocket
leaves and serve with crusty bread.

TUNA WITH BEANSPROUT SALAD

Mix the soy sauce, oil and ginger in a shallow dish. Add the tuna steaks and turn to coat in the marinade. Cover and leave to marinate for 1 hour at room temperature.

Heat a cast iron griddle pan until very hot. Drain the tuna steaks from the marinade and place in the hot pan. Cook for 2 minutes then turn over and cook for a further 1–2 minutes until the steaks are well seared but still a little pink in the middle. Cook for a further 2–3 minutes if you prefer the tuna well done.

To make the dressing, place all the ingredients in a small pan and heat gently, stirring, until just warmed through.

Mix the alfalfa sprouts, beansprouts and mustard and cress in a bowl and toss together with the lime juice. Season with salt and pepper.

Divide the sprouting salad between 4 serving plates and top with the tuna steaks. Drizzle over the warm dressing. Garnish with lime wedges and serve immediately.

SERVES 4

2 tbsp soy sauce

1 tbsp sunflower oil

1 tsp fresh ginger, grated

4 tuna steaks, about 175 g/ 6 oz each

55 g/2 oz fresh alfalfa sprouts

55 g/2 oz fresh beansprouts

25 g/1 oz mustard and cress

squeeze of lime or lemon juice

salt and pepper

lime wedges, to garnish

dressing

3 tbsp sunflower oil

2 tbsp soy sauce

1 tbsp clear honey

2 tbsp rice vinegar

SALT CHILLI
SQUID SALAD

To make the dressing, mix all the ingredients together in a bowl to taste, cover and refrigerate until required.

Cut the squid tubes into 5-cm/2-inch pieces, then score diamond patterns lightly across the flesh with the tip of a sharp knife. Heat the oil in a wok or large frying pan over a high heat, add the squid pieces and tentacles and stir-fry for 1 minute. Add the chillies and spring onions and stir-fry for a further minute. Season to taste with salt and pepper and add a good squeeze of lemon juice.

Mix the watercress and spinach together, then toss with enough of the dressing to coat lightly. Serve immediately with the squid, together with the lemon wedges to squeeze over the squid.

SERVES 4

12 squid tubes and tentacles (about 700 g/1 lb 9 oz total weight), cleaned and prepared

2–3 tbsp olive oil

1–2 red chillies, deseeded and thinly sliced

2 spring onions, finely chopped

lemon wedges, for squeezing and to serve

3 good handfuls watercress

2 handfuls baby spinach or rocket

salt and pepper

dressing

100 ml/3½ fl oz olive oil

juice of 1 lime

1 tsp caster sugar

2 shallots, thinly sliced

1 tomato, peeled, deseeded and finely chopped

1 garlic clove, crushed

SPICY WARM
CRAB SALAD

SERVES 4

2 sprays sunflower oil

1 fresh serrano chilli, deseeded
and finely chopped

115 g/4 oz mangetout,
cut in half diagonally

6 spring onions, trimmed and
finely shredded

25 g/1 oz frozen sweetcorn
kernels defrosted

150 g/5½ oz white crabmeat,
drained if canned

55 g/2 oz raw prawns, peeled and
deveined, thawed if frozen

1 carrot, about 85 g/
3 oz, peeled and grated

115 g/4 oz beansprouts

225 g/8 oz fresh baby spinach
leaves

1 tbsp finely grated orange rind

2 tbsp orange juice

chopped fresh coriander,
to garnish

Heat a wok and when hot, spray in the oil and heat for
30 seconds. Add the chilli and mangetout then stir-fry
over a medium heat for 2 minutes.

Add the spring onions and sweetcorn and continue to
stir-fry for a further 1 minute.

Add the crabmeat, prawns, grated carrot, beansprouts
and spinach leaves. Stir in the orange rind and juice and stir-
fry for 2–3 minutes, or until the spinach has begun to wilt and
everything is cooked. Serve divided between 4 bowls, sprinkled
with the chopped coriander.

FRUIT

CHILLED BERRY BREAKFAST SALAD

Place all the berries in a shallow bowl. Stir in the orange juice and sugar. Cover and chill in the refrigerator for at least 2 hours or overnight.

Put the yogurt in a small bowl and fold in the orange rind and honey.

Divide the chilled salad between 4 serving bowls. Top each with a dollop of the yogurt and sprinkle with the sunflower seeds and hazelnuts. Serve immediately.

SERVES 4

225 g/8 oz small strawberries, halved

140 g/5 oz raspberries

115 g/4 oz blackberries

115 g/4 oz blueberries

juice and finely grated rind of 1 orange

1 tbsp caster sugar

6 tbsp Greek yogurt

1 tbsp orange blossom honey

1 tbsp sunflower seeds

1 tbsp toasted chopped hazelnuts

GREEN FRUIT SALAD

To make the syrup dressing, pare the rind from the lemon using a potato peeler.

Put the lemon rind in a saucepan with the white wine, water and clear honey. Bring to the boil, then simmer gently for 10 minutes.

Remove the syrup from the heat. Add the sprigs of mint and leave to cool.

To prepare the fruit, first cut the melon in half and scoop out the seeds. Use a melon baller or a teaspoon to make melon balls.

Core and chop the apples. Peel and slice the kiwi fruit.

Strain the cooled syrup into a serving bowl, removing and reserving the lemon rind and discarding the mint sprigs.

Add the apple, kiwi fruit, grapes and melon to the serving bowl. Stir through gently to mix.

Serve the fruit salad, decorated with sprigs of fresh mint and some of the reserved lemon rind.

SERVES 4

1 honeydew melon

2 green apples

2 kiwi fruit

125 g/4½ oz seedless green grapes

fresh mint sprigs, to decorate

syrup dressing

1 lemon

150 ml/5 fl oz white wine

150 ml/5 fl oz water

4 tbsp clear honey

few sprigs of fresh mint

TROPICAL FRUIT SALAD

SERVES 4

1 papaya

1 mango

1 pineapple

4 oranges, peeled and cut into segments

125 g/4½ oz strawberries, hulled and quartered

single or double cream, to serve (optional)

syrup dressing

6 tbsp caster sugar

400 ml/14 fl oz water

½ tsp ground mixed spice

grated rind of ½ lemon

To make the syrup dressing, put the sugar, water, mixed spice and lemon rind into a saucepan. Bring to the boil, stirring continuously, then continue to boil for 1 minute. Remove from the heat and leave to cool to room temperature. Transfer to a jug or bowl, cover with clingfilm and chill in the refrigerator for at least 1 hour.

Peel and halve the papaya and remove the seeds. Cut the flesh into small chunks or slices, and put into a large bowl. Cut the mango twice lengthways, close to the stone. Remove and discard the stone. Peel and cut the flesh into small chunks or slices, and add to the bowl. Cut off the top and bottom of the pineapple and remove the hard skin. Cut the pineapple in half lengthways, then into quarters, and remove the tough core. Cut the remaining flesh into small pieces and add to the bowl. Add the orange segments and strawberries.

Pour over the chilled syrup, cover with clingfilm and chill until required. Serve with single or double cream, if using.

EXOTIC FRUIT COCKTAIL

Cut 1 orange in half and squeeze the juice into a bowl, discarding any pips. Using a sharp knife, cut away all the peel and pith from the second orange. Working over the bowl to catch the juice, carefully cut the orange segments between the membranes to obtain skinless segments of fruit. Discard any pips.

Cut the passion fruit in half, scoop the flesh into a nylon sieve and, using a spoon, push the pulp and juice into the bowl of orange segments. Discard the pips.

Using a sharp knife, cut away all the skin from the pineapple and cut the flesh lengthways into quarters. Cut away the central hard core. Cut the flesh into chunks and add to the orange and passion fruit mixture. Cover and refrigerate the fruit at this stage if you are not serving immediately.

Cut the pomegranate into quarters and, using your fingers or a teaspoon, remove the red seeds from the membrane. Cover and refrigerate until ready to serve – do not add too early to the fruit cocktail as the seeds discolour the other fruit.

Just before serving, peel and slice the banana, add to the fruit cocktail with the pomegranate seeds and mix thoroughly. Serve immediately.

SERVES 6

2 oranges

2 large passion fruit

1 pineapple

1 pomegranate

1 banana

PAPAYA SALAD

To make the dressing, whisk together the oil, Thai fish sauce, lime juice, sugar and chilli. Set aside, stirring occasionally to dissolve the sugar.

Shred the lettuce and white cabbage, then toss together and arrange on a large serving plate.

Peel the papayas and slice them in half. Scoop out the seeds, then slice the flesh thinly. Arrange on top of the lettuce and cabbage.

Soak the tomatoes in a bowl of boiling water for 1 minute, then lift out and peel. Remove the seeds and chop the flesh. Arrange on the salad leaves.

Scatter the peanuts and spring onions over the top. Whisk the dressing and pour over the salad. Garnish with basil leaves and serve at once.

SERVES 4

1 crisp lettuce

¼ small white cabbage

2 papayas

2 tomatoes

25 g/1 oz roasted peanuts, chopped roughly

4 spring onions, trimmed and sliced thinly

fresh basil leaves, to garnish

dressing

4 tbsp olive oil

1 tbsp Thai fish sauce or light soy sauce

2 tbsp lime or lemon juice

1 tbsp dark muscovado sugar

1 tsp finely chopped fresh red or green chilli

MOROCCAN ORANGE SALAD

SERVES 4

5 large oranges

1 small red onion, finely sliced

½ tsp ground cumin

½ tsp ground coriander

1 tbsp roughly chopped fresh flat-leaf parsley

1 tbsp roughly chopped fresh coriander

salt and pepper

Using a serrated knife cut away the peel and all the white pith from 4 of the oranges. Cut the flesh into thin slices removing any pips. Place the orange slices in a shallow dish with the onion.

Halve and squeeze the juice from the remaining orange. Mix the juice with the cumin and coriander and pour over the orange slices. Cover and chill in the refrigerator for 1 hour.

Add the parsley and coriander to the orange slices and mix gently. Pile onto a serving dish and season lightly with salt and pepper before serving.

FRUIT

279

FENNEL &
ORANGE SALAD

Arrange the orange slices in the bottom of a shallow dish. Place a layer of fennel on top and then add a layer of onion.

To make the dressing, mix the orange juice with the vinegar and drizzle over the salad. Season with pepper and serve.

SERVES 4

2 oranges, peeled and sliced

1 bulb Florence fennel, thinly sliced

1 red onion, peeled and sliced into thin rings

dressing
juice of 1 orange

2 tbsp balsamic vinegar

pepper

MELON & MANGO SALAD

To make the melon dressing, whisk together the yogurt, honey and ginger in a small bowl.

Halve the melon, scoop out the seeds with a spoon and discard. Slice, peel and dice the flesh. Place in a bowl with the grapes.

Slice the mango on each side of its large flat stone. On each mango half, slash the flesh into a criss-cross pattern, down to but not through the skin. Push the skin from underneath to turn the mango halves inside out. Now remove the flesh and add to the melon mixture.

Arrange the watercress and lettuce leaves on 4 serving plates.

To make the salad leaves dressing, whisk together the olive oil and vinegar with a little salt and pepper. Drizzle over the salad leaves.

Divide the melon mixture between the 4 plates and spoon over the melon dressing.

Scoop the seeds out of the passion fruit and sprinkle them over the salads. Serve immediately or chill in the refrigerator until required.

SERVES 4

1 cantaloupe melon

55 g/2 oz seedless red grapes, halved

55 g/2 oz seedless green grapes

1 large mango

1 bunch watercress, trimmed

handful iceberg lettuce leaves, shredded

1 passion fruit

melon dressing

150 ml/5 fl oz natural yogurt

1 tbsp clear honey

1 tsp fresh ginger, grated

salad leaves dressing

2 tbsp olive oil

1 tbsp cider vinegar

salt and pepper

MELON & STRAWBERRY SALAD

½ iceberg lettuce, shredded

1 small honeydew melon

225 g/8 oz strawberries, sliced

5-cm/2-inch piece cucumber, thinly sliced

fresh mint sprigs, to garnish

dressing

200 g/7 fl oz natural yogurt

5-cm/2-inch piece cucumber, peeled

a few fresh mint leaves

½ tsp finely grated lime or lemon rind

pinch of caster sugar

3–4 ice cubes

Arrange the shredded lettuce on 4 serving plates.

Cut the melon lengthways into quarters. Scoop out the seeds and cut through the flesh down to the skin at 2.5-cm/1-inch intervals. Cut the melon close to the skin and detach the flesh.

Place the chunks of melon on the beds of lettuce with the strawberries and cucumber slices.

To make the dressing, put the yogurt, cucumber, mint leaves, lime rind, caster sugar and ice cubes into a blender or food processor. Blend together for about 15 seconds until smooth.

Serve the salad with a little dressing poured over. Garnish with sprigs of fresh mint.

FRUIT

285

MINTED PEA & MELON SALAD

Cut all the melon flesh into even-sized chunks removing any seeds. Place the chunks in a bowl with the cucumber.

To make the dressing, place all the ingredients in a small bowl and whisk together.

Pour the dressing over the melon and cucumber and toss well to coat. Cover and chill for 1 hour.

Add the pea shoots to the chilled melon and cucumber and gently toss together. Transfer to a serving bowl and serve garnished with mint leaves.

SERVES 4

350 g/12 oz wedge of watermelon

½ small honeydew melon

½ Charentais or cantaloupe melon

½ cucumber, peeled and diced

55 g/2 oz fresh pea shoots

fresh mint leaves, to garnish

dressing

3 tbsp light olive oil

1 tbsp white wine vinegar

½ tsp caster sugar

1 tbsp chopped fresh mint

salt and pepper

PROSCIUTTO WITH MELON & ASPARAGUS

Trim the asparagus, cutting in half if very long. Cook in lightly salted, boiling water over a medium heat for 5 minutes, or until tender. Drain and plunge into cold water then drain again and reserve.

Cut the melon in half and scoop out the seeds. Cut into small wedges and cut away the rind. Separate the prosciutto slices, cut in half and wrap around the melon wedges.

Arrange the salad leaves on a large serving platter and place the melon wedges on top together with the asparagus spears.

Scatter over the raspberries and Parmesan shavings. To make the dressing, put all the ingredients into a small screw-top jar and shake until well blended. Pour over the salad and serve.

SERVES 4

225 g/8 oz asparagus spears

1 small or ½ medium-sized Galia or cantaloupe melon

55 g/2 oz prosciutto, thinly sliced

150 g/5½ oz mixed salad leaves, such as herb salad with rocket

85 g/3 oz fresh raspberries

1 tbsp freshly shaved prosciutto

salt

dressing

1 tbsp balsamic vinegar

2 tbsp raspberry vinegar

2 tbsp orange juice

CANTALOUPE & CRAB SALAD

SERVES 4

350 g/12 oz fresh crabmeat

5 tbsp mayonnaise

50 ml/2 fl oz natural yogurt

4 tsp extra virgin olive oil

4 tsp lime juice

1 spring onion, finely chopped

4 tsp finely chopped fresh
   flat-leaf parsley

pinch of cayenne pepper

1 cantaloupe melon

2 radicchio heads, separated into
   leaves

flat-leaf fresh parsley sprigs,
   to garnish

fresh crusty bread, to serve

Place the crabmeat in a large bowl and pick over it very carefully
to remove any remaining shell or cartilage, but try not to break
the meat up.

Place the mayonnaise, yogurt, olive oil, lime juice, spring
onion, chopped parsley and cayenne pepper into a separate bowl
and mix until thoroughly blended. Fold in the crabmeat.

Cut the melon in half and remove and discard the seeds. Slice
into wedges, then cut off the rind with a sharp knife.

Arrange the melon wedges and radicchio leaves in 4 serving
bowls, then arrange the crabmeat mixture on top. Garnish with
a few sprigs of fresh parsley and serve with crusty bread.

FRUIT

FIG &
WATERMELON
SALAD

Cut the watermelon into quarters and scoop out and discard the seeds. Cut the flesh away from the rind, then chop the flesh into 2.5-cm/1-inch cubes. Place the watermelon cubes in a bowl with the grapes. Cut each fig lengthways into 8 wedges and add to the bowl.

To make the syrup dressing, grate the lime and mix the rind with the orange rind and juice, maple syrup and honey in a small saucepan. Bring to the boil over a low heat. Pour the mixture over the fruit and stir. Leave to cool. Stir again, cover and chill in the refrigerator for at least 1 hour, stirring occasionally.

Divide the fruit salad equally between 4 bowls and serve.

SERVES 4

1 watermelon, weighing about 1.5 kg/3 lb 5 oz

115 g/4 oz seedless red grapes

4 figs

syrup dressing

1 lime

grated rind and juice of 1 orange

1 tbsp maple syrup

2 tbsp clear honey

SPRING CLEAN
SALAD

Core and dice the apples, place in a bowl and pour over the lemon juice. Mix well to prevent discoloration.

Add the rest of the fruit and vegetables to the bowl and mix gently. Pour in the walnut oil, mix again and serve.

SERVES 4

2 dessert apples, cored and diced

juice of 1 lemon

large chunk of watermelon, deseeded and cubed

1 head chicory, sliced into rounds

4 sticks celery with leaves, roughly chopped

1 tbsp walnut oil

RASPBERRY & FETA SALAD

SERVES 6

350 g/12 oz couscous

600 ml/1 pint boiling chicken stock or vegetable stock

350 g/12 oz fresh raspberries

small bunch of fresh basil

225 g/8 oz feta cheese, cubed or crumbled

2 courgettes, thinly sliced

4 spring onions, trimmed and diagonally sliced

55 g/2 oz pine kernels, toasted

grated rind of 1 lemon

dressing

1 tbsp white wine vinegar

1 tbsp balsamic vinegar

4 tbsp extra virgin olive oil

juice of 1 lemon

salt and pepper

Put the couscous in a large, heatproof bowl and pour over the stock. Stir well, cover and leave to soak until all the stock has been absorbed.

Pick over the raspberries, discarding any that are overripe. Shred the basil leaves.

Transfer the couscous to a large serving bowl and stir well to break up any lumps. Add the cheese, courgettes, spring onions, raspberries and pine kernels. Stir in the basil and lemon rind and gently toss all the ingredients together.

To make the dressing, put all the ingredients into a small screw-top jar and shake until well blended. Pour over the salad and serve.

FRUIT

STRAWBERRY & WATERCRESS SALAD

To make the balsamic glaze, place the vinegar and sugar in a small saucepan. Heat gently, stirring, until the sugar dissolves. Simmer gently for 5–6 minutes until syrupy. Cool for 30 minutes.

Place the watercress in a serving dish. Scatter over the strawberries. Halve, stone, peel and slice the avocado and toss gently in the lemon juice. Add to the salad. Scatter over the cucumber and walnuts.

Drizzle the glaze over the salad. Season lightly with salt and pepper and serve immediately.

SERVES 4

115 g/4 oz watercress, tough stalks removed

350 g/12 oz strawberries, sliced

1 ripe avocado

1 tbsp lemon juice

¼ cucumber, finely diced

1 tbsp chopped walnuts

salt and pepper

balsamic glaze

100 ml/3½ fl oz balsamic vinegar

2 tbsp sugar

FETA, MINT & STRAWBERRY SALAD

To make the dressing, mix the vinegar, sugar, mustard and salt together in a bowl until smooth. Slowly pour in the oil, whisking constantly.

Bring a large saucepan of water to the boil, add the beans and cook for 5 minutes, or until just tender. Remove with a slotted spoon and refresh the beans under cold running water. Hull and halve the strawberries, then add to the beans. Stir in the pistachio nuts and mint leaves. Toss the salad with enough of the dressing to coat lightly.

Break the feta cheese into chunks and scatter over the salad. Add a good grinding of pepper and serve immediately.

SERVES 4–6

500 g/1 lb 2 oz French beans

500 g/1 lb 2 oz strawberries

2–3 tbsp pistachio nuts

1 small bunch fresh mint leaves

500 g/1 lb 2 oz feta cheese
(drained weight)

pepper

dressing

2 tbsp raspberry vinegar

2 tsp caster sugar

1 tbsp Dijon mustard

pinch of salt

125 ml/4 fl oz olive oil

WARM PEACH & GOAT'S CHEESE SALAD

SERVES 4

4 just ripe peaches, halved,
    stoned and cut into 6 slices

1 tbsp olive oil

2 tsp lemon juice

55 g/2 oz lamb's lettuce

55 g/2 oz curly endive

125 g/4½ oz mild goat's cheese,
    crumbled

4 slices Serrano ham

1 tbsp toasted hazelnuts, chopped

dressing

4 tbsp olive oil

2 tbsp hazelnut oil

2 tbsp red wine vinegar

½ tsp sugar

salt and pepper

To make the dressing, place all the ingredients in a small bowl and whisk together well.

Place the peach slices in a bowl and add the olive oil and lemon juice. Turn to coat and season lightly with salt and pepper.

Heat a cast iron griddle pan and add the peach slices. Cook over a medium heat for 2–3 minutes, turning once, until lightly charred and just starting to soften.

Mix the lamb's lettuce and curly endive together in a bowl and add half the dressing. Toss well to coat and divide between 4 serving plates. Top with the warm peach slices and crumbled goat's cheese. Place a ruffled slice of ham on the top of each salad.

Drizzle over the rest of the dressing and scatter over the toasted hazelnuts. Serve immediately.

PEAR & ROQUEFORT SALAD

To make the dressing, place the cheese in a bowl and mash with a fork. Gradually blend the yogurt into the cheese to make a smooth dressing. Add the chives and season with pepper to taste.

Tear the lollo rosso, radicchio and lamb's lettuce leaves into manageable pieces. Arrange the salad leaves on a large serving platter or divide them between individual serving plates.

Cut the pears into quarters and remove the cores. Cut the quarters into slices. Arrange the pear slices over the salad leaves.

Drizzle the dressing over the pears and garnish with a few whole chives.

SERVES 4

few leaves of lollo rosso
few leaves of radicchio
few leaves of lamb's lettuce
2 ripe pears
whole fresh chives, to garnish

dressing
55 g/2 oz Roquefort cheese
150 ml/5 fl oz natural yogurt
2 tbsp snipped fresh chives
pepper

PEAR & STILTON SALAD

Bring a large, heavy-based saucepan of lightly salted water to the boil. Add the pasta, return to the boil and cook for 8–10 minutes, or until tender but still firm to the bite. Drain, refresh in a bowl of cold water and drain again.

Place the radicchio and oakleaf lettuce leaves in a salad bowl. Halve the pears, remove the cores and dice the flesh. Toss the diced pear with the lemon juice in a small bowl to prevent discoloration. Top the salad with the Stilton, walnuts, pears, pasta, tomatoes, sweetcorn, onion slices and grated carrot. Add the basil and lamb's lettuce.

To make the dressing, mix the olive oil, lemon juice and vinegar together in a bowl, then season to taste with salt and pepper. Pour the dressing over the salad, toss and serve.

SERVES 4

250 g/9 oz dried orecchiette pasta
1 head radicchio, torn into pieces
1 oakleaf lettuce, torn into pieces
2 pears
1 tbsp lemon juice
250 g/9 oz Stilton cheese, diced
55 g/2 oz chopped walnuts
4 tomatoes, quartered
55 g/2 oz canned sweetcorn
1 red onion, sliced
1 carrot, grated
8 fresh basil leaves
55 g/2 oz lamb's lettuce

dressing
4 tbsp olive oil
2 tbsp lemon juice
1 tbsp white wine vinegar
salt and pepper

BEANSPROUT, APRICOT & ALMOND SALAD

SERVES 4

115 g/4 oz beansprouts

small bunch seedless red and
  green grapes, halved

12 unsulphured dried apricots,
  halved

25 g/1 oz blanched almonds,
  halved

pepper

dressing

1 tbsp walnut oil

1 tsp sesame oil

2 tsp balsamic vinegar

Place the beansprouts in the bottom of a large salad bowl and
sprinkle the grapes and apricots on top.

  To make the dressing, put all the ingredients into a small
screw-top jar and shake until well blended. Pour over the salad.
  Scatter over the almonds and season.

CHICKEN & GRAPEFRUIT SALAD

Place the chicken in a large saucepan and pour over enough water to cover. Add the bouquet garni and peppercorns and bring to a gentle simmer. Cover and simmer for 25–30 minutes until just cooked through. Leave the chicken to cool in the liquid.

Using a serrated knife, cut away the peel and pith from the grapefruit. Holding the fruit over a bowl to catch any juice, segment the flesh. Reserve 2 tablespoons of the juice.

Toss the salad leaves in a bowl with the grapefruit segments.

To make the dressing, place all the ingredients in a small bowl with the reserved grapefruit juice. Whisk together until thoroughly blended.

Drain the poached chicken and pat dry with kitchen paper. Tear into bite-sized strips or thinly slice. Arrange on top of the salad. Drizzle over the dressing and garnish with chervil sprigs.

SERVES 4

2 skinless, boneless chicken breasts, about 175 g/6 oz each

1 bouquet garni

few black peppercorns

2 pink grapefruit

3 Little Gem lettuces, separated into leaves

1 head chicory, separated into leaves

fresh chervil sprigs, to garnish

dressing

1 tbsp light olive oil

3 tbsp Greek yogurt

1 tsp wholegrain mustard

pinch of sugar

1 tbsp chopped fresh chervil

salt and pepper

CHICKEN & CRANBERRY SALAD

Carve the chicken carefully, slicing the white meat. Divide the legs into thighs and drumsticks and trim the wings. Cover with clingfilm and refrigerate.

Put the cranberries in a bowl. Stir in the apple juice, cover with clingfilm and leave to soak for 30 minutes.

Meanwhile, blanch the mangetout, refresh under cold running water and drain.

Separate the lettuce hearts and arrange on a large serving platter with the avocados, mangetout, watercress, rocket and the chicken.

To make the dressing, put all the ingredients into a small screw-top jar and shake until well blended.

Drain the cranberries and mix them with the dressing, then pour over the salad. Serve immediately.

SERVES 4

1 smoked chicken, weighing 1.3 kg/3 lb

115 g/4 oz dried cranberries

2 tbsp apple juice or water

200 g/7 oz mangetout

4 lettuce hearts

2 ripe avocados, peeled, stoned and sliced

1 bunch watercress, trimmed

55 g/2 oz rocket

dressing

2 tbsp olive oil

1 tbsp walnut oil

2 tbsp lemon juice

1 tbsp chopped fresh mixed herbs, such as parsley and lemon thyme

salt and pepper

PRAWNS WITH PINEAPPLE & PAPAYA SALSA

FRUIT

315

SERVES 8

4 tbsp sunflower oil

1 fresh red chilli, deseeded and chopped

1 garlic clove, crushed

48 prawns

chopped fresh flat-leaf parsley, to garnish

pineapple & papaya salsa

1 large papaya, halved, deseeded, peeled and cut into 5-mm/ ¼-inch dice

1 small pineapple, halved, cored, peeled and cut into 5-mm/ ¼-inch dice

2 spring onions, very finely chopped

1 red chilli, or to taste, deseeded and finely chopped

1 garlic clove, very finely chopped

2½ tsp lemon juice

½ tsp ground cumin

¼ tsp salt

pepper

To make the pineapple and papaya salsa, put the papaya in a large bowl with the pineapple, spring onions, chilli, garlic, lemon juice, cumin, salt and pepper. Adjust the lemon juice, cumin, salt or pepper to taste, if necessary. Cover and chill until required, ideally at least 2 hours.

Heat a wok over a high heat. Add the oil and swirl around, then add the chilli and garlic and stir-fry for 20 seconds. Add the prawns and stir-fry for 2–3 minutes until the prawns are cooked through, become pink and curl.

Tip the prawns, garlic and any oil left in the wok into a heatproof bowl and leave the prawns to cool and marinate in the chilli oil. When the prawns are completely cool, cover the bowl and chill for at least 2 hours.

When ready to serve, give the salsa a stir and adjust the seasoning, if necessary. Arrange a mound of salsa on each of 8 plates. Remove the prawns from the marinade and divide between plates. Sprinkle with parsley and serve.

INDEX

COMPUTERS AS A TOOL IN LANGUAGE TEACHING

Editors

BILL BRIERLEY

IAN KEMBLE

School of Language and Area Studies
Portsmouth Polytechnic

ELLIS HORWOOD
NEW YORK   LONDON   TORONTO   SYDNEY   TOKYO   SINGAPORE

First published in 1991 by
ELLIS HORWOOD LIMITED
Market Cross House, Cooper Street,
Chichester, West Sussex, PO19 1EB, England

A division of
Simon & Schuster International Group
A Paramount Communications Company

Printed and bound in Great Britain
by Hartnolls, Bodmin, Cornwall

British Library Cataloguing in Publication Data

Brierley, B. and Kemble, I.
Computers as a tool in language teaching
CIP catalogue record for this book is available from the British Library
ISBN 0–13–159427–3 (Library Edn.)
ISBN 0–13–151812–7 (Student Pbk. Edn.)

Library of Congress Cataloging-in-Publication Data available

COMPUTERS AS A TOOL
IN LANGUAGE TEACHING

ELLIS HORWOOD SERIES IN COMPUTERS AND THEIR APPLICATIONS

Series Editor: IAN CHIVERS, Senior Analyst, The Computer Centre, King's College, London, and formerly Senior Programmer and Analyst, Imperial College of Science and Technology, University of London

Series continued at back of book

CONTRIBUTORS

Alida Bedford is a Research Student in the School of Information Science, Portsmouth Polytechnic.

Bill Brierley is Principal Lecturer and Information Technology Coordinator for the Faculty of Humanities and Social Science, Portsmouth Polytechnic.

Jim Coleman is Reader in French Studies and Associate Head of the School of Languages and Area Studies, Portsmouth Polytechnic.

Bob French is Head of the School of Languages and Area Studies, Portsmouth Polytechnic.

Ray Gallery is Senior Lecturer in French at Bristol Polytechnic.

Mike Harland is Lecturer in Portuguese and Spanish at the University of Glasgow.

Ian Kemble is Senior Lecturer in German in the School of Languages and Area Studies, Portsmouth Polytechnic.

Günter Minnerup is Senior Lecturer in German at the University of Birmingham.

CONTENTS

Contents

1 INTRODUCTION

Ian R. Kemble and William Brierley

This book is primarily designed for the teacher of foreign languages (including English as a foreign language) in further and higher education whose interests have hitherto not been the most amply served by the literature on the application of information technology to the teaching and learning of foreign languages. However, it should also be of interest to all teachers of foreign languages who already use primary computer applications packages such as word processors in their work. The target audience is both the interested novice and the teacher with some experience.

In the introduction to their book *CALL*, Hardisty and Windeatt (1989) comment that, compared with the language laboratory, it has taken far less time for language teachers to perceive what the computer has to offer to language learning. "It took the profession fifteen or more years to find effective ways of utilizing language laboratories. ... It has taken CALL a considerably shorter time to move from its crude beginnings ... to a stage where the use of computers is both innovative and truly appropriate." (1989, p. 3). This statement reflects closely our own experience and sentiments on the use of information technology in the learning of foreign languages. We have in many respects reached a crossroads in the use of computers in language teaching, a phase of both consolidation and development. On the one hand, we are able to review the developments in information technology over the past five years (1985-90) and assess their application to the learning of foreign languages. On the other, we are already entering a phase of further new developments whose potential application we are in the process of evaluating. But it is important to recognise that the two phases are not unrelated and do not mean that, as we move forward, an entirely new technology has to be accommodated. On the contrary, recent developments such as hypertext and interactive video use existing technologies, but in a new and exciting way.

For teachers, the problem is simply expressed: which computer do you use in the classroom and what software do you use? For many, the issue of hardware is the one which has been addressed first, and may even be the decision over which they have least (and sometimes no) control. Some may even have seen a succession of machines - Commodores, BBCs and IBM PC compatibles - and have then had to spend a great deal of time adapting materials and methods to keep pace with the technology. Many will have experienced the frustration of having a machine (perhaps bought by a different department for different purposes) and no appropriate software; others might spot an exciting software development in the catalogues, only to discover that it is not available for the equipment to which they have access. The chaotic developments of the 1980s seem now to have settled down and a small number of standards have become accepted. The hardware standard assumed in this book is the IBM PC AT compatible with 640k RAM and hard disk, running MS or similar DOS, version 3 or higher.

Software has also undergone rapid development during the same period. In the early days, many language teachers felt obliged to tackle computer programming languages, learning BASIC and producing simple drill exercises (based on a pedagogical model they had long ago rejected as unsound in the language laboratory). Then came dedicated software for the teaching of English and foreign languages. This has been on the market since the mid-1980s, thanks in no small measure to the WIDA and CAMSOFT software publishing houses. These dedicated CALL (Computer-Assisted Language Learning) packages are essentially language testing programs in a variety of forms such as gap-filling, multiple choice, text reconstruction and so on. Many will have an authoring facility to allow teachers to use their own materials. Flexible authoring packages of this type have been used in imaginative ways by ingenious teachers, but whilst there is little to dispute in C. Jones' assertion "It's not so much the program, more what you do with it..." (Jones 1986, pp. 171ff), some of the teaching uses to which dedicated CALL programs have been put raise some doubts - for example, using text reconstruction packages to test translation skills. "Learners are given a piece of paper on which is written an English translation of Dante, and are asked to discover the original Italian on the STORYBOARD screen." (Jones 1986, p. 173) If this method of teaching 15th century Italian is to be successful, then it must surely depend to a high degree on energetic teacher input, which raises the question: Is the computer really performing a useful function in this context?   Moreover, as Phillips (1987, p. 279) puts it, "Programs written within this model tend to be small-scale and, as it were, 'stand-alone'".   While they embody some flexibility for the language teacher they create inflexibility for the student user since the machine will accept one response only. [This is a considerable limitation of such programs and one which tends to restrict their use to the testing of language accuracy.] Hardisty and Windeatt (1989, p. 10), however, view this attribute in quite positive terms. "This limitation can in practice be very useful, since it provides a motivation for the student to use the language as accurately as possible."

In the early days the problem facing a number of teachers was the availability of hardware.   Where teachers had access to a larger number of machines, the problem of distribution and control of materials arose.   Machines which were not joined in a network provided the teacher using a dedicated CALL exercise with the problem of having to make the exercise available to every single student on a separate disc.   Just as the language teacher using the language laboratory can very quickly transfer the foreign language listening materials to every student booth - either just before the lesson gets under way or during the warm-up phase - so too should the teacher who uses computer equipment be able to transfer quickly and efficiently any computer-based language learning materials to a group of students.   In other words, in certain modes there is a need for a network of computers.

A significant development was the widespread availability of word processing facilities.   This opened up a new range of activities to the imaginative teacher, such as the drafting of a script for a video film, which is an ideal exercise for the computer as word processor.   Word processing, the most widely used application of the computer in foreign language teaching, has come to typify our approach to the use of information technology in language teaching.   Let us consider some of the reasons for this.

Firstly, there is its emancipatory effect.   Anyone who has moved from a typewriter to a word processor will know exactly what is meant by this statement.   In our own department, numbering over 40 staff, even the Luddites, or some of them at least, have adopted the word processor with a noticeable increase in productivity - pedagogical, administrative and academic.   Secondly, the word processor is a very powerful device.   Not only can substantial amounts of text be stored, accessed and processed, but there is an ease with which text can be altered and corrected as it is being entered, or saved to disc to be worked on later.   In addition, there are facilities such as the search facility which allows the processed text to be used rather like a book.   As the cursor moves from one example to another, so the activity begins to resemble that of flicking through the pages of a book to find a series of references. Thirdly, there is its versatility. There is a whole range of facilities offered to writers for text manipulation which can help readers engage with texts and learn from them. (In language teaching, the word processor can be used to enhance the development of both accuracy and fluency (see Chapter 2).

word program

As what word processing could offer began to be appreciated, so the word processor was used increasingly to complement or replace dedicated CALL packages, as it was realised that most of the exercises offered by dedicated CALL programs could, on the one hand, be duplicated to some high degree using a primary applications package such as word processing and, on the other, a whole range of additional possibilities exploited. This approach has been termed the "prosthetic paradigm" by Phillips (1987, pp. 275ff). He distinguishes three models of CALL activity. (Firstly, the games model "CALL programs ... fashioned on the pattern of the computer game" with characteristic features of games such as "intrinsic motivation, ... competition, ... constitutive and regulative rules." He considers this model to have a number of inherent difficulties and limitations, described by Higgins (1983) as "artificial unintelligence". What is primarily meant by this is that most programs of this type, which include less obvious ones such as text reconstruction exercises, involve some degree of 'intelligence' on the part of the computer, i.e. an ability to respond to the user's input by means of a more or less sophisticated set of diagnostic programming routines. However, the 'intelligence' of the machine is severely restricted to inflexible sets of data provided by the programmer. This explains the restriction of its use to the domain of language testing or accuracy. For example, in the well-known STORYBOARD text reconstruction package, the text to be reconstituted first appears on the screen and is then replaced by a series of dashes or dots. The task of the student is to reconstitute the text using simply memory and a knowledge of grammatical structures. Where the student types in a response which makes sense and is acceptable to a native-speaker, but does not represent a word or expression in the original text and hence the program, this is rejected by the computer, usually without explanation.

Phillips' second model is the expert system or AI (Artificial Intelligence) paradigm. This displays two features: "The first would be its ability to draw upon encyclopedic knowledge of the world, to draw inferences and form judgements. The second would be its facility for handling natural human language" (p. 280) (natural language processing, i.e. input parsing and speech recognition and synthesis). Phillips goes on to sketch out a language learning system of the future: "It is possible to conceive of an integrated intelligent language learning system at the heart of which would be a real-time diagnostic model. This would adjust flexibly to the student's responses in open-ended natural language interaction. The net result is that it would present the student with an individualised sequence of learning experiences. This may sound a somewhat far-fetched scenario but many of the elements of such a system are already being worked out." (p. 281). It is far from clear that any real progress in this direction is being made. While the Artificial Intelligence community is, indeed, working towards this goal, its achievements hitherto have been modest and are likely to remain so for the foreseeable future.

The third model, Phillips calls the prosthetic paradigm. This envisages a "more modest" role for the computer in language teaching, based on the acknowledgement of a very fundamental role of the computer, namely its function as a tool. Within this paradigm, "the instrumental uses of the computer are exploited. This is to take advantage of what, in a sense, is its natural role and the one which has allowed it to become so firmly established in society. The word processor, the database and other data processing techniques such as the spreadsheet are now indispensable tools in a wide range of applications." (p. 282). Concluding his article he writes: "Of the approaches discussed here, I would feel least unhappy if the prosthetic model were to achieve, albeit provisionally, paradigmatic status."

This, indeed, is the assumption on which this book is based, namely that it is in the use of primary applications packages, e.g. word processing and database packages, and what might be called secondary applications packages, that is to say, powerful and versatile, often commercially produced, text-based packages such as glossary compilation or machine translation packages, that the language teacher can make the best use of information technology.

There is a growing amount of evidence to suggest that the instrumental approach has achieved paradigmatic status, i.e. has become the prevailing model. Three recent publications in the UK for schools: *Learning Languages with Technology* (1988), S. Hewer's *Making the Most of IT Skills* (1989) and Hardisty and Windeatt's *CALL* (*op. cit.*) are based substantially on the use of primary applications packages. A similar approach is outlined in the 1986 volume of the Longman Applied Linguistics and Language Teaching series *Computers in English Language Teaching and Research* (Leech & Candlin). See also *CALL in Great Britain* (Wolf 1988). The present volume embraces the prosthetic or instrumental approach much more comprehensively. It stresses that the computer is not used to replace what teachers do, but to complement what they do. Its role in teaching is analogous to that of the language laboratory and the video camera, two other items of modern technology which form part of most modern foreign language teachers' repository of learning tools.

Chapter 2 Word Processing seeks first to examine the issue of the particular functional and design specifications of word processors for use in foreign language teaching, for example to display and print out foreign language characters such as accented characters and alphabets such as the Russian and Greek. There then follows an account of basic word processing facilities, illustrated by some examples of how word processing functions might be incorporated into a language programme. The chapter also examines how packages for text and style analysis might be used to enhance the learning process.

The boundaries between word processing and desktop publishing (DTP) are becoming increasingly blurred as enhanced word processing packages appear, offering a number of DTP features. In many respects DTP can broadly be seen as second-generation word processing. Chapter 3 on Desktop Publishing starts by looking at the hardware and software requirements and the working methods of desktop publishing. Creative writing and image processing as learning experiences in undergraduate language and area studies courses are then examined. DTP applications are illustrated by means of simulations of, for example, election posters, newspapers, tourist guides, business reports, and the production of teaching materials. The chapter includes descriptions of possible student projects.

All undergraduate students of foreign languages are engaged on a continuous basis in the production of dictionaries of one sort or another. Increasingly, we find that word processors include a dictionary facility either for purposes of checking the spelling of words or for providing the user with a ready-made database, such as a thesaurus. At the same time, commercially-produced, mono- or bi-lingual CD-ROM-based dictionaries are becoming more and more available for use in translation. Chapter 4 on Lexicography outlines some relevant issues in modern lexicography and then shows how the foreign language user may set about the compilation of a computer-based, bi-lingual dictionary in a systematic way. The established and widely used Oxford Concordance Program (OCP) is contrasted with a more recent and innovatory dictionary generator package, INKTextTools.

The availability of PCs and the spread of word processing has brought tachine translation out of the domain of the computer specialist or military, international or multi-national organisations and into the higher education environment. Chapter 5 on Machine Translation starts with an introduction to machine translation with particular reference to languages and codes, restricted languages and automated dictionaries. Using machine translation in the classroom, and particularly for student-centred learning, is then illustrated by the comparison of two commercial machine translation programs. Possible group and individual activities built around a machine translation program are described in terms of four stages:

- pre-editing: predicting and resolving problems inherent in the source text, mainly complexity and ambiguity;
- dictionary entries: providing syntactic information for both analysis and synthesis and addressing the particular problems of homographs and idioms;
- post-editing: using a split screen, the student post-edits a machine-produced text with particular attention to determiners, pronouns, prepositions, word order and words used with a new sense;
- review: the information gathered in the dictionary entry and post-editing stage is scanned for use in further pre-editing exercises and amendments are suggested for dictionary entries.

Commercial machine translation systems are, generally speaking, expensive. Prolog, on the other hand, is inexpensive and relatively easy to learn and can run on any IBM compatible. Most books on Prolog contain a chapter or two on Natural Language Processing and/or parsing, which is the subject of Chapter 6. The use of the two types of package vary in that machine translation systems tend to focus on the lexico-grammatical level, requiring the user to define each word in a dictionary in terms of a series of grammatical features; whereas the parsing approach using Prolog focuses on the syntactic level, requiring the user to define all the acceptable components of, for example, noun and verb phrases - but in each case learners are required to call on large reserves of untapped and often unappreciated reserves of grammatical knowledge, and they are thus forced to explore and make explicit all their assumptions about the rules of grammar.

The computer offers individualised, user-controlled learning which is flexible and inexhaustible; expanding storage capacities make on-board dictionaries, reference grammars and drill-and-practice activities easily accessible. Video, with its authenticity and predominantly spoken language, is ideally matched to communicative objectives and methods. It is reassuringly familiar, yet highly motivating to the learner. It is flexible in use - as stimulus, model, comprehension task - and gives a maximum of clues to understanding, from lip movements and gestures to the context of communication. With video, teachers have the same control of real target-language speech as they have of written language in a book or newspaper. In combination, video and computer offer an unmatched teaching and learning tool.

Chapter 7 on Interactive Multimedia describes recent developments in the field of interactive video (IV). It begins with a specification of what an interactive video workstation normally consists of, and what useful add-ons are available. It discusses those technical standards which are current and those which are approaching the horizon. It evaluates the advantages and drawbacks of tape as opposed to disc (topicality and the DIY approach versus non-linearity, durability and professional standards).   In a survey of existing software, it describes the approaches and techniques employed in school-level experiments and in commercial discs for business English and Spanish, as well as the research into its effectiveness in language training. The further potential of IV in different teaching/learning situations is explored in the final section of the chapter.

Chapter 8, Database, describes the basic functions of databases and how they are constructed and organised. It then goes on to explore examples of how databases can be used for simulation purposes in the language classroom. The database adds a new dimension to language teaching and learning by linking into the business applications of language. Effective simulations of commercial operations, such as order processing, stock control, and invoicing, bring the world of business activity into the classroom.

Computers can, of course, 'talk' with one another. In Chapter 9, Electronic Communication, the potential of this increasingly important mode of communication is explored. The chapter starts with an account of electronic mail systems such as TTNS, JANET and EARN, which not only offer the possibility of access to both national and international databanks, for example automated dictionaries such as Eurodicautom in Luxembourg and press agencies such as Agence France Presse, but can be used to support collaborative work with overseas institutions through the development of joint projects such as technical glossaries and Joint Study Programmes with European partner institutions.

In a second section the application of electronic communication to student learning is examined. Illustrations range from the delivery of learning materials by means of in-house systems (networked micros and minis) to the innovative notion of the network as a virtual classroom in which both tutor and learner are liberated from the constraints of the timetable. The chapter concludes by exploring the possibilities of the more structured learning environment offered by computer conferencing systems

HyperText, HyperMedia and MultiMedia are very recent additions to the linguistic inventory of the applied computer specialist. Chapter 10 on HyperMedia sets out to make sense of the confusion which these terms have generated for the learner and the teacher. A few examples of HyperText applications currently available are described. This is followed by an examination of the idea of "browsing" as an interactive learning technique and an assessment of the freedom and constraints of such a technique. 'Linear' and 'non-linear' forms of presenting information are then discussed and the problems involved in designing hypertexts and in familiarising users with them (so as to avoid the phenomenon of getting "lost in HyperSpace"!) are outlined. The chapter concludes with an assessment of the advantages and disadvantages of HyperText for CALL authoring and the possibilities afforded by integrated sound and graphics.

The final chapter addresses some of the methodological issues raised in the previous chapters. Most language teachers would probably acknowledge that their teaching practice draws on several different methodologies; that whilst one approach may dominate (perhaps the communicative approach), techniques from other systems (and none) will occasionally intrude. It is not the purpose of the final chapter to suggest the development of a new language teaching methodology to supersede existing ones, but rather to suggest that a methodology needs to be developed to manage the complexity and speed of change in the language teacher's environment, and to identify information technologies (and the computer in particular) as major agents of change. Given that methodologies exist to analyze and manage the introduction of new technologies into other work environments, it is suggested that the same methodologies might be used in the teaching situation, and the systems approach is offered as an appropriate structured method for coping with the complex issues involved.

Bibliography

Hardisty, D. & Windeatt, S. (1989) *CALL*, Oxford University Press.

Hewer, S. (1989) *Making the Most of IT Skills*, Centre for Information on Language Teaching and Research.

Higgins, J. (1983) Computer assisted language learning, *Language Teaching* **16** 102-114.

Jones, C. (1986) It's not so much the program, more what you do with it. The importance of methodology in CALL, *System* **14**,2 171-178.

Kenning, M-M. (1990) Computer-assisted language learning, *Language Teaching* **23** 67-76.

Learning Languages with Technology (1988), Microelectronics Education Support Unit.

Phillips, M. (1987) Potential paradigms and possible problems for CALL, *System* **15**,3 275-287.

Wolf, W. (1988) CALL in Great Britain. In U. O. H. Jung (ed.) *Computers in Applied Linguistics and Language Teaching*, Verlag Peter Lang, 315-324.

2 WORD PROCESSING

Ian R. Kemble and William Brierley

Introduction

Of all the computer tools available to the language teacher, the most liberating and enabling by far is the word processor. Given a little imagination and preparation, a whole new range of activities can be made available to the student, both in the classroom and as group or private study activity. Almost all word processors can be used for the activities described later in this chapter, but it is worth pausing for a moment to describe the basic technical and functional specifications that the language teacher should look for in a word processor. Teachers able to influence institutional purchasing decisions should put at the top of the list of their demands the ability to display and print the full range of characters required by the target language(s). Given that the functionality of word processors (see next section) differs little from package to package, compromise on the issue of accented characters will undermine the usefulness of word processors as a language teaching and learning tool.

Given that most word processors are designed to cope with American English, the first thing to check is that your word processor will actually cope with British English (some word processors for example have difficulty with displaying the £ sign; others may be supplied with spelling checkers for American not British English). But for languages other than English, the principal requirement must be the availability and ease of use of accented characters. Most word processors will have at least one way of allowing accented characters to be typed, but a fairly common "default" method is the combination of ALT key plus a number corresponding to the accented character in the IBM extended character set. For example, holding down the ALT key and keying 138 on the number pad will produce the letter è on the screen. Most west European languages can be handled in this way, though Portuguese (e circumflex) is not available. Special punctuation marks (¿ ¡), currency symbols (¥ ₧), graphics characters, and Greek characters used in mathematical notation (α Σ) are also available. For languages using relatively few accented characters (Italian, German) this method is usually acceptable, but for languages using relatively large numbers of accented characters (French, Spanish), teachers should explore the extent to which their keyboard can be reconfigured.

Keyboard reconfiguration can be achieved at the operating system level. MS-DOS and PC-DOS have command files that may be run before the word processor is loaded to reconfigure the keyboard to behave like a typewriter keyboard for the country in which the language is spoken. This will not only make accented characters available via one key stroke (or SHIFT keystroke), but will allow the switch from the British QWERTY keyboard to the continental AZERTY keyboard. Some word processors will also allow the programming of specific keys, thus allowing accented characters to be assigned to function keys, for example. One thing is certain, no two word processors will solve the problem in the same way, so choice of keyboard represents a compromise between authenticity and convenience.

What is likely to infuriate the language teacher even more than the keyboard layout and the display, is the printing of accented characters. Most cheaper printers will only print the basic (American) 128 character ANSI set. This set does not even include the £ sign, let alone accented characters. More expensive printers will print the full ANSI set or the IBM Extended Character Set (256 characters), but will often require extensive reconfiguration from the pre-set default configuration. This may involve simply the re-setting of dip switches, but with more complex systems and printers, considerable programming skills may be required to achieve the desired results.

None of the above, of course, applies to languages which do not use the Latin alphabet. Other languages (Greek, Russian, Hebrew, Japanese, etc) are catered for by specialist word processors which will, in various ways, allow the user to switch between English and foreign language keyboards. Vuman and Nota Bene are two examples.

Word processor design features and functionality

In evaluating a word processor for use in the classroom, the language teacher should examine both the design principles of the word processor and its functionality. In terms of design principles, the language teacher must assess at least the following features:

■   on-line help / tutorial: students must have easy access to a good tutorial package (preferably self-instructional, and on the machine, rather than book-based), to introduce them to and familiarise them with the operation of the package. Similarly, the word processor should have an on-line help facility, so that new users can refresh their memory of particular commands or functions without constant reference to either the teacher or a manual. Some word processors (not normally PC-based) also allow the tailoring of on-line help facilities to specific needs.

■   menus versus clean screen: the choice between word processors which are menu-driven (at each stage of the operation the user is presented with options in a menu which remains displayed on the screen) and those which use function keys without on-screen menus (and therefore leave more of the screen for the document display) is largely an aesthetic one. Less proficient users may prefer the security of a menu display, whereas more experienced ones may prefer to see more of the document.

■   commands (function keys versus CTRL + key combinations): again, the choice between the various command accessing methods is largely one of aesthetics. Most word processors will use a combination of function keys and/or CTRL (control) key plus a "mnemonic" letter key combination.

■   file saving and retrieval: normally, when the user saves a word processed text to disk, the file thus created will also contain computer codes relating to formatting or printing operations (underlining, indentation, etc). This is necessary to enable the word processor to present text in a variety of ways. However, for many of the more advanced computer operations such as style analysis or glossary compilation, it is much more convenient to work with text files without these additional embedded commands. The word processor should therefore be able to save and retrieve plain (ASCII) text files.

■   WYSIWYG or not: a final aesthetic consideration is whether your word processor automatically displays the text as it will appear on the page (WYSIWYG - what you see is what you get), or whether it displays the page as part of a print routine, or not at all (you only find out what it looks like by printing out).

In terms of functionality the word processor must have:

■   insert/delete: all word processors offer insertion and deletion facilities, and there is only a limited range of ways in which this can be accomplished. The only consideration, therefore is again an aesthetic one: should the word processor be set normally in insertion or overstrike mode? A further consideration might be: how does the word processor deal with reformatting after insertion/deletion (automatic reformatting, or after the issue of a format command)?

■   split screens/windows/no. of documents open at once: in more advanced word processing activities, the student may require to use two or more text files at the same time, and will therefore require a word processor with windowing and/or split screen facilities.   Where such facilities are required, switching between windows and documents should be achieved with the minimum number of key strokes.

■   working with blocks of text: given that many of the suggested uses of word processors in language teaching make use of block manipulation (and block may refer to word, phrase, sentence, paragraph, etc), the ease with which blocks may be marked and then moved is of some importance.

■   moving, copying, pasting text: similarly, once the text has been marked it should be cut, stored and recalled with the minimum of effort.

■   formatting: changing page and line lengths, indenting paragraphs, altering layouts and so on should also be easily achieved to create "real" situations: converting notes into minutes; an instruction into a letter; a transcript of an interview into a news report.

■   spelling checkers, thesauruses: most word processors now come with spell checkers for British as well as American English; many come with thesauruses. A few are available with foreign language spell checking dictionaries and thesauruses.   Using a spelling checker sensitises students to spelling mistakes in a way that the traditional red mark has failed to.   Even so, students need to be made aware of the limitations of spelling checkers (the inability to check correct usage of words, such as, for example, the difference between dependent and dependant), and of the need for careful proofreading of the final text.

■   graphics, fonts, DTP aspects: again, for more adventurous and wide ranging language teaching needs, the availability of desk-top publishing facilities can open up new avenues for exploration: for example the production of a news-sheet based on notes taken from recordings of the week's news broadcasts in the target language.

Basic applications of word processing
In what follows, four basic word processing facilities are considered: formatting, cut and paste, insertion/deletion and search and replace.   A brief explanation of each facility is followed by examples of possible use in the classroom.

Exercises using the word processor differ from those involving dedicated CALL packages in that the computer does not provide the answer.   Instead the student is dependent on one or more sources for appropriate information: they are other students, the teacher, native speakers, sample written documentation such as answer sheets or more sophisticated documentation such as reference books.   The word processor may therefore be used for activities which encourage accuracy (in the fashion of traditional CALL packages), but it can also be used to develop fluency.   So, for example, in a transcription exercise the focus is on the accurate reproduction of the original text. In the case of an editing exercise, e.g. turning an informal press text into a more formal one, the focus is on producing a text with the appropriate stylistic features. For a full discussion of the distinction between fluency and accuracy in language teaching methodology, see Brumfit (1984, pp. 52-54).

Formatting

Formatting in computer terminology is ambiguous. It can refer either to a process which prepares the disc for use on the computer or to the layout of text on the page. Here it is being used in the latter sense.

A punctuation exercise can be set by removing all punctuation devices from the text. Given the limited attention which is often paid to punctuation, the exercise may provoke at the very least some useful discussion on the rules governing punctuation devices. In languages like German, where the comma marks an important clause structure boundary, the split screen facility of the advanced word processor could be used to compare and contrast punctuation conventions in two languages. An extreme version of this exercise would involve the removal of all spaces and punctuation between words in a text. Students are then presented with a solid block of letters and asked to insert spaces between the words once again and insert the punctuation. This exercise could be used effectively in a foreign language course focusing on the development of reading skills, where in the initial stage the student is acquiring an ability to recognise word boundaries. At the other end of the scale, paragraph divisions could be removed so that the student saw only continuous text on the screen and was confronted with the task of deciding upon paragraph divisions. It would clearly be possible to use a variety of different formats to produce a suite of exercises based on a taxonomy of language structures: from word to clause to sentence to paragraph to text.

Cut and paste

The cut and paste function allows a section of text to be blocked or highlighted so that it can be moved to another part of the document.

One of the important functions of advanced language teaching is to raise the student's awareness of textual cohesion and coherence. Cohesion refers to the grammatical and lexical devices which are used by a writer to link information both within and across sentences so as to produce a text that 'hangs together' or 'fits together' well. While cohesion operates primarily at clause, sentence and paragraph level, coherence operates exclusively at text level in that it is concerned with the logical presentation of ideas. The basic linguistic textbook on cohesion is *Cohesion in English* (Halliday & Hasan 1976); excellent practical examples, also in English, are to be found in *Think and Link* (Cooper

1979) and *Writing Skills* (Coe, Rycroft & Ernest 1983). A common exercise which is employed to develop this awareness is to ask the student to sort out a jumbled-up text into the correct sequence. The units chosen for re-arrangement can vary; for example, letters within words; words within a phrase, clause or sentence; lines of lists, recipes or processes; paragraphs of logical argument, narrative or exposition. Theoretically, there are no limitations to the linguistic items which can be jumbled up using the word processor. In practice, however, working within a line, e.g. jumbling up words or letters within a word, can result in an exercise which involves the student in a laborious and time-consuming solution process. It is, therefore, recommended that the basic unit for text-jumbling should be the sentence or the paragraph. Despite this limitation, the use of the word processor to develop the student's awareness of textual cohesion has much to recommend it on account of the ease with which the text on the screen can be re-ordered.

Insertion and deletion

These are self-explanatory word processing functions which can be applied to the entire hierarchy of language units from the individual letter or character of a word to an entire text.

To the language teacher the term insertion immediately suggests the cloze test, an exercise which has an almost universal application to language teaching in that it can be used to test all descriptive levels of language and uses of language - morphological, grammatical and syntactic; lexical, semantic, stylistic and pragmatic. Using the deletion keys, words can be deleted from the text and replaced by markers (a series of dashes or dots) either at regular intervals in the strict sense of the cloze test or irregularly depending on which feature of the text the teacher wishes to test. The answers produced by the student can then be compared with a printout of the original version and their validity established in discussion. A variety of exercises can be developed using a combination of the cut and paste and insertion/deletion functions, particularly where the emphasis is on cohesion and coherence - linguistic notions which, as we have suggested above, play an important role in advanced language teaching.

Search

This feature of the word processor allows the user to instruct the computer to search for a particular word or phrase.

It may be used to test or explore grammatical or grammatico-lexical structures, that is, the word formation features of a text. For example, in a language testing situation, the teacher first deletes particular repeated spelling patterns (such as 'ie' and 'ei' in English), and replaces them by a series of dashes or dots. Students then work through the text using the search function to identify the series of dashes or dots, they then delete them and replace them by the correct spellings as appropriate. In a language exploring situation, the search function may be used to find examples of particular grammatical feature of a text, such as conditional sentences, passive sentences, modal verbs. This exemplifies the use of the computer as a storage and information retrieval system in that texts stored on the computer - and these can be quite substantial given the rapidly increasing storage capacity of even floppy discs - can be examined on the screen. Some word processors such as WordPerfect allow basic concordance files (see Chapter 4) to be created which contain examples of a particular text feature, such as 'if' clauses. Johns (1986, pp. 151-162) describes an early experiment with concordances. "One of the first experiments ... was to use concordances of the half-dozen commonest prepositions, getting students to underline on the printout the head word colligating with the preposition (e.g. 'depending on', 'on demand'), and then to develop a system of classification for the examples they found. The reaction of students was that this was far more helpful than the usual exercise involving 'filling in the missing prepositions'. With the computer on hand, they soon began to investigate such further questions as whether, judging from the contexts in which they occur, 'on the contrary' could be distinguished from 'on the other hand', and then whether these could in turn be distinguished from 'however' and 'nevertheless'."

In addition to the above facilities, the word processor can be used in a fundamental way as a text editor. Here we may identify three editing processes: 'editing up', in other words, producing a longer, more developed text from notes or other textual prompts; 'editing down', the reverse process -- producing a shorter text from a longer one; and 'editing across', or producing a text in a different form or format.

Editing up
An exercise could be devised based on an information-gathering activity. English students could be asked to interview foreign exchange students on their attitude towards a particular issue: for example, German students on the question of German relations with the Soviet Union. The notes are then written into a series of text files on the computer and used to produce a report. Using the split screen facility of the word processor allows the student to access a particular text file in the bottom half of the screen and to use the information contained therein to draft the report in the top half of the screen. Alternatively, a text file can be produced by the teacher containing biographical details of an important personage or the sequence of events of a particular development. Students, working individually or in small groups, are then asked to produce a detailed text. Again, an appropriate exercise for further examination of the ways in which items of information in a text may be linked to produce a coherent whole.

Editing down

The obvious exercise here is the summary. Once again the split screen facility of the word processor can be used to allow the student to write the summary in the top half of the screen and survey the original text in the bottom half. Where the emphasis is on training as in the first year of an undergraduate course, a two-stage procedure might be adopted. The students are asked to highlight - for example, where the word processor allows, this could be done in a different colour - those parts of the text which encapsulate the main points made by the writer. When they are satisfied that they have identified the main points, the rest of the text can be deleted and the various points checked so that they are clear and easy to follow. In the second part of the exercise the summary is written, using the notes produced by the students in the first part of the exercise.

Editing across

Many undergraduate courses in foreign languages are developing industrial placement schemes which allow their students to spend part or all of the year abroad in commerce or industry in the foreign country. In many cases it is the students themselves who take responsibility for establishing contact with a foreign company and negotiating an employment contract. To help them, the computer can be used as an information retrieval system in that sample correspondence, both to and from the foreign company, can be provided in text files which students can then adapt to meet their own requirements.

Modern undergraduate courses in foreign languages use newspaper articles as a major source of information on current affairs. To sensitise students to the variety of journalistic texts being used, stylistic exercises among others can help to raise awareness of the style of the newspaper report or commentary. For example, students can be asked to edit an existing text stored in the computer which, let us say, is written in the style of a popular daily in order to produce a new text which is more formal in style. Typically, some of the direct speech of the existing text will be re-cast in indirect speech, involving changes to the verb in particular. Moving to a different text type, namely advertising, students could be asked to change a sexist advertisement for a job into a non-sexist form. Besides pronoun changes, 'he' and 'she' forms to 'they', students can look for more sophisticated forms of discrimination. A very advanced group may like to discuss ways of avoiding clumsy 'non-sexism', for example, through the use of the passive voice.

Each of the above activities has its place in the language teaching environment. A scheme is reproduced below which could be used to form the basis of an introductory word processing course for advanced students of foreign languages in the first year of their undergraduate course. There are two objectives: firstly, to enable students to become conversant with word processing and thereby develop a basic word processing competence and, secondly, to encourage the perception on the part of students that the computer can be a useful tool in the language learning process.

Introduction to IT for the advanced learner
Aims
>(a) to introduce students to information technology
>(b) to acquaint students with word processing and its application to writing skills
>(c) to acquaint students with data retrieval techniques

General Objectives
>(a) to develop keyboard skills
>(b) to develop students' awareness of the computer as an information store
>(c) to practise language structure manipulation
>(d) to develop students' awareness of textual cohesion

Specific Objectives
>Specific objectives take the form of a series of exercises, tasks or assignments which the student will be expected to complete during the course. The exercises will be integrated with other components of the language teaching programme.

A.   Familiarisation Exercises
>1.   copy a text into the computer
>2.   edit a text
>3.   format a text

B.   Structure Manipulation
>1.   edit a text from the polite ('vous') form to the familiar ('tu') form
>2.   edit a text for correct tense
>3.   edit a text from direct speech to indirect speech and vice versa, where appropriate
>4.   adapt a text from active to passive, where appropriate

C.   Sentence Connection
>Link sentences using:
>1.   proforms
>2.   conjunctions
>3.   logical connectors

D.   Text Production
>1 Letters
>>(a)   compose a formal letter to a high degree of accuracy
>>>(i) requesting information
>>>(ii) making an enquiry
>>>(iii) making a complaint

        (b)   respond to a formal letter (as above)
        (c)   compose an informal letter
        (d)   respond to an informal letter

2 Advertisements
        (a)   produce an advert from information received in text form
        (b)   produce an advert from a glossary of terms
        (c)   edit an advert (see *Editing across* above)

3 Minutes
        (a)   produce the minutes of a meeting
        (b)   edit minutes of a meeting

4 Transcription
        (a)   edit a transcription of a recorded text
        (b)   produce a transcription of a recorded text

5 Summary
        (a)   edit a summary of a short television or radio broadcast
        (b)   produce a summary of a television or radio broadcast.

Advanced text processing

If language teaching is to be effective it must be relevant to the needs of learners. If computers are to be used effectively in language teaching and learning, they must be used in ways which complement or enhance the range of techniques and tools already in use. An essential part of any learning process is analysis of outcomes and review. In the language learning environment, this might take the form of analysis of the learner's output against criteria of style, register and coherence; comparison with a model (native speaker production, for example); then review and revision of the learner's output so that it conforms more closely with the model.

Computers can play an important role in objectively establishing standards for various types of written output, against which learners' output can be measured. In all of this, however, it must be borne in mind that computer programs offer qualitative judgements ("this is a good/bad piece of writing") based almost exclusively on quantitative analysis (measures of word length, sentence length, percentage of common words, and so on). The computer's calculations should therefore always be seen as precisely what they are, and the final judgement about what is good or bad in written production should be left as a matter of negotiation between reader and writer (in this case, teacher and learner). Some commercial packages currently available for these sorts of analysis are Grammatik, Readability and PC-Proof. We discuss the latter two packages.

Readability (from Scandinavian PC Systems) uses a range of statistical measures and tests to analyze texts (in ASCII and some word processor formats) and compares the results against models of "readability". The basic measures used are word lengths, sentence lengths and percentage of commonly used words. The manual points out that readability is also affected by other factors, such as the reader's prior knowledge of the subject, syntax and clarity of reference, none of which can be measured by the program.

Readability's first principle is that languages (in this case English) are made up of 'bricks' and 'mortar'. Mortar refers to the 400 most commonly used words in English, and these will normally constitute about 80 per cent of a text; the bricks are the words that carry the information the author wishes to convey. In English, commonly used words are also short, which leads to the inference that sentences with lots of short words are likely to be easy to understand. Thus the relationship between length of word and length of sentence is central to Readability's analysis. On analysis, Readability assigns each sentence in the text to one of nine categories (simple, normal, narrative, foggy, elegant, difficult, complicated, pompous, and wordy), then compares the result of analysis against nine models (normal, children's book, newspaper article, advertising copy, novel, magazine story, technical manual, government report, and bureaucratic report). The computer will offer basic advice about readability and can print out sentences which do not conform to the desired pattern. Whilst the manual points to "language flow contaminants" (such as nominalisation, the passive voice, excessive details, abstractions, status enhancement and prolonging words, jargon, dependent clauses), Readability has no way of identifying these; it is left to the user to identify these for him/herself. (The Unix multi-user operating system, by contrast, does have style analysis tools which can identify many of these features.)

Readability is a useful tool in carrying out initial analysis and initiating discussion about issues of style, register, appropriacy, coherence and cohesion, and so on. It has the advantage over the human critic of appearing objective and neutral. All the students in the class know that their output has been treated in exactly the same way. Its limitations lie in the range of measures it uses, and in its limited capacity for output. There is no facility for editing texts within Readability, or for comparing directly two versions of the same text.

PC Proof (from Lexpertise Linguistic Software) is an English proofreading tool that scans text for potential errors and provides suggestions for corrections. Unlike Readability, it works interactively, showing the text on the screen as analysis proceeds, stopping at potential problems, flashing a message in a window and allowing instant editing. PC Proof looks for problems in three main areas: mechanics (spelling, punctuation, capitalization and double words); usage (offensive, often confused, formality, imprecision, wordy, non-standard, user-defined); and style ("be" verbs, and nominalisation). It also has a further facility to analyze document structure (sentence list, sentence beginnings, document structure, repetitions, word counts and averages).

There are additional versions of PC Proof which have been designed specifically to assist native speakers of French and German to write English. These versions additionally look for "false friends", and typical native speaker errors. These French and German versions are useful to native speakers of English in checking translations from either of the languages.

These, and similar packages, could be relatively easily integrated into a language teaching programme of activities: for example, with students whose primary interest in learning a language is the study of literary texts. Such students are required at an early stage to give close attention to aspects of coherence and cohesion in texts. The teaching strategy might begin with a survey of literary book reviews, to establish notions of form, style, purpose, structure, etc. The students could then be asked to do several short recomposition exercises (where the paragraphs of a book review are jumbled together and have to be sorted into the correct order) to explore for themselves the structures of sample reviews. Where possible, these reviews could then be submitted to style analysis packages (such as those described above) for comparison (and evaluation of style analysis packages themselves). After this exercise, students could be asked to compose their own literary reviews of set texts, either imagining themselves in the situation of a contemporary reviewer, or of a writer of a retrospective celebrating the anniversary of the author's death. Further exercises might include comparisons with original reviews of the given text, or compilation of class reviews into a literary review journal.

Bibliography

Brumfit, C. (1984) *Communicative Methodology in Language Teaching*, Cambridge University Press.

Coe, N., Rycroft, R. & Ernest, P. (1983) *Writing Skills. A Problem-Solving Approach*, Cambridge University Press.

Cooper, J. (1979) *Think and Link. An Advanced Course in Reading and Writing Skills*, Edward Arnold.

Halliday, M. A. K. & Hasan, R. (1976) *Cohesion in English*, Longman.

Hardisty, D. & Windeatt, S. (1989) *CALL*, Oxford University Press.

Hewer, S. (1989) *Making the Most of IT Skills*, Centre for Information on Language Teaching and Research.

Johns, T. (1986) Micro-Concord: a language learner's research tool, *System*, 14,2 151-162.

3 DESKTOP PUBLISHING

Günter Minnerup

Introduction
All too often, the meaning of "computer literacy" is confused with keyboard familiarisation.   In arts and humanities faculties, in particular, expensively acquired hardware is under-used as little more than sophisticated typewriters and most students never really deepen their understanding of computer technology beyond the word processing level. This article is inspired by the conviction that there is considerable merit in educating even arts faculty students in what computer literacy should really mean: some understanding of how not only numerical, but also textual and pictorial information can be stored, communicated and displayed by (and between) machines. Equipped with such an understanding, they will be much more able to keep up with the pace of innovation in the field of information technology, communication and automation. Science and engineering students have long accepted the relevance of computing to their chosen careers, but in the arts and humanities the passive resistance to IT remains strong and computer awareness continues to lag far behind the degree to which traditionally "low-tech" fields of human activity are being affected by microchip technology.

Furthermore, and on a perhaps slightly more controversial note, anything that imposes the rigours of binary logic onto the often somewhat fuzzy thought processes of arts and humanities students can only be beneficial. Under the

British school system with its early specialisation, language and literature students tend to be raised on a one-sided diet of intellectual problems with a heavy emphasis on intuitive-speculative modes of thought - often to a point of virtual innumeracy, unfamiliarity with the rigid rules of formal logic, and sometimes even a snobbery that considers the world of applied technology as an entirely "lower" form of intellectual life.

The following considerations are therefore not simply concerned with desktop publishing (DTP) as a language-learning tool in the narrow sense, but are designed to suggest a way by which students can be exposed to the potential and the pitfalls of IT more deeply than is possible by employing computers merely as word processing, number-crunching or data recall and manipulation tools.   DTP is very well suited to this because it engages the natural instincts of arts and humanities students to communicate, to see their work in print, and to judge output by aesthetic criteria, while at the same time posing practical problems which cannot be solved easily without entering into the nuts and bolts of binary information management.   Above all, DTP is an integrative pursuit because it involves collaboration within a well-defined division of labour (avoiding the solitary confrontation of an individual with the machine which applications like word processing, spreadsheets, and databases tend to engender), as well as the integration of different items of hard- and software, different input and output devices and different data types and file formats (rather than the one-dimensional, "black box", fingers-keyboard-file-printer-paper path in word processing).

The aims of a DTP module as suggested below can therefore be broadly defined as follows:
- the language skills involved in using foreign-language sources such as radio, television, newspapers and magazines for information and inspiration, and in writing similar material in the foreign language as copy for the publication project;
- the "Area Studies" skills of analyzing the media market of a particular country and researching the political, social, economic and cultural issues to be covered in the project;
- the computer literacy skills involved in generating and combining output from different hardware devices and software packages, understanding the various formats in which machines can read, store and exchange textual and graphical information, and solving the practical problems associated with handling these formats.

In addition, of course, students will develop some familiarity with the problems of typography, page layout and graphic design, although this is purely coincidental to the exercise and not a major aim in itself.

What is desktop publishing?
There is a common misunderstanding that DTP is simply an extension of word processing. This may be a result of the fact that most DTP work has a predominant textual element in it, and it is a confusion promoted by the vendors of advanced word processing software wishing to add another marketable dimension to their products. One day, perhaps, advances in the processing power of commonly available microcomputers may indeed overcome the divisions between text editing, page layout and graphic illustration packages, but on the current hardware platforms such all-purpose software would be impossibly slow and unwieldy. The fastest and most flexible word processors operate in text mode, whereas DTP software is essentially graphics-oriented, so that it is still common practice to import entire text files prepared in a dedicated word processor beforehand - even on micro-computers such as the Apple Macintosh with its graphic user interface.

Although most DTP programs do have at least rudimentary text and graphics editing functions, their chief purpose is not the creation of textual and pictorial data, but the integration and arrangement of such data on the pages of a document. In fact, "desktop publishing" is itself a bit of a misnomer insofar as the actual publishing process will rarely begin and end on the same desktop - at the input end, the operator of DTP software will rarely also be the author of the textual and pictorial material being published, while on the output side most so-called DTP systems can only provide the camera-ready artwork for the printer/platemaker, via dot-matrix, laser or typesetter output.

Properly understood, desktop publishing is a creative process involving a chain of diverse activities: the gathering, preparation, processing, presentation and dissemination of information. Depending on the actual project, it can involve an extremely broad range of skills - those of the researcher, writer or journalist; the editor, production manager and proofreader; the illustrator and graphic designer; the typographer and printer; the computer programmer and hardware technician; even the promoter, accountant and distributor. It is against this background, and on this understanding rather than that of DTP as "word processing with pictures", that the role of DTP is discussed here.

The production of mock-up newspapers and magazines in a foreign language is, of course, not a new idea in language teaching, although more recently, with the spread of video technology ("desktop video"), newsreading and interviewing techniques appear to have become more popular. With video, it is possible to simulate the real-life production of television items to a fairly high degree of authenticity, and this must be part of its appeal to both students and teachers. Traditional publishing, however, was either prohibitively expensive or unsatisfactory in the extent to which it could come up with plausibly realistic procedures and results.   Until the advent of DTP, that is.

Software

This is another reason why extended word processing should be regarded as a poor substitute, as should the very low-end, self-styled "DTP" applications whose only real attraction is their price.   Students have a very fine sense of distinction between unsatisfactory ersatz activities and the real thing: conversation exercises between themselves never arouse as much enthusiasm as a meeting with real foreigners, for instance.   By the same token, any such "high-tech" projects as DTP and video work should generally be as near to the real thing as possible.

The use of DTP in language teaching suggested here is therefore concerned with creating a project-oriented learning situation in which the lines of distinction between the various linguistic, technical, creative and organisational skills being practised are as blurred as possible and always overshadowed by the demands of the practical task at hand.   The example given - the production of a foreign-language newspaper - is merely illustrative and could be extended by many other, similar applications.   But before this is discussed in detail, some consideration needs to be given to software and hardware requirements.

Hardware

DTP programs are available for almost every type of computer, but some are better suited for the task than others.   Eight-bit computers such as the once ubiquitous BBC and Amstrad PCWs are really too underpowered for serious consideration: as an essentially graphics, rather than character, oriented task, DTP is something that such slow CPUs with their restricted memory-handling abilities are just not up to.   For the same reason, the still quite common IBM PCs and compatibles of the first, XT generation (i.e. those with Intel 8086/8088 processors) are far from ideal.   In MS-DOS terms, the minimum standard for the comfortable handling of high-resolution graphics is an Intel 80286 with a minimum of 640k and a Hercules or VGA screen (monochrome is quite acceptable, colour processing still being confined to the very high end of professional DTP).

The only DOS machines really comfortable with DTP, however, are the still quite expensive 80386 PCs with several megabytes of RAM, running a graphical user interface (GUI) such as Windows 3.   Serious consideration should therefore be given to breaking with the "industry standard" and acquiring a computer which was specifically designed to operate in graphics mode, such as the Apple Macintosh or even the Atari ST, Commodore Amiga or Acorn Archimedes.   The Apple Macintosh is the standard platform for DTP with a wealth of advanced software available for it, and of the latter machines the

Atari ST, in particular, makes quite a capable, low-cost DTP workstation. The decision to break with the common "IBM compatibles only" institutional acquisition policies should not be too difficult considering that only one DTP platform will usually be required: the word processing side of things can be done on whatever other computers are already present, from Amstrad PCWs to dumb terminals on a Unix network.

Non-textual input, such as line art illustrations and photographic material, makes an image scanner pretty much essential. These have come down in price quite considerably, and for very restricted budgets a hand-held device of the HandyScanner type might well suffice, although an A4 flatbed is preferable and one with a true grey-scale capability ideal for photographic halftones. Video images (sourced from television or video camcorders) can be imported into DTP software through video digitisers, with low-end models available for even the most restricted budgets.

A modem can be useful in a variety of ways. Sometimes it offers the only method of transferring text or graphics files from remote machines of a different type, when direct serial links are not feasible and disk formats totally incompatible. Access to on-line information services can be a valuable source of news data, and modem links can also be used to output the finished pages to a remote laser printer or typesetter.

Most important on the hardware side, however, is the final output device. Printed output is, after all, what DTP is all about and student motivation is likely to suffer if the end product is going to be crude dot-matrix output on continuous tractor-feed paper. It is true that reasonable results can be achieved with modern 24-pin dot matrix printers, but as these tend to be very slow, noisy and ribbon-consuming, a laser printer is really essential. Lasers basically fall into two categories: those with built-in PostScript interpreters and those without. Not surprisingly, the latter are a lot cheaper than the former, and the HP LaserJet compatibles, in particular, are supported by most DTP software. The industry standard, however, is PostScript, and most DTP packages support this page description language and its associated, huge catalogue of fonts, clip art and graphic illustration software. If a true PostScript printer is beyond departmental means, PostScript emulation in software (Freedom of the Press, GoScript, UltraScript) may provide a more affordable alternative.

The project
The most obvious and in many ways most attractive DTP exercise is the production of one or more look-alikes of foreign newspapers or magazines. The most obvious, because newspapers and magazines are, of course, the *raison d'être* of DTP software. The most attractive, because students can easily relate to this

and it integrates a number of activities which are (or should be) part of a modern languages/area studies course anyway: current affairs and media studies. The project could, for example, be to produce mock issues of the *Bildzeitung*, the *Frankfurter Allgemeine* and the *Frankfurter Rundschau* - or, perhaps more realistically, the front pages of each - based on the same raw materials of events on one particular day (or even week, see below).

A different approach is to take the students' own environment as a starting point and produce, for example, a departmental newspaper/newsletter in the foreign language. Again, it should not be difficult to motivate students and one advantage compared to the "foreign newspaper" variant is that a freer reign can be given to the visual design as it is not necessary to simulate a particular model in style, typeface etc. On the other hand, the "area studies"/ "media studies" aspects fall by the wayside and it is also less possible to prescribe particular language levels and registers to be used, thus perhaps also reducing the language-learning dimension.

A third obvious application of DTP in language learning is the generation of teaching materials by groups of students themselves, for use by themselves and subsequent years. Such a project would differ from the two previous suggestions in that its format could be more like a book rather than a newspaper/magazine, in which case the graphics element might be absent and an advanced word processing package may well be sufficient. To include the typical DTP aspects, care would have to be taken to include illustrations such as photos and maps. A German Studies group might, for example, have monitored the process of German re-unification between the collapse of the GDR in autumn 1989 and the first all-German elections in December 1990 and then be given the assignment of compiling a Reader for use by future generations of students. There are really no limits to the possible applications.

In the following, the "foreign newspaper" project will be assumed because it offers the broadest range of tasks and activities.

Organisation and division of labour

It is desirable that the DTP module should, as far as possible, be planned and managed by the students themselves and not simply be executed as a sequence of pre-defined exercises designed by the teaching staff. Ideally, the lecturer should act primarily as a technical advisor - and even in this role he/she should be prepared to give way to any students who, as will be increasingly the case given the advances of computer education in secondary schools, show a measure of IT knowledge (or other specialist skills such as graphic design etc).

On the other hand, however, timetable pressures and other factors necessitate a very high degree of organisation and discipline if the exercise is not to overrun its allocated time schedule or even descend into chaos. The key to such organisation and discipline is a thorough discussion of the nature and purpose of the project and agreement on a well-defined division of labour.

In many, if not most, departments, the number of graphics-capable computer terminals will be strictly limited, and in the vast majority of cases these will be single-user terminals not connected to a network. In what follows, we shall assume the availability of no more than one DTP workstation (that is, a graphics-capable computer with a hard disk, sufficient RAM and a laser printer, running a page layout software package), alongside more character-based systems, either stand-alone or linked in a local area network cluster. A well-defined division of labour is therefore necessary in the first place because the number of students involved in a project will almost always be greater than the number of available page-layout platforms. Functionally, this is of course not a setback at all because there are far more tasks involved in preparing and producing a publication than page layout, but from the point of view of student motivation it is desirable that every participant gets an opportunity to practice what is, arguably, the most "glamorous" of the tasks. Also, no student should be excluded from a hands-on experience of the complex page layout stage, so if at all possible some form of task rotation ought to be established, with small groups/individuals switched from one job to another during the course. There are basically two ways of achieving this: rotation from issue to issue (assuming that more than one issue is produced), or rotation within the division of labour by assigning to one group/individual different functional tasks in relation to different parts of the publication to be produced: writing the sports page, designing the front page, illustrating the features page, or whatever.

The functional division of labour will be largely suggested by the real-world situation being emulated. A publication has to be designed, the copy (reports, features, comments etc) obtained and written up, the copy sub-edited and fitted into the allocated space, illustrations produced, the pages made up and finally the production organised. On this basis, it is probably best to employ two principles of division of labour concurrently: a vertical division of labour following these stages of production, and a horizontal division of labour as suggested in the previous paragraph (i.e. by pages/rubrics, issues, or different types of publication) - the latter principle permitting an equal share of all participants in all aspects of the project.

Specific IT-related tasks

A general description of the jobs involved can be gleaned from a number of specialist publications on journalism and periodical production, so we shall take a knowledge of these for granted and will concentrate here on the specifically IT-related aspects, the problems likely to be encountered, and their possible solutions in a low-budget context.

Reporting, writing, editing

The main problem here is obtaining enough information about the main stories to be covered. This leaves radio and television as the main sources, and it is obviously desirable that the department has access to satellite television and video facilities for this purpose. The "reporters" will write up the articles based on audio and video recordings of the foreign media, supplemented by any coverage of the events by the British media, while others can compose items such as editorials, features, weather forecasts, horoscopes, letters to the editor and other matter. A special case, particularly suitable for first or second year students, may be to take a "digest" publication such as the *Guardian Weekly* as a model and produce a weekly edition of one of the leading newspapers of the country, drawing heavily on one week's issues for material to be rewritten and summarised.

From the computer point of view, the chief task is to get the copy into machine-readable form, that is ideally, word-processed text files in one of the import formats supported by the DTP software. This is not absolutely essential, as it is always possible to fall back on pure ASCII files, but text attributes like bold, italics, underline and so on are quicker to generate in word processing than in DTP programs. The best solution is the use of DTP software which supports style sheets and "tagging", allowing much of the formatting of the text to be done on character-based word processing terminals. Even if the software does not support "tagging", it is often possible to simulate it by identifying the appropriate control codes and defining these as macros in the word processing package. The more of the text-based editing work can be done within a word processing environment the better, as it is always superior to the editing facilities offered by DTP software.

The physical transfer of the word-processed files to the DTP workstation can often be a problem, given the profusion of disk formats, especially in the world of MS-DOS. Nothing is more frustrating than saving an article to a 1.44Mb, 5¼in disk on a PC-AT, only to find that the "other side" only reads, say, 720k, 3½in disks. Things can be even more intractable between two different operating systems - such as a UNIX network and an Apple Macintosh computer. If all else fails, there is always the option of by-passing disks altogether and resorting to serial data transfer via a serial null modem cable or even modem/telephone - which may be the only solution with very large files exceeding disk capacities, such as those created by high-resolution scanners (see below). Special difficulties can arise from the fact that many word processing packages deal only inadequately with foreign languages.   Certain foreign characters may be difficult to generate, and spell-checking dictionaries may not be available.   Some languages such as German are not usually much of a problem as they are fully supported by the standard ASCII character set, but others with many accented characters, even non-Latin scripts (Russian!) may require a graphics-capable terminal and special software, perhaps a word processor imported from the country in question.   Foreign software is a good idea in any case as it may be the only way to obtain a suitable spell-checking dictionary, and it can only be beneficial if students have to consult a foreign-language manual to look up commands and solve problems.

One often under-rated feature of word processing software is the provision of a powerful and flexible search-and-replace function.   Virtually all word processors have search-and-replace in some form, of course, but few can search for non-printable control characters.   This is essential not only for global style changes, but also to solve any difficulties arising when different software packages, not to mention different operating systems, have different ways of handling foreign characters, linefeeds/carriage returns and so on.

Illustrations and pictorial material
One of the most rewarding aspects of DTP is the use of illustrations alongside the text.   Strictly speaking, of course, pictorial illustrations have little to do with language teaching as such, but apart from the motivational factor a number of hidden benefits can be associated with the work involved in obtaining such material, both in terms of research into the subject matter - searching through books and magazines for suitable illustrations, perhaps generating graphs and charts - and the computing skills demanded by their use in DTP.

Illustrations can be broken down into two broad categories: line art graphics (as in cartoons, diagrams, maps, pie and bar charts, logos etc), and photographic halftones.   Both can be used even in low-budget DTP but both also pose their own challenges.   Coming to grips with these challenges is one of the main contributions to the raising of computer literacy standards among students.

Computer graphics can be stored in two basic forms: as bit-image or pixel, and as vector graphics.   Bit-image graphics are made up of dots of fixed size but arranged in various patterns, with the overall size of the image dependent on the dot size and dot density of the output device - both on screen and when printed on paper.   When enlarged, such images will become coarser and when reduced, moire patterns can appear and subtle shades of grey be consolidated into dense blacks.   Vector graphics, by contrast, are stored as mathematical descriptions of one or more objects (which is why they are also referred to as "object-oriented" graphics) and are thus resolution-independent, but more difficult to create and suitable only for line art illustrations. Creating and handling both types requires a good understanding of the main principles of digital data storage.

The problems posed by photographic material relate closely to the limitations of the bit image file formats used by scanners (and much of what follows applies equally to working with video digitisers); the distortions introduced by rescaling, especially non-proportional rescaling, are intensified by the complexity of the dither patterns used to simulate grey shades, and the data volumes generated can be considerable: an uncompressed A4 scan at a resolution of 300 dots per inch will require close to one megabyte of disk storage and RAM space. On the other hand, the bit image file format makes it fairly easy - albeit tedious - to edit photos at pixel level, and there is now a growing range of image editing software allowing all kinds of interesting effects to be achieved. All in all, the complexities of graphics editing suggest that this task be assigned to a particular group of students, even though the source material may be provided in part by the "reporters" and final touching up be left to the page layout.

Page layout and printing
The textual and pictorial material prepared will then have to be made up into pages. If the project is a mock-up of a specific foreign publication, then it is obviously desirable to follow the original design as closely as possible - the same or very similar typefaces if available, an identical or strikingly similar masthead (this can be scanned and imported as a graphic), a similar column layout. Copy-fitting is likely to be the chief problem, so the operators of the DTP software will have to edit the text to size, experiment with different headlines, experience the pitfalls of cropping and scaling pixel graphics. Captions have to be written and graphical elements such as column guides and boxes created.

In essence, this is not a job for a committee, so individual students should be assigned responsibility for particular pages once the overall design has been discussed and agreed upon. This responsibility should also extend beyond the presentation to the linguistic quality of the page, at least to a final proofreading and spell-checking. If the text is set in narrow newspaper columns, hyphenation will be necessary to avoid white rivers of inter-word spacing, and since algorithmic hyphenation can be of dubious quality - especially with foreign languages in an English/American DTP program - and adequate hyphenation-exception dictionaries may not be available, hyphens may have to be inserted or amended by hand. Other manual corrections that may be necessary include the individual insertion of accented characters that may have got lost in the file import process.

Finally, printing. If everything has been set up properly, there should not be any technical problems with printer drivers and fonts (if there are, they will need to be resolved, of course), but a first hardcopy may well reveal shortcomings that were not apparent on a lower-resolution monitor screen: distorted aspect ratios or moire patterns in graphics, positioning of items, word or letter spacing, missing captions and so on.

In conclusion

This essay could only scratch the surface of the many opportunities offered by the ability of microcomputers and the appropriate software to produce sophisticated printed documents to very high standards. Because of the variety of possible applications, investment in desktop publishing capacities will have many benefits to a department in addition to their utilisation in teaching: in the preparation of more attractive teaching materials and handouts by staff, for example, or the production of departmental publications and stationery. To explore all these possibilities, it is necessary to overcome the narrow view of microcomputers as purely word- or number-crunching machines dating from the days of character-based displays and daisywheel printers, and recognise their potential as creative tools now that user-friendly, graphic environments and high-resolution displays and output devices are becoming commonplace.

4 LEXICOGRAPHY

Ian R. Kemble

Introduction

Underlying the following considerations is the notion of a semi-integrated model of a translator's workbench (see Levy 1990, pp. 177-188). The model consists of two levels of integration, in which the text or text file functions as the linking element between all the parts of the system. The first level of integration is a fully integrated word processing environment consisting of the following tools: word processor, thesaurus, spell-checker and bilingual dictionary. The second level of integration is a semi-integrated set of resources which includes the concordancer, the dictionary generator and the style-checker. In what follows, the focus is on the 'dictionary' components of the model, namely the bilingual dictionary, the concordancer and the automated dictionary generator, and their practical use in undergraduate foreign language teaching.

In language teaching we can identify two basic dimensions to vocabulary: the exposure to vocabularies in realistic or real language situations (vocabulary acquisition) on the one hand, and the learning of vocabulary which includes the use of vocabulary tools such as the mono- and bilingual dictionary and the thesaurus (vocabulary learning) on the other. In this chapter the focus will be on the former, and in particular the software tools which are available to enable students to compile their own dictionaries or glossaries.

The chapter is structured in two parts. It starts by looking at a number of background issues of interest to undergraduate lexicographers, with particular reference to technical glossaries or dictionaries, before evaluating two fundamental software tools available to the undergraduate user.

Lexicography: some background issues

The recent evolution of the dictionary

It is only comparatively recently that "the lexicographer has looked beyond one type of user - persons of cultivated literary tastes, sharing the same educational and linguistic background as themselves", so writes Jean Dubois (1981, p. 236). In an article entitled "Models of the dictionary: evolution in dictionary design" he traces the various stages in the development of French monolingual dictionaries over the past four decades.

-     The traditional model. The model is characterised by its emphasis on word meaning. Prominence is given to the definition, supported by specially constructed examples designed to refer the user to his own educational background.

-     The traditional model in evolution. The second stage is marked by a gradual shift towards the description of the present-day language in response to changes in the educational background of dictionary users. Greater emphasis is given to syntactic patterns and collocations (groups of words which occur repeatedly). A new criterion is introduced to determine the different senses of a word: frequency of use in the twentieth century.

-     The pedagogical model. The model is governed by the following criterion: the function of the dictionary as a facilitator of competence in oral and written expression. Hence the emphasis is exclusively on present-day usage; the sentence takes precedence over the word in terms of illustrating both the syntactic environments in which a lexical item may occur and the sense(s) in which it is used. The dictionary is no longer merely a reference tool but an integral component of language learning as taught in French schools. "Its sample sentences are often used as a starting-point for composition; it acts as a check on grammatical accuracy..." (Dubois 1981, p. 242).

-     The learners' dictionary. Dubois concludes with a reference to the need to respond to the needs of non-native speakers of French, particularly those in French-speaking Africa. However, in contrast to the English-speaking world, French monolingual learners' dictionaries remain few in number and are difficult to identify. A notable example of this genre is the *Dictionnaire Larousse du Français Langue Étrangère (Niveau I et Niveau II)*, 1979 (Lamy 1985, p. 33).

In the English-speaking world the progression from the traditional to the modern dictionary has followed a similar pattern with two exceptions. Firstly, there has not been any attempt on the part of government to make the dictionary an indispensable and officially-sanctioned aid to study in schools.

Secondly, the worldwide dominance of EFL (English as a Foreign Language) has resulted in the publication of a number of learners' dictionaries, the aim of which is not only to help users "grasp meanings" (Bolinger 1965, p. 572) but to provide them with a learning aid for the language itself and hence integrate lexicography with pedagogy. Examples include the *Longman Dictionary of Contemporary English*, the *Oxford Advanced Learner's Dictionary of Current English* and, more recently, the *Collins Cobuild English Language Dictionary* (see below). In a review of four English-language dictionaries Hartmann (1981, pp. 297-303) expresses his admiration for five positive features of the new dictionaries:

- their up-to-dateness,
- the comprehensiveness of their coverage,
- the amount of linguistic information they contain,
- the attention paid to problems of appropriacy in usage,
- the consistency of arrangement and cross-referencing, made possible by word-processing and computer-typesetting technology.

Indeed, the computer is beginning to play an increasingly significant role in modern lexicography. Firstly, advances in data storage and retrieval techniques have resulted in the appearance of dictionaries stored on compact disc. The CD-ROM (text only) disc is a very powerful storage medium, making it possible to hold on a single five-inch disc an amount of data equivalent to about 250,000 A4 pages of text. It offers high-speed flexible access to a vast amount of text which can be searched in a variety of innovatory ways. Thus, for example, the CD-ROM version of the *Oxford English Dictionary* allows access by the definition of the word, by the etymology, by parts of speech or subject categories, and by the illustrative quotations, keyed to date, author, word, or the text of the quotation. The information gathered may be stored in a file and subsequently printed. Although the CD-ROM-based dictionaries currently available show a heavy English bias (Fox 1990, p. 27), there are some exceptions, notably *Le Robert Electronique*, the CD disc version of the *Le Grand Robert*, containing 80,000 records. In the bilingual or multi-lingual dictionary context two dictionaries can be mentioned: the *Harrap's Multi-Lingual Dictionary Database* and the *Collins On-Line Electronic Dictionary*.

Secondly, lexicographers are beginning to make increasing use of computer-stored corpora. The best-known example of such corpora is the most recent addition to the available learners' dictionaries, the *Collins Cobuild Dictionary*, which first appeared in 1987. The principal contribution of the computer here is the availability in machine-readable form of a concordance based on 7.3 million words (the Main Corpus), supplemented by a further concordance of 13 million words (the Reserve Corpus), a total of 20 million words. The main corpus exists in two separate forms: a spoken corpus and a written corpus. The potential main advantages of such corpora are:

- citations are not made-up examples, but are based on actual usage and are attestable by reference to a major corpus of texts.
- concordancing techniques enable the user to discover patterns that exist in natural language by grouping text in such a way that they are clearly visible.

A typical KWIC (keyword in context) concordance not only reproduces all the instances of the keyword (i.e. the word you ask the computer to search for) in the corpus in a straight column down the middle of the page, but does so in a way which makes it very easy to see what words occur immediately before and after it in each case. A further concordance technique allows particular combinations of keyword and co-word or co-words to be grouped together and reproduced, for example, in descending order of their frequency. The information this provides helps the lexicographer to make decisions about which collocational patterns, word senses and examples to include in the dictionary entry.

The technical dictionary

By the 'technical' dictionary is meant the dictionary for a special register or the 'segmental' dictionary, which "refers to language use that differs somewhat from the way in which the 'common' language is employed and hence is in need of explication to outsiders." (Opitz 1983a, p. 56). Just like many other dictionaries the 'technical' dictionary is user-orientated in that it is compiled on the basis of criteria provided by particular target groups and their professional or special interest needs. What sets it apart from other dictionaries is the additional factor of subject specialisation. And just as in the case of the general dictionary the distinction can be made between dictionaries for the general user and dictionaries for particular groups of users, so too in the context of the technical dictionary can the distinction be made between dictionaries for large groups of users, e.g. engineers, and smaller groups of users, e.g. navigators. But the definition of user groups is never a clear one and it is rare to find a technical dictionary which caters exclusively for the specialist and ignores other groups with whom the specialist is associated, be it the student, the translator or the secretary. This variety of functions inevitably translates itself into a multiplicity of dictionaries and an assortment of styles.

The nub of the problem facing the technical lexicographer resides in the interaction between the 'common' language (the language of everyday speech) and its use by the subject specialist. While there is no problem in categorising as technical terms such low-frequency, specialised terms as parabola, paradigm, quadrille and quadraphony, the problem begins when common words are imbued with a new meaning, such as in computing terminology, hard disk, file, buffer, memory, register, bus. The problem gets worse as a number of different technical spheres adopt the same word for their own, e.g. hard (as in hard water), and is compounded by the inclusion in technical registers of words from the 'common' core. "One of the most intractable problems of 'content-user fit' in special glossaries concerns the user's failure -- frequent enough particularly among technical occupations -- to sufficiently differentiate between technical and general lexemes, thus expecting to find in a technical dictionary much more material than would be warranted from a strictly linguistic point of view." (Opitz 1983b, p. 168.   See also Opitz 1979, pp. 89-95.)

Two important lexicographical techniques for overcoming the problem of polysemy, which may result from the adoption of a particular term by more than one technical register, are tagging and referencing.   Tagging means attaching labels to terms to indicate their use in a particular specialist sphere (smelting, welding, brewing, tourism), whereas referencing means providing authentic examples of the use of technical terms in context, for example: extracts from legal documents, government papers, professional journals, or specifying the source of a definition of a technical term.   Neither of these two techniques can be effective without the bringing together of the linguist-lexicographer and the subject specialist and supporting their deliberations with the results of enquiries, surveys and statistical data of language used by specialists so that the right choice of lexical items can be made.

According to Opitz, the good technical dictionary or glossary distinguishes itself above all in terms of four important presentational features dictated by user needs:
- simplicity (e.g. a straightforward alphabetical ordering),
- clarity (use of different fonts and typefaces, regular spacing),
- consistency (in the listing of multi-term words (e.g. compounds)),
- brevity (avoidance of "overstuffing" entries with information relating to syntactic structuring and pronunciation).

The dictionary entry
In his article "LSP Dictionaries for EFL Learners", Moulin reacts to Opitz's fourth point above (Moulin 1983) by listing some of the questions LSP (Language for Special Purposes) students commonly ask of their teachers: "Why do most bilingual dictionaries work on the principle of one equivalent (or translation) for each headword?   Why are examples in bilingual and monolingual dictionaries so rare, so sketchy and so consistently obsolete?   Why are full and meaningful citations the exception rather than the rule?   Why is phonetic transcription always omitted?   Why do compilers of special-purpose dictionaries never seem to bother about problems of grammar and usage?"   Moulin envisages a need for two types of dictionary: the first a kind of learners' dictionary for a specialist field, and the second an advanced, fully-fledged specialist dictionary.   He then goes on to outline the ideal entry for both kinds

of dictionary, compiled by a team of specialists and LSP teachers. He envisages an up-to-date data-base, supplemented by frequency lists of special terms and phrases, with the selection of entries based on two criteria: (a) frequency of occurrence, and (b) the team's information and experience. The ideal entry is characterised as follows:

- Headword, with spelling variants, where appropriate.
- Pronunciation, with variants.
- Grammatical information, similar to that in the LDOCE (*Longman Dictionary of Contemporary English*).
- Foreign language equivalents of the headword's basic non-specialised meanings, accompanied, where appropriate, by an indication of the context in which they typically occur; cross-references to synonyms, antonyms, etc. which encourage the learner to make paradigmatic explorations; register labels (e.g. formal/informal/familiar; written/spoken; derogatory/appreciative/humorous).
- Definition of the concept in clear, complete and accurate language, followed by its translation.
- Examples (with FL translations), preferably consisting of sentences, selected on the grounds not only of their authenticity and frequency, but chiefly of their usefulness for learners. "Thus, if apart from their informative interest, they also illustrate a very frequent grammatical pattern, all the better."
- Illustrations. "A clear and easily comprehensible chart will enhance the value of the information supplied in the rest of the entry."

While context has an important role to play in Moulin's model, for the Cobuild team, context is "crucial" (Sinclair 1987, p. 87). By concentrating on the formal features of a lexical item and the contexts in which it appears, the lexicographical team aims to arrive at "a reasonable analysis" (Sinclair 1987, p. 89) of the various sense distinctions of the lexical item. The editor expresses the operating principle thus: "Every distinct sense of a word is associated with a distinction in form" (*idem*). The axiom has particular, in part innovatory, consequences for the way in which the dictionary team approaches the questions of the dictionary definition and examples. In Cobuild, for example, the more traditional definition is replaced by the explanation. Each explanation, written in prose style, consists of two parts. The second part consists of a more traditional-looking dictionary definition. The first part, however, illustrating the use of the word in context, is more innovatory in its intention. For example, explanations which start:

A brick is ...

Calligraphy ...

are intended to illustrate the words in use as a count and non-count noun. (The information is duplicated in an extra column adjacent to each entry in the dictionary, which provides grammatical information.)   Explicit contextual restrictions can also be catered for, such as:

A brick of ice cream is ...

In the case of the verb the first part of the explanation is used to indicate the valency of the verb or its 'selectional restrictions' in the transformational-generative sense.   For example, the fact that large numbers of verbs take a human subject is indicated by addressing the reader directly; 'If you...' or 'When you ...'.   The wording can be varied to reflect different selection restrictions:

When the sun sets, ...

When a horse gallops, ...

The traditional infinitive citation form is used for verbs where the selection preferences on the subject are general, but note the collocates:

To dam a river means...

To pedestrianize a street or shopping area means...

To kill a person, animal, plant, or other living thing means ...

As with explanations, so the attempt is made to choose examples which illustrate particular syntactic patterns - thereby reinforcing the syntactic pattern used in the definition - or typical collocations, again possibly duplicating some of the information given in the explanation of the word.   "Examples must thus show words used in their most typical contexts, most frequent grammatical structures, and with other words that are used at the same time in the same sentence." (Sinclair 1987, p. 140).   Account is also taken of the fact that sentences do not as a rule occur in isolation, but as part of a text, and typically contain words which either refer back to previous parts of the text (anaphoric elements) or refer forward to parts of the text which follow (cataphoric elements).   The example chosen for the phrasal verb 'back down on something' ("Eventually he backed down on the question of seating") reveals the typical syntactic pattern associated with the verb: + preposition + noun phrase, but also contains a number of text-linking elements such as 'eventually' , 'he' and 'the question of'. In some cases the examples are much longer, as in the case of 'reason': 'Public pressure is towards more street lighting rather than less: the reason is, of course, that people feel safer in well-lit streets.'

Lexicography in practice

The question: How can lexicography best be taught? is answered in the following in a purely practical way.   Students are invited to undertake a series of exercises culminating in the compilation of a specialised dictionary or glossary. A useful starting-point is the student's own dictionary.   All students keep vocabulary notes of one form or another, rarely organised in any systematic way. These form the starting-point of a discussion on the dictionary needs of the undergraduate.   Small groups of students are formed and asked to assess the purpose and format of the vocabulary notes produced by the various members of the group. Each group chooses an 'ideal' set of vocabulary notes which is then presented as a 'model' to the other groups. A second stage involves students looking at a specified number of entries from a series of commercially-produced, bilingual dictionaries, both general and specialist, printed and electronic, with the aim of identifying differences and similarities in terms of organisation, layout and presentation. The discussion concludes with a summary of user needs and the production of dictionary entries for two definable user groups.

The second stage of the exercise involves the student in compiling a bilingual glossary of specialist terminology of his/her own. This problem-solving approach is recommended since students have to rely on their own initiative not only for exploring a new subject field, but for organising the knowledge acquired and presenting it in a user-friendly way. The completed glossary is in three sections:

- a preface, which describes the work involved, the difficulties encountered, experience gained, etc.
- an introduction, which outlines the scope of the glossary, its purpose, user types, the range and quality of information etc.
- the glossary entries in alphabetical order.

The concordancer

Concordances have a long history. The earliest known complete concordance is of the Latin Bible, compiled by the Benedictine Hugo de San Charo in the thirteenth century with the assistance of no fewer than 500 monks (Tribble and Jones 1990, p. 7). Although the corpora used in the undergraduate teaching context do not begin to approach the order of magnitude of the corpora used in the research context, there can be little doubt that, without the advent of powerful micro-computer technology, we would not be discussing the analysis of corpora in teaching at all. Concordances provide an excellent illustration of the use of the computer as a tool in language teaching. The concordance program is characterised by two basic features: (a) the storage of very large amounts of information and (b) simple operations of searching, sorting and counting. For readers unfamiliar with concordances five basic texts can be recommended. For a brief introduction there is Sinclair (1986); a more extensive introduction to the subject is to be found in Butler (1985, chapters 2 and 3). Hockey (1980) provides the fullest account of the use of concordances in humanities teaching, although the book is no longer in print. A discussion of concordance applications, firstly to language teaching and secondly to lexicography, is to be found in Tribble and Jones (1990) and Sinclair (1987) respectively.

No student can be asked to commit his/her time to a major computing task unless the task in question is either real in the sense that it is of immediate use to the student in the real world or realistic in the sense that its objectives are perceived as having some intrinsic application to the real world. A realistic task can be provided, for example, within the framework of a one-year course on technical translation, in which the student is required, among other things, (a) to produce a glossary on an area of science or technology which s/he has selected him/herself, and (b) to translate a foreign-language text on the same subject area into English. The glossary produced by the student is thus not an end in itself, but a means towards an end, namely an accurate English translation of a foreign-language text (see Kemble & Brierley, 1990). Using a concordance program to compile a glossary is just one area of application of a concordance program. See Hockey (1980) for a description of the full range of applications. In lexicographical applications the computer functions as a major labour-saving device, but there is also considerable human input. As Hockey puts it: "The making of concordances and word indexes is ... a largely automatic task well-suited to the computer. ... Lexicography, on the other hand, demands human effort on a much larger scale." (Hockey 1980, p. 69).

Zgusta (1971) defines the work of the lexicographer in terms of four major tasks:
- the collection of material;
- the selection of entries;
- the construction of entries;
- the arrangement of entries.

In the following the role of the concordance program in the first two of Zgusta's stages will be examined.

Stage one is to collect the material. This may be done by asking the student to contact a company operating in an international context, and hence producing materials in both English and the foreign language. The document-ation can relate to any business function such as marketing (sales literature, advertising) or production (the operating manual for a particular piece of equipment). The minimum corpus size is 5,000 words. An important consider-ation for the teacher will be whether data from a series of student corpora can be sensibly merged to form a more general corpus.

Having collected the materials to build the corpus the next stage is to transfer them to the computer by creating text files in ASCII format. This can be done in one of two ways (a) keyboarding (typing the text on a word processor and saving it), or (b) by means of a scanner or OCR (optical character recognition) device. Keyboarding is ideally suited to the experienced typist. For the less experienced typist OCR devices are currently available at acceptable cost. Although a good degree of accuracy can be achieved with less expensive devices, the original text must ideally be characterised by mono-proportional spacing, i.e. each letter or character should occupy the same amount of space on the page to enable accurately scanned texts to be reproduced on the computer screen. It is, therefore, likely that some post-editing will be necessary at some stage of the text file creation process.

Concordance programs produce three kinds of list:
- a concordance: a list of keywords in context (KWIC format), see above;
- an index: a list of words followed by their frequency and a list of line numbers to indicate their place in the text corpus;
- a word list: a list of words with their frequency.

For glossary compilation the word list and the concordance are of primary interest. The first requirement is to get the computer to produce a list of all the words (i.e. word-forms) in the text in descending order of frequency. This will permit an initial identification of suitable single words for inclusion in the glossary based on their frequency of occurrence. However, the decision to include items in the glossary cannot be based on frequency alone. In small undergraduate corpora there will be many items listed with a frequency even as low as 1 which are in fact important terms. Here knowledge of the subject area is crucial.

Having decided on a selection of items for inclusion in the glossary the next stage is to produce a number of different concordances which will throw light on the syntactic and/or lexical environment of the terms in question. In addition to the KWIC format there are two further basic concordances: the right-sorted concordance which produces a concordance in which the words immediately to the right of the keyword are listed alphabetically, and the left-sorted concordance which lists in alphabetical order all the words immediately to the left of the keyword. In this way all the instances of a particular phrase can be grouped together.

While concordance programs are an exciting tool to use, in the sense that they reveal information about patterns in a text in a novel, exciting and sometimes unexpected way, a number of limitations of such programs have to be borne in mind.

The computer can only deal with word-forms (take, takes, taking, took, taken) rather than words in the sense of lexical items or dictionary headwords (take). Hence the computer will not group together all the various word-forms of a particular lexical item under the dictionary headword or lemma. Instead, they will appear on the printout in alphabetical order, between other intervening word-forms. Hockey does not consider the lack of a lemmatizer -- a computer program which removes the suffixes from the various word-forms of a particular word and groups all occurrences of the word under a headword -- a particular problem, although she is quick to point out that the extent of the problem will vary from language to language: "I would say that for most concordances lemmatization is not worth the effort involved. In most cases words from the same lemma are grouped fairly closely together. It is only in languages where there are prefixes and infixes that real difficulties arise." (Hockey 1980, p. 63). German is clearly one of those languages. As Butler points out, the German verb 'aufnehmen' can appear in any of over 30 forms; in Finnish there are verbs with over 60 forms (Butler 1985, p. 14). While this is potentially a considerable problem for scholars working with literary texts, in which a variety of word-forms of a particular lexeme may occur, the problem is much less severe in the case of the technical text where it can be predicted that the verb will almost certainly be exclusively used in the third person singular or plural and in a specific number of tenses, often in the passive voice. It is in the context of identifying the various word-forms of a word that the wildcard or dummy element of the concordance program can be used to advantage.

Wildcards are symbols such as the "at" sign @ or the asterisk * that have an "open" meaning, i.e. they can be used for one or many things. A simple example of the use of the dummy element would be to ask the computer to produce a list of words containing a particular prefix or suffix, e.g. in German be* or *ung. The wildcard may be used to help reduce the problems created by the occurrence of verbs in languages such as German which have the form: separable prefix + verb, e.g. auf + nehmen. The issue is further complicated by the fact that 'aufnehmen' is an irregular verb (its various forms include: nimmt = 3rd person singular present tense; nahm = 3rd person singular preterite tense; aufgenommen = past participle). Furthermore, it is a characteristic feature of German that in the main clause the two parts of the prefixed verb do not appear adjacent to one another, e.g. Sentence 1. 'Die beiden Staatsoberhäupter nahmen erst nach einem mehrwöchigen Schweigen die Verhandlungen wieder auf.' When a subordinate clause is embedded into the main clause the separation of the two parts of the verb is even greater. Sentence 2. 'Die beiden Staatsoberhäupter nahmen erst nach einem mehrwöchigen Schweigen, das nur durch den regen Briefwechsel der jeweiligen Aussenminister gebrochen wurde, die Verhandlungen wieder auf.' (Literal translation: 'The two heads of state started only after a prolonged silence, which by a hectic exchange of letters interrupted was, the negotiations again.'

Using the wildcard feature of the concordance program a command can be formulated which instructs the computer to look for all occurrences of word-forms containing the stem variants 'nahm', 'nehm', 'nimm' and 'nommen'. For the time being, the prefix 'auf' is ignored. Using the micro-computer version of OCP (Oxford Concordance Program) a command can be issued under *ACTION to PICK WORDS *nahm* *nehm* *nimm* *nommen*. This will, of course, produce a printout with a whole series of other word-forms which contain one of the above stem variants, e.g. other verbs of the form: prefix + nehmen.

The example above (Sentence 2) serves to illustrate a further problem, namely that of context. The minimum span of a concordance is normally one printed line, typically 79 characters long. "The dictionary-maker does not wish to refer back to the original text in order to determine the meaning of a word. He must therefore have at his disposal sufficient context for this purpose, which may be up to seven or eight lines." (Hockey 1980, p. 71). While it is reported that most concordancers will allow the user to print out contexts consisting of a complete sentence, or a fixed number of words, or a whole paragraph (Tribble & Jones 1990, p. 32), Davidson (1990, p. 83) comments in the case of OCP that this is not as straightforward as the user manual suggests. This is one clear advantage of INKText (see below) which, at the press of a key, reveals the context of each occurrence of a particular word-form. Context here means the sentence containing the term plus one sentence before and after.

To sum up, the concordancer is potentially a very useful tool for the first two stages of the glossary compilation process. Although there are problems with lemmatization and the identification of homographs (words which are spelt the same, but have different meanings), procedures can be adopted such as the use of the wildcard which allow the word-forms of a particular lexeme or lemma to be identified and printed relatively adjacent to one another. Any superfluous data can be removed with a word processor. Above all, the operations employed are simple and straightforward: 1. the production of word lists with frequency indications and 2. the production of a series of concordances. The primary purpose of the concordances will be to identify significant collocations or multi-word terms. As Jones and Sinclair put it, "Significant collocation is most significant in the span positions immediately next to the node." (Jones & Sinclair 1979, pp. 15-61). The "node" is like the keyword, the "span" is the amount of text within which collocation between items occurs. Once a series of concordances has been produced by the computer the undergraduate lexicographer is faced with the task of deciding which collocations warrant inclusion in the glossary. As research has shown, collocational restrictions operate in clines (gradable degrees of fixedness) from (a) less fixed (e.g. to harbour doubt / grudges / uncertainty / suspicion) to (d) more fixed (e.g. dead drunk; pretty sure; stark naked; pitch black). "As far as the relative fixedness of fixed expressions is concerned, it will be seen ... that all the above expressions are in some way fixed but that some are more fixed than others." (Carter 1987, p. 61). In some cases the decision whether to include a particular multi-word term will not be a straightforward one. Evidence will have to be adduced that an expression is of the "more fixed" variety and hence warrants inclusion in the glossary.

The automated dictionary generator

Like the concordancer, the automated dictionary generator can be employed to help the user identify potential source language vocabulary and terminology for inclusion in the glossary. This is done by submitting a text file in ASCII format to the dictionary generator for analysis. In the following section, explicit reference is made to the automated dictionary package INKTextTools, which consists of two elements, a dictionary generator and a dictionary lookup facility. INKText produces relevant information to help the user select dictionary entries in a variety of formats, all of which can be accessed at the touch of a key on the computer keyboard. Initially, INKText produces three word lists. They are:

- Stem Forms
- All Forms
- Multi-word Terms

The Stem Forms list is of relevance to texts in English only since the package is furnished with a lemmatizer for English which provides for the morphological reduction of inflected forms. Where the text is in a foreign language, such as German, no lemmatizer is available. However, the English lemmatizer appears to operate on the German text, producing some curious results, suggesting for example that 'ab' is a reduced form of 'aber'. One improvement to the system would be to allow for disconnection of the lemmatizer whenever a foreign language text is submitted to the machine for analysis.

The foreign language user is, therefore, dependent on the All Forms list for basic information. The All Forms list is an alphabetical list with no frequency indication. On the one hand, groups of words which have in common the same initial configuration of letters appear adjacent to one another. For example:

belichter	bild	daten
belichtereinheit	bildauflösung	datenaustausch
belichtet	bilder	datenbank
belichtung	bildern	datenbanken
belichtungen	bildschirm	datendatei
	bildschirmfarben	datenfelder
	bildschirms	datenmengen
	bildschirmseite	

Note that all nouns appear on the screen in lower case, whereas in reality all German nouns are written with a capital letter.

An initial analysis of the data above would suggest 'belichten' and its derived forms 'belichtung' and 'belichter', 'bild' and 'bildschirm', 'daten' and 'datenbank' as candidates for inclusion in the glossary. Further investigation, e.g. information on the frequency of occurrence of the above items, could result in the list being extended to include further compounds.

However, word-forms of the same lexeme do not always appear adjacent to one another. In the following example of the German verb 'geben', the absence of a lemmatizer was not a serious issue in a number of cases. For example, in the All Forms list the following word-forms appeared at the following distances from one another: 'gab' was separated from 'geben' by a distance of nine words, followed six words later by 'gegeben'. Post-editing the list and deleting the intervening words, could therefore be accomplished quickly. However, the present tense form 'gibt' which was next on the list appeared 58 word-forms later. While the inflected forms will not, of course, find their way into the glossary, it is important to have access to all occurrences of the verb in order to identify any collocational patterns, i.e. typical combinations of subject and verb or verb and object.

INKText will also provide the user with information on the frequency of occurrence of a word and contextual information. However, in both cases the information provided is in relation to an individual word. So, for example, the computer can be asked to provide information on how many times the word 'datenmengen' occurs, followed, at the press of a key, by information on the context in which the same word occurs. Although moving between different sets of information, e.g. identifying an item on the All Forms list, requesting first frequency data and then contextual information, can be effected very rapidly, the overview of a whole set of data, e.g. all the words in a text with an indication of their frequency, which is provided by a concordancer, is not possible. This is why it is recommended that the concordancer is first used to select items for inclusion in the dictionary. Further detailed analysis can then be carried out using the dictionary generating facilities of INKText, including the Multi-Word Terms list.

The Multi-Word Terms list is a particular feature of INKText. It consists of a list of terms of two to four consecutive words, e.g. 'file name extension', 'technical terminology database system', which often merit their own entries in the dictionary, distinct from the entries for their component words. They are basically a series of left of keyword concordances and again can be used to supplement the data on collocations provided by the concordancer.

Effective use of the Multi-Word Terms list is related to a further feature of INKText, the noise file. The noise file is a user-defined list of determiners, pronouns, prepositions, conjunctions and the like which do not normally play a role in a terminology database. Use of the noise file is necessary because it keeps processing speeds and memory consumption within acceptable limits. The larger the noise file the greater the processing speed. However, inclusion of 'of' in English, 'de' in French and Spanish, and 'di' in Italian would mean the exclusion of a large number of multi-word terms because the preposition 'of' and its foreign language equivalents would be ignored during processing. The foreign language noise file has, therefore, to be constructed carefully by the student, to achieve a balance between a range of useful multi-word terms on the one hand and sufficient memory to allow the processing of a long text on the other. Alternatively, the text submitted for processing may have to be divided up into smaller sub-texts.

Tasks three and four of the lexicographical process, the construction of entries and the arrangement of entries respectively, have now been reached. INKText comes with a ready-made dictionary entry format, consisting of four fields as follows:

Transl.   a field of up to 65 characters for the translation
Form.   a field of five characters for information on the part of speech and/or noun gender
Usage.   a field of up to 63 characters for linguistic or contextual information
Info.   a field of up to 63 characters for further relevant information, e.g. file name of the source text or the name of the translator operating INKText on the one hand or more linguistic information on the other.

The last two fields are of particular interest. The 'usage' field provides a clear opportunity to give an example of the use of the technical term in context in keeping with modern lexicographical practice, e.g. to show typical collocates of nouns, typical subjects and/or objects of verbs etc. The 'info.' field can be used quite flexibly. For example, the entry could take the form of a translation in the target language of the example presented in the 'usage' field or a further example of the word in context. Alternatively, it could be used to log information about a document or a particular user. This might be important at a later stage where it was considered desirable to merge a series of dictionaries in order to produce a larger, more general dictionary. Given that this general dictionary would be the product of the labours of a series of different lexicographers, it is predictable that the problem of inconsistent terminology would emerge. Decisions would then have to be made, for example, to allow for a series of synonyms, e.g. 'hard disk', 'fixed disk', 'Winchester disk' or to standardise on 'hard disk'. Other problems which would require a decision would be those of homonymy and polysemy.

Polysemy is not a problem for INKText which allows up to fifteen translations per entry. This is done by calling up the translation entry screen repeatedly and filling in up to three translations per screen. This greatly facilitates the compilation of a dictionary with entries for each part of speech of each base form , e.g. in English-French 'market' (n) = 'marche', 'market' (v) = commercialiser.

The final lexicographical task, namely the arrangement of entries, is accomplished automatically by INKText which arranges the entries in alphabetical order.

A particular design feature of INKText, which has been referred to above, is the facility which allows dictionaries to be merged. INKText uses a hierarchy of dictionaries: the general dictionary; the project dictionary, which allows the creation of a more specialised dictionary; and the document dictionary, which, as the name implies, relates to the vocabulary of a particular document only. Dictionaries can be merged to form larger ones; so for example two document dictionaries can be merged to form a project dictionary. In addition, dictionaries can be swopped, i.e. source and target language terms reversed.

Methodology

In conclusion, consideration is given to the methodology to be used in the production of a bilingual dictionary or glossary. This is presented in the form of a series of procedures:

- Identify source text terminology by submitting a large sample of typical text to computer analysis, first to the concordancer and then to the dictionary generator. The text should ideally have already been translated so that equivalent terms can be found from the translations. The alphabetical lists, frequency indications and contextual information provided (in particular the concordances) can be used to identify potential entries, both single and multi-word terms.

- Using INKText, consult the list of multi-word terms to see if there are any further potential multi-word terms for inclusion in the dictionary and transfer them to the All Words list.

- Using the system-generated lists as a basis, build a monolingual dictionary containing usage examples for each part of speech of every source language headword.

- Peruse existing translations of the source documents and extract from them the "equivalent" of each item of source text terminology. Existing translated material is almost certain to be the best source for initial target terms.

- Discuss the target language 'equivalents' gleaned from the translated texts with as many experts as possible. These may include students and staff of the scientific and technological disciplines in question.

- When the target terms for all source items have been checked, the bilingual dictionaries can be completed using the system's dictionary updating facility.
- Documents awaiting translation can then be submitted to the system. Any words they contain which do not already figure in the system's dictionaries will be isolated and equivalents found along the lines suggested above, and entered.
- The final stage is to translate the texts in a word-processor with on-line dictionary look-up.

It is obvious that a computer-based dictionary is only useful if it can be used in conjunction with the other elements which make up the translator's workstation. The dictionary will be consulted when the translator is unsure as to how a particular term should be rendered. This will normally occur when s/he is keying-in the translation in a word processor. It follows therefore that the dictionary should be accessible from the word processor. In the case of INKText this is achieved through a RAM-resident program which is invoked through a simple combination of keystrokes making use of a 'window', which allows the user to view elements of more than one file simultaneously through superimposition. The dictionary lookup of INKText makes it possible to instantly 'paste in' the selected dictionary term, i.e. transfer the term from the dictionary database to the word processor. The lookup facility also allows new words or terms to be added to a dictionary.

It is assumed that the translator will either be using the whole screen for typing the translation, whilst looking at a hard-copy of the source text, or will be working in synchronised split-screen mode with both source and target texts visible (see Chapter 2 Word Processing). Whichever approach is used, the RAM-resident portion of the system will be accessible whenever a terminological query arises and the desired target language equivalents can be 'pasted' directly into the text.

Conclusion
Using a modern word processing package like WordPerfect, the translator has access to a variety of tools. Not only is the system equipped with a spell-checker and thesaurus, but it also has considerable potential for concordancing. Although not so quick or versatile as a dedicated program such as Micro OCP, WordPerfect is nevertheless ideal for editing concordances produced by other programs such as OCP. When the word processor is linked to a dictionary database such as INKText the result is a very powerful set of tools for the translator.

By loading onto the hard disk of the modern micro-computer a series of packages such as a concordancer (Micro OCP), a word processor with spell-checker and thesaurus (WordPerfect), a terminological database generator like INKText, which includes a dictionary lookup facility which can be accessed via the word processor, and a style-checker such as PC Proof, the translator has at his/her disposal a range of tools which can be invoked in the following sequence:

- submit sample texts for analysis (a) to a concordancer and (b) a dictionary generator;
- compile a document or project dictionary;
- translate a text using a word processor with access to a terminological database;
- check the translation for spelling with a spellchecker and finally
- check the text for stylistic appropriacy using a style-checker.

Although not fully integrated one with another, the various tools are easily accessed through simple combinations of keystrokes and currently represent the best the 'instrumental' approach to IT in foreign language teaching is able to offer to the translator/lexicographer.   While for the time being machine translation systems continue to produce less than satisfactory output, the effective use of the automated dictionary through continual revision and updating of the dictionary entries constitutes the most effective way of helping the translator to produce an accurate rendering of the source-language text in the target language.

Bibliography

Bolinger, D. (1965) The atomization of meaning, *Language*, **41**.

Butler, C. (1985) *Computers in Linguistics*, Basil Blackwell.

Carter, R. (1987) *Vocabulary*, George Allen & Unwin.

Davidson, T. T. L. (1990) Teaching with the Oxford Concordance Program, *Literary and Linguistic Computing*, 5,1.

Dubois, J. (1981) Models of the dictionary: evolution in dictionary design, *Applied Linguistics*, 2,3.

Fox, J. (1990) *Educational Technology in Modern Language Learning*, The Training Agency.

Hartmann, R. R. K. (1981) Dictionaries, learners, users: some issues in lexicography, *Applied Linguistics*, 2,3.

Hockey, S. (1980) *A Guide to Computer Applications in the Humanities*, Duckworth.

Hockey, S. (1988) *Micro Oxford Concordance Program: Users' Manual*, Oxford University Computing Service.

Jackson, H. (1990) OCP and the computer analysis of texts: the Birmingham Polytechnic Experience, *Literary and Linguistic Computing*, 5,1.

Jones, S and Sinclair, J. (1979) English lexical collocations: a study in computational linguistics, *Cahiers de Lexicologie*, 24,1.

Kemble, I. and Brierley, W. (1990) Computers and translation. Integrating IT into undergraduate FL learning, *Computer Assisted Language Learning*, 2.

Lamy, M-N. (1985) Innovative practices in French learners' dictionaries as compared with their English counterparts. In R. Ilson, *ELT Documents 120, Dictionaries, Lexicography and Language Learning*.

Levy, M. (1990) Concordances and their integration into a word-processing environment for language learners, *System*, 18,2.

Moulin, A. (1983) LSP dictionaries for EFL learners. In Hartmann, R. R. K., *Lexicography: Principles and Practice*.

Newton, J. (1989) The terminology database in the translation department, *The Linguist*, 28,2.

Opitz, K. (1979) Technical dictionaries: testing the requirements of the professional user. In *Dictionaries and their Users*, papers from the 1978 BAAL Seminar on Lexicography, Exeter Linguistic Studies, 4.

Opitz, K. (1983a) On dictionaries for special registers. In Hartmann, R. R. K., *Lexicography: Principles and Practice*.

Opitz, K. (1983b) The terminological/standardised dictionary. In Hartmann, R. R. K., *Lexicology: Principles and Practice*.

Sager, J. C. (1981) Approaches to terminology and the teaching of terminology, *Fachsprache*, 3,3-4.

Sinclair, J. M. (1986) Basic computer processing of long texts. In Leech, G. & Candlin, C. N. (eds) *Computers in English Language Teaching and Research*.

Sinclair, J. M. (1987) *Looking Up. An account of the Cobuild Project in Lexical Computing*, Collins.

Tribble, C. & Jones, G. (1990) *Concordances in the Classroom*, Longman.

Zgusta, L. (1971) *Manual of Lexicography*, Mouton.

5 MACHINE TRANSLATION

J. Robert French

Whatever the shortcomings of today's machine translation systems, there is no doubt that the translator's world has been changing rapidly over the last ten years. The changes which we are experiencing are not in the main due to any great theoretical breakthrough but have come about primarily as a result of the almost universal availability of word and data processing in the developed world. Today's translator is likely to be working directly on a word processor with all that implies for facility of re-drafting and revising. The translator's personal glossary, instead of being laboriously compiled in card indexes, can be stored on floppy disks. A library shelf's worth of mono- or multi-lingual dictionaries can be stored on CD-ROM and at a humbler level the traveller's electronic pocket phrase book with liquid crystal display and audio output is available by mail order.

The effect of these changes can be clearly seen already in the translator's work station but there is a further development in text handling which should not be overlooked when considering how best to cope with the increasing demand for translations and that is the actual mode of storage and transmission of the source text. Hard copy can be converted to machine readable form with considerable success using optical scanners but, more important still, most text is now produced and stored electronically. Machine readable copy is easier to store, transmit and edit than the hard copy which has been the traditional way in which source texts arrive on the translator's desk.

It is important therefore in this changing world for students specialising in languages and particularly for students of translation to be aware of the range of systems available for handling natural languages and, where possible, to be given the opportunity to work with machine translation in order to discover at first hand the potential and limitations of the systems offered.

At the simplest level and considering the systems available for classroom use it is probably best to divide the development of machine translation (MT) into two periods, pre- and post-1966. (Anyone wishing to follow in detail the history and development of translation systems should refer to Hutchins [1986].) The first period is marked by optimism and a spread of research projects on both sides of the Iron Curtain. Some indication of the attraction of the idea of MT and the skill of researchers in obtaining funding is given by the estimated total expenditure of approximately $13 million by the US government and military agencies on MT research at eleven US institutions and two foreign institutions during the period 1956-65 (Hutchins 1986, p. 169). It is also fair to say that many departments of linguistics although not themselves involved in MT projects were also indirect beneficiaries of this wave of enthusiasm.

The report of the Automatic Language Processing Advisory Committee (ALPAC) in 1966 with its conclusion that "there is no immediate or predictable prospect of useful machine translation" (Hutchins 1986, p. 167) is usually seen as a watershed after which it became more difficult to obtain funding and the impetus for further research was found only in situations where multilingual problems were acute enough to mean that existing translation services already absorbed substantial sums.

As Knowles points out in his review of Hutchins (Knowles 1990), the chronological and geographical approach to the development of MT has been supplemented by a differentiation of MT approaches into direct, transfer, interlingual and AI systems "which has fertilised thinking throughout the confraternity". These distinctions are described in detail in Hutchins (1986) or more briefly in Lewis (1985).

Working with two languages and in one direction only enables the designers of direct systems to take a very pragmatic approach to the solution of the particular problems arising between say Russian and English, where verbs will have to be marked as perfective or imperfective and some method will be needed to ensure that definite articles and copulas appear in the target output.

Interlingual systems represent a much more theoretically and intellectually satisfying response to the problem. Instead of limiting research to the resolution of problems raised by working in one direction between a pair of languages, researchers attempt to perform analysis and synthesis in terms of a "universal deep structure representation" which eliminates some of the rather *ad hoc* procedures of direct systems. The attractiveness of such projects for situations involving a multiplicity of languages and directions is obvious.

Transfer systems represent a step back from the attempt to use a universal deep structure by limiting analysis to language specific deep structures and making the transfer by substitution of target language (TL) lexical items with subsequent synthesis into TL sentences.

Eurotra is one of the most ambitious transfer projects and has a stratificational approach with the possibility of transfer at any stage once a proper match can be made. The raw source text is converted first to a Normalized Text which is then successively analyzed for Morphological Structure, Constituent Structure, Relational Structure and Interface Structure. In the latter stages syntactic, functional and semantic features can be taken into account. The categories of one level become the features of a subsequent level. Dictionaries are to be developed corresponding to each of the levels of analysis/synthesis.

Direct, interlingual and transfer systems are all directed at the goal of automatic translation and represent various strategies for the resolution of the inherent problems. No system has been able to achieve the ideal of high quality fully automatic MT and the most successful commercial systems are those which have accepted their limitations and "rely on human intervention at some stage and incorporate this into the design concept" (Lewis 1985, p. 46).

Although the requirement for human intervention may be considered as a defeat in terms of the goal of fully automated translation, use of an MT program in the language teaching context finds its justification in confronting the language user with the problems inherent in the process. Intervention may be in the form of pre- or post-editing and also by questions about the ambiguities being addressed to the operator during the running of the program.

The above analysis is postulated in terms of the operation of MT systems. However, it will be seen below that the major component of any MT system is the dictionary or dictionaries and much of the work of the language learner or trainee translator/terminologist is concerned with setting up dictionaries for either general or specific purposes.

The main consideration which faces the translation service or technical writing section when considering the purchase of hardware and software is the extent to which the use of the computer will cut down the time and effort which translation entails.   A report by Redmond (1990) gives some indication of the scale of the problem.   A Canadian company, faced with a major translation job, found that human translators could offer only 1500 words per day.   Assisted by the Lexitech MT system, with the computer doing 75 to 80 per cent of the work, the individual translator's output was increased to 2500 words per day, and revisers could scan 10,000 words per day.   Without the computer, the job would have taken thirty translators more than ten years; with the computer the job could be handled by 27 translators in three years.

The use of MT packages in the classroom has been treated in two recent articles.   The first by Rodney Ball of the University of Southampton appeared in the CTISS File/8 (1989) and reports on the use of MicroCAT. Ball distinguishes three different modes of application:

- using an MT system as a means of learning more about a foreign language (in this case the language, not the MT system, is the object of interest);
- using a particular MT system as a way of introducing students to the general concept of MT (MT as a field is the object of interest);
- showing students how to use the various facilities available on a specific system and encouraging them to evaluate the system's knowledge (the software itself - and its eccentricities - are the object of interest).

In discussing the rationale for the introduction of MT within a university languages course, he points to the danger that any course which requires too closely detailed hands-on experience of a particular type of software may turn "into a glorified course of instruction in word processing" (Ball 1989, p. 53).

Experience with a different system at Coventry Polytechnic is outlined in a paper by Patrick Corness in Picken (1986). Summing up on ALPS as a language teaching aid, Corness emphasises "the benefit of hands-on experience with a range of information retrieval and information processing techniques from word processing and database handling to computer assisted translation."   This he sees as providing students with "basic skills in these areas, which they are likely to need if they become professional linguists" (Corness, 1986 p. 126).

It is perhaps not surprising that the authors represented in the present volume tend to support the latter view, seeing the acquisition of skills and techniques as enhancing and liberating and the exploration of the limitations of existing technology as the stimulus to future discovery.   Perhaps it should also be emphasised that, although not normally conjured up by the term "professional linguist", the teacher of modern languages working with authentic materials is increasingly in the business of materials production where such skills are invaluable.

Translation and transcoding

The first important distinction to establish is the difference between transcoding and even cryptanalysis and translating. The original impetus for MT is usually taken to be the Warren Weaver memorandum in 1949 which puts the case as follows:

> one naturally wonders if the problem of translation could conceivably be treated as a problem in cryptography. When I look at an article in Russian, I say "This is really written in English, but it has been coded in some strange symbols. I will now proceed to decode".

It is not difficult to invent trivial exercises in decoding which will provide a useful opportunity to introduce simple programs to transfer, for example, from letters to ASCII codes or morse. The main point to underline in this connection is the potential two-way nature of the process which is determined by the one-to-one relationship between the symbol sets. Keeping at the level of transfer from one character set to another, the next stage to consider is writing programs for automatic transliteration and here the Russian-English example chosen by Weaver can be used to illustrate the unidirectional nature of the process and the loss of information which may occur. Moving from Russian to English is the simpler process because of the extra symbols in the Russian alphabet. However for a program to work in the opposite direction, rules would have to be developed to cope with the digraphs *ts, zh, kh, sh* (not to mention *shch*) and also to distinguish between *y* = Ы and *y* before *a* or *e* forming a digraph representing Я and Е respectively. Even without moving to the Cyrillic alphabet, potential loss of information can also be illustrated simply by moving from lower to upper case in French for instance, with the suppression of accents making it impossible to fully recreate the original lower case text automatically.

The challenge for the MT program is to find the unique solution for each and every translation unit. The third stage is therefore to consider the extent to which restricted languages can be reduced to the level of a code. In this connection students are asked to identify contexts in which the linguistic elements in a human/machine interaction are so strictly circumscribed that there is never a choice. The analogy with "user-friendly" computer programs is obvious and designs can be produced for multilingual timetables, automated teller machines for banks, telephone directory enquiry services and many others, through to quite extensive interchanges about specific products based on the development of expert systems and recognition of keywords. The main point of this type of exercise is to exemplify the need for restricted syntax down to the limit of only using set sentence patterns with slots for specific items and establishing the notion of standardised terminology.

Although at the linguistic and translation level these exercises may seem trivial, they have the great advantage of concentrating attention on accuracy and also standardised forms of expression, including reordering of information where necessary. With more user-friendly programs, questions of the level of familiarity also have to be resolved. In most situations, one quickly runs up against the onset of ambiguity and the limitations of the transcoding approach.

Pre-editing

For more that ten years the Technical Publications Department of Perkins Group Limited of Peterborough has been using a system called Perkins Approved Clear English (PACE). In 1987 with the help of Tony Hartley, then at the University of Bradford, when they were moving over to use the MicroCAT system, they discovered that it was possible to increase the number of words in PACE provided that it was done in a controlled manner. The aim is to use all words in one sense only. For example, "In PACE *right* is defined as 'when facing north, right is east' and *correct* is used to mean 'conforming to a standard, opposite of wrong'" (Pym 1990, p. 85).

It is interesting to note that pre-editing of technical texts in this instance was originally prompted by consideration of communicating in English on technical subjects with engineers who were working in English but for whom English is not a mother tongue. Application of the same principles to texts for MT goes a long way to resolving the unique solution problem alluded to above. The Perkins system also incorporates ten rules for simplified writing (Pym, *op. cit.*, pp. 85-86).

Ten Rules of Simplified Writing

	Keep it short and simple		*Make it explicit*
1.	Keep sentences short.	6.	Avoid elliptical constructions.
2.	Omit redundant words.	7.	Don't omit conjunctions or relatives.
3.	Order the parts of the sentence logically.	8.	Adhere to the PACE dictionary.
4.	Don't change constructions in mid-sentence.	9.	Avoid strings of nouns.
5.	Take care with the logic of 'and' and 'or'.	10.	Do not use '-ing' unless the word appears thus in the PACE dictionary.

There is no need to comment here on the usefulness of an exercise designed to ensure that a source text is comprehensible. It may not be such an intellectually demanding exercise as the précis or abstracting but it has the advantage of being based upon a rigorous understanding of the original and a clear appreciation of what might potentially be ambiguous. In the context of an MT program it is often immediately rewarded by the production of a usable translation.

Of course the idiosyncrasies of the computer program may well confound all efforts in this connection. For instance, it is not possible on either of the systems considered below to alter the basic syntactical analysis and synthesis programs, but that too can be used to advantage to provide the student a practical problem in linguistics: how to define precisely the difficulty which the machine is facing at this point.

The Weidner MicroCAT system

The main characteristics of the system are word processing, translation, and dictionary management.

Word processing

As this has been fully covered in an earlier chapter, it is sufficient to say that word processing facilities are available. Diacritics are achieved either by a single key stroke e.g. for ç, ñ etc., or by the use of a dead key for accents which then appear on the screen above the next character entered.

The text is given a name e.g. SOURCE and can be called up at any time. Control + Z writes the text to memory. For pre-editing, texts may be saved first in their original form and then copied into a new file e.g. SOURCE.REV which can be amended to make them easier for the machine to handle. In split-screen mode the reference file SOURCE is displayed in the top half of the screen with SOURCE.REV displayed in the bottom of the screen so that the operator can check that no information has been lost in the pre-editing process. This type of split screen working obviously becomes even more important after translation has been carried out and the raw translation is being post-edited.

As the use of spelling checkers becomes more and more widespread, so users must be increasingly on their guard against the covert errors which cannot be detected by the spelling check program. The *Grauniad* may be assured of getting its name spelled correctly but nevertheless it may still occasionally interchange 'there' and 'their'. Spelling checkers do little to ensure quality control on agreements. Furthermore, although modern communicative approaches to language teaching present many advantages of increased fluency and speed of language processing, it is useful to find occasions on which attention can legitimately be drawn to such problems. Short transcription exercises as described in Chapter 2 above can also be used as input to an MT process at which point it will become clear that the responsibility for corrupt TL versions does not always lie with the machine. Garbage in, garbage out.

Increased use of optical scanners will not obviate the necessity for careful proof reading at some stage.

Translation

The system has three modes for translation: Immediate Translation, Translation, and Deferred Translation.

In Translation and Deferred Translation mode the messages "Preprocessing" and "Translation in Progress" appear on the screen with an indication of the number of words processed. Deferred Translation enables files to be stored for subsequent translation at a time when the machine is not in use for entering texts, updating dictionaries and pre- or post editing. This obviates the necessity for the operator to waste time waiting for the translation process to be completed.

In Immediate Translation mode, the machine will accept a phrase of up to 80 characters in length and this is normally translated in a few seconds. The purpose of the Immediate Translation mode is to enable dictionary entries to be checked for efficiency without having to wait until they appear in a longer text.

In all translation modes there is a facility for tagging 'unknown' words, that is, words which do not occur in any of the dictionaries being consulted. The program also provides a Vocabulary search facility to give advance warning of items which will have to be entered in the dictionaries. When the machine is being used for language teaching purposes with students working on relatively short texts and being invited to suggest improvements in pre-editing, post-editing and dictionary entries, it is often more useful to set the machine a task and then examine the output with a view to determining what modifications would be needed to make the text more machine friendly (pre-editing), what supplementary dictionary items should be added or what modifications are required to existing dictionary entries and what shortcomings in the raw translation should be left to the post-editing phase.

There is a further spin-off in this process and that is the necessity for the student to decide at what point the translated text becomes usable. One of the miseries of translation as an academic exercise can be a hollow feeling that perfection has proved elusive. Anyone working as a translator in "real time" has to match the needs of communication with the time available, and it can be a useful discipline to define as far as possible the requirements and the abilities of the end user. Translations may not be thought of as being for bilinguals but in a multilingual community there is inevitable interaction between languages. With electronic methods of data retrieval it may even be that some users of translations will in future switch into the translation only where they wish to check on specific items causing problems, using it in effect as an interlinear crib. Raw translations of minutes produced by MT which would need considerable post-editing for outside consumption may prove to be of quite an acceptable standard of usefulness for members of the committee involved.

This should not be construed as an argument for lowering standards in translation. High quality is a prerequisite where translations are being produced for publication or used as evidence of near native command of two languages. For in-house purposes, on the other hand, particularly where speed is of the essence, the law of diminishing returns should be rigidly applied. With the spread of language skills among technical and professional people texts which are not quite fully englished or frenched may well be perfectly usable provided they are not ambiguous or misleading.

Dictionary entries

The MicroCAT dictionary is divided into two sections, a core dictionary of some 20,000 words and a general dictionary. The core dictionary is fixed and cannot be amended. The general dictionary on the other hand can be built up and added to by the operator. It is also possible to add further dictionaries to cope with specific registers or domains or even for specific customers (Perkins-speak). For instance it would be possible to set up separate dictionaries for meteorology and medicine containing different preferred translations for Fr. *front*: Eng. 'front' or 'forehead'. This is a very useful aspect of the system when it is made available to student-centred learning. Each student works on his or her own glossary and does not therefore impinge on any other. Careful thought needs to be given to the naming of dictionaries, so that they can be easily referenced for future use. Where the entries are successful they can later be merged into the general dictionary.

When the source word has been entered, the program asks for guidance about the number of meanings and proposes a comprehensive list of possible types of homograph. It may well be objected here that no human language processor is ever going to be forced to reflect on whether *l'interprète* is a noun phrase consisting of a determiner and a singular noun or the present tense of a verb preceded by a third person singular pronoun. However, for anyone seriously considering using electronic devices to process natural language such questions are crucial.

Homographs can, in fact, only be distinguished in this system if the different meanings can be assigned to different parts of speech as in the case of *interprète* above. There is no way of distinguishing *échelle* (ladder) and *échelle* (scale), *feu* (fire) and *feu* (light), or *marche* (stair) and *marche* (march).

If such distinctions have to be made the separate meanings must be listed in separate dictionaries so that *char* (mil) is distinguished from *char* (agri). How effective such a procedure will be depends on the precision with which register can be specified. For the type of exercises outlined below, it is not crucial as students normally work on a single text of restricted length.

Once the number and type of homographs has been decided - and here decisions have to be made which are very similar to the thinking behind the development of PACE - further information has to be entered for each part of speech to facilitate morphological and syntactic analysis: gender, animacy of nouns, inflections of adjectives and verbs.

Further data is required to facilitate synthesis in the TL, providing an opportunity for goal directed reflection on grammatical categories. Detailed consideration of the rules of the native language occurs at best spasmodically in foreign language courses and given the immediacy of feedback there is often an interesting learning experience connected with this task. Items entered into the dictionary can be tested by Immediate Translation.

The final stage in the compilation of the dictionary is the entering of idioms. The program has no facility for monitoring collocations other than by having items of two or more (up to nine) words specially entered as idioms. Entry of idioms can be a time-consuming procedure as all the details of individual words have to be entered first before the complete phrase can be specified. Nevertheless it is frequently possible to copy single lexical entries from the core dictionary and this provides a useful check on how well the specifications have been drawn up.

Post-editing
When Translation or Deferred Translation has been completed, the translated text goes immediately into a file e.g. SOURCE.OUT and can then be called up onto the screen with or without the reference text (SOURCE). At this stage unknown words will appear in their original form and may have been tagged with an "unknown word marker". For example,

$l'interprète$ speaks too fast.
Such items can then be listed for entering into the dictionary.

This is the most interesting phase and the point at which the operation comes closest to the standard translation exercise. Words and phrases have to be reordered and amendments made to agreements, prepositions, determiners and pronouns to take account of the inherent limitations of the MT program, concentrating attention on contrasts between the two grammatical systems but also revealing the general rules that have been built into the program's syntactic and morphological analysis and synthesis procedures. All such procedures are looked at to work out whether it would have been possible to make alterations at the pre-editing stage which would have eliminated the problem. Such recommendations are then tried out for generality on other texts.

MicroCAT and ALPS were both expensive packages which are no longer available but it is noticeable in 1990 that much cheaper systems have become available. Anyone who has had experience of the MicroCAT system will find many familiar features in the Globalink system for instance.

The Globalink Translation System

Advances in text handling are immediately obvious from the fact that the source text input can be made through one of the standard word processing packages. This means that material provided on disk can be used without any need for manual input. The PC can then convert the Wordperfect text, for example, into ASCII code ready for translation or pre-editing. The split screen facility is, however, only available during the translation process. Diacritics are achieved by holding down 'Alt' and striking a single specific key. For example, Alt + 2 gives é.

The two translation modes available on Globalink are Interactive Translation and Batch Translation. Interactive translation operates on one sentence at a time and is the mode in which to test the effectiveness of dictionary entries. It is also possible to interrupt the Batch Translation process at any time and edit the source language (SL) text along the lines of Perkins-speak. The edited SL text can then be saved for future use.

The system comes equipped with a general dictionary which contains a number of reserved items which cannot be modified or even displayed. Micro-dictionaries are being developed and may be developed by the user. All dictionaries have a 3 letter identification code e.g. GEN, WEL. Any single micro-dictionary can be given precedence over the general dictionary.

In addition to the single word dictionaries there are also a semantic units dictionaries taking multi-word entries. In both batch and interactive modes the SL and TL texts appear together on the split screen, although in Batch mode the TL text is only displayed momentarily, unless interrupted. However, this does allow the operator to monitor progress. For post-editing, interactive mode is selected and amendments can be made on screen.

Dictionary entry is very simple. The complete range of possibilities appears on the screen. The cursor is moved to the relevant position and the appropriate entry is made. However, there is some lack of flexibility as only N, V, Adj. are available as potential homograph variants.

The French and English dictionaries work independently and so entries have to be made in both and, although there are a large number of variant forms built into the program for some verbs, all irregular forms which are likely to be encountered have to be entered as separate words.

One very useful feature for classroom use is the browse function which enables the user to inspect other dictionary entries and consequently flip through any dictionary. However, there is a set of reserved terms which cannot be inspected in this way and the present handbook provides inadequate information on some aspects of coding.

Browsing through the semantic unit dictionary gives a good insight into the limitations of the basic translation program. Insertion of an adverb such as *également* necessitates the inclusion of the complete phrase as a separate unit. Nevertheless it is a fairly straightforward matter to set up a dictionary to provide a reasonably useful translation.

The following extracts represent raw translations of the same source text on MicroCAT and Globalink. The fourth text is the same source text translated by Globalink after a first run of dictionary updates, but before post-editing. For use in the classroom, the TL texts could be accompanied by a commentary on a particular aspect.

Text for translation

Les postes de soudage se présentent sous plusieurs formes différentes. Néanmoins, ils sont toujours entièrement capotés de façon à protéger les organes internes de l'appareil. Sur le tableau de commande, on trouve des appareils de mesure tels qu'un ampèremètre et un voltmètre. Ces cadrans indiquent au soudeur l'intensité du courant fourni par l'appareil et la tension à laquelle il est débité. Avant de mettre l'appareil en marche, le soudeur doit normalement consulter la plaque signalétique située à l'avant de l'appareil de soudage. Cette plaque a pour objet de faire connaître à l'utilisateur le caractéristiques électriques indispensables qui lui permettent d'en faire le meilleur usage. On y retrouve notamment la catégorie de l'appareil (transformateur de soudage, transformateur-redresseur de soudage, générateur, etc.) la nature de la caractéristique statique voltage-ampérage, la nature du courant de soudage, la tension à vide, la gamme de réglage de la machine, le facteur de marche, etc. Après avoir réglé l'intensité du courant à l'aide d'un levier, volant ou commutateur, le soudeur met l'appareil en marche en appuyant sur le bouton marche situé également sur le tableau de commande.

Raw MicroCAT translation

The $soudage$ posts present themselves under different several forms. Nevertheless, they always are completely manner $capotes$ to protect the internal organs of the gear. On the order painting, one finds measure gear such that a $ampère-mètre$ and a $voltmètre$. These faces indicate to the $soudeur$ the intensity of the furnished current by the gear and the tension to which it is $débité$. Before placement the gear walks, the $soudeur$ has normally to consult veneers situated $signalétique$ for it to the before $soudage$ gear. This veneers has for fact object to know to the user the electric indispensable characteristics which allow for him of in to do the better usage. One finds there notably the category of the gear ($transformateur$ $soudage$, $transformateur$-$redresseur$ $soudage$, generator, etc.) the nature of the static characteristic $voltage$-$ampérage$, the nature of the current $soudage$, the tension to empties, the range $réglage$ machine, the postman market, etc. After to have regulated the intensity of the current to the help of a lever, flying or switch, the $soudeur$ puts the gear walks while leaning on the button walks situated equally on the order painting.

Raw Globalink translation

Positions of @@soudage appear under several different forms. Nevertheless, they are always entirely @@capote's of manner to protect internal bodies of the machine. On the table of order, one finds machines of measure such that an ammeter and a @@voltme'tre. These dials indicate in the solderer the intensity of the current provided by the machine and the tension which it is debited. Before to put the machine in step, the solderer has normally to consult the plate @@signale'tique situated to the before the machine of @@soudage. This plate has for object to make to know to the user the indispensable electrical characteristics that allow it to make some the best usage. There @@retrouve notably the category of the machine (transformer of @@soudage, transformer - rectifier of @@soudage, generator, etc.) the nature of the static characteristic voltage - @@ampe'rage, the nature of the current of @@soudage, the tension to void, the range of adjustment of the machine, the factor of step, etc. After having ruled the intensity of the current with the assistance of a lever, wheel or switch, the solderer puts the machine in step by supporting on the bud walks situated equally on the table of order.

Globalink translation after dictionary up-date

Power sources appear under several different forms. Nevertheless, they are always entirely enclosed so as to protect internal parts of the machine. On the control panel, one finds measuring equipment such that an ammeter and a voltmeter. These dials indicate in the welder the intensity of the current provided by the machine and the tension which it is debited. Before to start the machine, the welder has normally to consult the name plate situated in front of the welding machine. This plate has for object to make known to the user the indispensable electrical characteristics that allow it to make the best use of it. One there finds notably the category of the machine (transformer of welding, transformer - rectifier of welding, generator, etc.) the nature of the static characteristic voltage - amperage, the nature of the current of welding, the tension to void, the range of adjustment of the machine, the factor of step, etc. After having controlled the intensity of the current with the assistance of a lever, wheel or switch, the welder starts the machine by supporting on the situated on button equally on the control panel.

Conclusion

The MT system in the classroom is not subject to the economic considerations which apply in commercial use but students working with these programs will not find it difficult to believe that the cost of researching, coding and checking terminology in a computerized dictionary has been estimated at $32 per word pair (Mayorcas-Cohen, 1986, p. 76). Many professional linguists in the future will be faced with deciding on the viability and cost effectiveness of packages now being developed. They will be able to do that so much more reliably if they have had an opportunity to get inside the systems and explore their strengths and weaknesses.

A great deal has been written about MT by both enthusiasts and critics. Whatever the shortcomings of the systems at present available, the advances in text handling mean that the translator of the future will be relying on the computer not only for word processing but also for dictionary, thesaurus and encyclopedia look-up. Which parts of the translation process can suitably be automated will be a matter of judgment and personal preference but the evidence of comparatively crude systems at present operation-al is sufficient to show that computer assisted translation is already a reality.

No attempt has been made here to evaluate the usefulness of either of these systems for their primary purpose, the rapid production of usable TL text. With the increased emphasis in language teaching on the use of authentic material and engaging students in authentic translation tasks, computer assisted text handling of all sorts should be a commonplace for students of languages, whether as linguists and therefore potential co-producers of translations or as specialists in other disciplines who are the end users of translations. Accessing dictionaries on CD-ROM should soon be as normal for linguists as the use of the computer for scientists and engineers. They should also be expected to engage in computer assisted translation to explore just how much of the process can be automated and be asked to make judgments about whether raw MT is usable as it stands and what improvements could be achieved by pre-editing or dictionary up-date. The real test of a translator is not the drudgery of writing the translation and searching for an unknown word but in the self-critical process of creating a coherent text. In the post-editing phase the student is faced with precisely that challenge.

In the translation bureau, revision and quality control are the most important and cost effective activities. Too often in academic translation this aspect can be seen as the responsibility of the teacher. Human assisted MT provides an opportunity for the student to act as revisor, taking control of both source and target text and contributing to dictionary management.

Bibliography

Ball, R. (1989) Computer-assisted translation and the modern languages curriculum, *The CTISS File* 8.

Corness, P. (1986) The ALPS computer-assisted translation system in an academic environment. In Picken, C. (1986) *Translating and the Computer: 7th International Conference on Translating,* ASLIB.

Hutchins, W. J. (1986) *Machine Translation: Past, Present, Future.*   Ellis Horwood.

Knowles, F. (1990) Language and IT: rivals or partners?, *Literary and Linguistic Computing,* 5,1.

Lehberger, J. & Bourbeau, L. (1988) *Machine Translation. Linguistic Characteristics of MT Systems and General Methodology of Evaluation,* John Benjamins.

Lewis, D. (1985) The development and progress of machine translation systems, *ALLC Journal,* 5.

Mayorcas-Cohen, P. (1986) The translator as information user. In Picken, C. (*op. cit.*).

Pym, P. J. (1990) Pre-editing and the use of simplified writing for MT: an engineer's experience of operating an MT system. In Mayorcas, P. (ed.) (1990) *Translating and the Computer 10.   The Translation Environment 10 Years On,* ASLIB.

Redmond, M. (1990) Computer-assisted translation on an ocean-going scale, *Financial Times,* 28/2/90.

6 NATURAL LANGUAGE PROCESSING

William Brierley

Natural language processing (NLP) means different things to different people. One definition of NLP would concern itself with the theories and techniques that address the problem of communicating with computers using natural (human) language. The focus of the research is to design computer programs to allow people to interact with computers in natural conversational dialogues. This aspect of NLP is of limited interest to the language teacher, since humans do not need to be able to communicate with computers in foreign languages. Other definitions might include the range of problems associated with speech recognition, though strictly speaking speech recognition and NLP are two distinct problem areas. Programs and hardware for speech recognition are likely to be well outside the resources of the readers of this book and it is not proposed to tackle this issue here. From the language teacher's point of view, a description of NLP should focus on that aspect of the field which concerns itself with developing programs which analyze natural language input from a user and generate appropriate responses; the interaction may or may not require the computer to exercise a corrective function.

Many descriptions of the application of NLP techniques to the teaching of foreign languages begin with ambitious objectives but end with discrete disclaimers. "Computer programs", we are told (Cook & Fass, 1986, p 163), "have been developed that describe the structure of sentences, that answer questions about selected subjects, and that engage in extended dialogue with humans". But "The applications described here are largely potential rather than actual; the teaching programs are small-scale and experimental" (*ibid.* p 169). Such descriptions are often of research projects, and it is often difficult to see what relevance such experiments might have to the practising language teacher since they rarely spawn commercially available products, and few language teachers will have the time to develop the programming expertise required to write applications of their own.

This chapter seeks rather to do the opposite: to argue that NLP has little to contribute at present to the development of communicative competence in learners of foreign languages and that therefore the communicative language teacher will better employ her time in the development of other computer applications. Nevertheless, sufficient work has been done in the area of NLP to justify an exploration of its objectives and achievements to date in the field of language teaching and to examine the extent to which it may be justifiable to claim that NLP does have a limited but important role to play in the consolidation of grammatical awareness (and therefore of accuracy as opposed to fluency) in advanced learners and students of linguistics and translation and that teachers and students with a linguistic orientation may therefore derive benefit from pursuing these issues.

The development of natural language processing

In the early days of computing, NLP consisted of simply counting the occurrences of particular words in computer-readable texts, and later of deriving indexes and concordances from the same sorts of texts. Nowadays, sophisticated word processors and other dedicated programs can handle many of these tasks, and NLP has moved on. Similarly, much early work was done (and many early hopes dashed) in the area of machine translation (but this is the subject of another chapter). An apparently promising early piece of work was Joseph Weizenbaum's ELIZA language analysis program (1966, see Weizenbaum, 1976). ELIZA consisted of a language analyzer and a script which allowed the computer to maintain a "conversation" (via keyboard and screen) on a specific topic. ELIZA was programmed with a series of "scripts" or conversational situations, the best known of which was called DOCTOR. In this script, the computer took the role of a Rogerian psychotherapist in an initial interview with a client. (The essence of Rogerian psychotherapy is that the counsellor should not intervene actively to direct the conversation, but should simply ask open-ended questions or "play back" the client's own statements, thus simply keeping the conversation going.)

In fact, DOCTOR does not engage in any form of conversation at all. It merely parrots ready-made phrases in response to keywords in the client's input (an example is given below). In view of this, the reaction of the psychotherapy community (many of whom hailed the program as a major advance in the automation of psychotherapy!) seems almost bizarre, but is perhaps more deeply symptomatic of the desire or need of computer scientists to reduce complex human interactions to the lowest common denominator of "information processing". In another context, Theodore Roszak (Roszak, 1986) observes:

> Because the ability to store data somewhat corresponds to what we call memory in human beings, and because the ability to follow logical procedures somewhat corresponds to what we call reasoning in human beings, many members of the (information) cult have concluded that what computers do somewhat corresponds to what we call thinking. (p 11)

In a similar way, and despite Weizenbaum's protestations, ELIZA is often quoted as an example of the computer being able to process natural language (which it may do in an extremely naive sort of way) and to converse (which it certainly does not, since conversation requires understanding and awareness of an interlocutor).

A more significant advance in the area of NLP was Terry Winograd's SHRDLU program (1971), which was the first demonstration that natural language understanding was possible for a computer, even if in a very restricted domain. Winograd developed a system to enable humans to instruct a robot to manipulate small blocks of wood. The computer/robot could engage in conversation with the human about this world and explain its actions. Despite the astonishing successes of this early attempt at NLP, Winograd himself is refreshingly modest about the limitations of his approach. It does not deal, he says,

> with all the implications of viewing language as a process of communication between two intelligent people. A human language user is always engaged in a process of trying to understand the world around him, including the person he is talking to. He is actively constructing models and hypotheses, and he makes use of them in the process of language understanding... A realistic view of language must have a complex model of this type, and the heuristics in our system touch only the tiniest bit of the relevant knowledge. (quoted in Weizenbaum, 1976, pp. 195-196)

Neither the humility of Winograd nor the recantations of Weizenbaum have prevented the artificial intelligentsia from continuing to make inflated claims for their discipline. And yet, this problem of understanding must, for the communicative language teacher, always be the obstacle to the adoption of teaching aids based on this AI approach to language analysis, since the cognitive model employed, if it ignores understanding, must at best be the mechanistic and behaviourist model embodied in the worst applications of the language laboratory, and long since rejected.

More recently, attention has focused on rather more limited objectives. There have been developments of "expert systems", such as syntax checkers, which will parse a limited range of input sentences and feed back comments on grammatical errors. But beyond their limited research value in the development of expert systems, such programs would seem to have little practical value to the language teacher in the classroom. From the program developer's point of view, the problem is once again that of meaning and understanding. Imlah and du Boulay (1985), having described their relatively simple syntax checker, observe:

> It is clear that methods based only on syntax must severely limit what can be achieved. Incorporating word meanings into the system immediately brings in all the standard, hard problems of natural language processing. (p 146)

With the general qualification, therefore, that from the teacher's point of view, any program which cannot handle meaning can have only limited use in the normal teaching situation, it may nevertheless be of use to describe in more detail some of the developments of NLP and their applications, especially those using the computer programming language Prolog. (For a fuller account of the history of NLP see Lehnert and Wringle [1982]).

Prolog

Most computer programming languages (Pascal, BASIC, COBOL, FORTRAN) work on the principle that problems can be broken down into sub-problems which can then be solved by the execution of a step-by-step procedure (or algorithm). The procedure is quite separate from the data which is to be processed. The computer programmer's function is to define the procedure for solving the problem in a very precise way.

Prolog uses a very different approach. In a Prolog program, there is no differentiation between program and data. A Prolog program consists simply of a description of all that is known about a particular problem: the facts of the situation and the rules which are known to apply to them. To run a program, one formulates a query in the form of a fact, which Prolog then seeks to prove by searching its database of facts and rules to find a matching fact or a rule whose conditions can be satisfied.

A very simple program might take the following form:

```
brother(charles,mabel).
father(david,jim).
```

mother(mabel,jim).

uncle(X,Y):-parent(Z,Y),brother(X,Z).
parent(X,Y):-father(X,Y);mother(X,Y).

The first three statements are facts in the form of predicate and arguments. The predicate name describes the relationship between the related objects (arguments). The uncle and parent relationships are defined as rules: a person (Y) has an uncle (X) if (:-) person Y has a parent (Z) and (,) that parent (Z) has a brother (X). The second rule states that X is the parent of Y if X is the father of Y or (;) if X is the mother of Y. Constants in Prolog begin with a lower case letter, variables begin with an upper case letter.

If we now wish to establish whether Charles is Jim's uncle, we state the fact:

uncle(charles,jim).

which Prolog will then attempt to prove using the facts and rules available to it. Since there is no fact in the database which matches the statement, Prolog applies the rule about uncles, and then seeks to prove the sub-goals, firstly to establish that Jim has a parent Z, and subsequently that Z is the brother of Charles.

It is important to note that Prolog has no "real world" knowledge except that which is given to it by the programmer. Thus, from the above facts we cannot establish that Mabel is the sister of Charles, since no sister relationship is defined in the database.

The most useful data structure in Prolog is the list. A list is used to combine various data items into a single structure, particularly when the number of items is either unknown or subject to variation. Hence, sentences may be represented in Prolog as lists of words:

sentence([the,cat,sat,on,the,mat]).
sentence([the,boy,stood,on,the,burning,deck]).

A list is contained between square brackets, and the elements of a list are separated by commas. Lists may also contain lists. A list may also be empty, in which case it is represented thus:

[].

Prolog allows a useful distinction to be made between the head of the list and the tail, by using the list separator |. If we use the above sentence lists as our example, we could establish the first element of each sentence by posing the query:

sentence([Head|_]).

The underscore character (_), or anonymous variable, is used to indicate that the values found are to be ignored. In processing this query, Prolog would bind the value of the first element of each sentence list to the variable Head, and ignore the remainder of the list, no matter what it contained. If however, we wanted to know about the remainder of the list, having discarded the first element, we could query thus:

sentence([_|Tail]).

In which case, Prolog would bind the end of the list to the Tail variable, giving new lists:

Tail = [cat,sat,on,the,mat]
Tail = [boy,stood,on,the,burning,deck].

One of the most commonly used list processing functions is to establish whether a named element is a member of a list. Here two rules are used: the first states that an element is a member of a list if it is at the head of the list; the second, that an element is a member of a list if it is a member of the tail of the list.

member(Head,[Head|_]).
member(Head,[_|Tail]):-member(Head,Tail).

The second rule here is recursive, or self-referential. A predicate is recursive if it is governed by a rule whose body contains a reference to the same rule. All substantial programs in Prolog make use of recursion.

Naive language processing

A conversation can be simulated with a series of fairly simple techniques (as for example in the DOCTOR script for ELIZA, described above). The computer could have a stock of set phrases to interject irrespective of the input, or it could convert a statement into a question, or it could search the input phrase for certain words for a more specific response.

A database of stock phrases might take the following form:

response('How are you? ').
response('Did you have a happy childhood? ').
response('Did you hate your father? ').
response('Do you have any friends? ').

The simple rules of conversation may be specified as follows:

> converse:-
>> patient(S),
>> doctor(S),
>> converse.

The patient's part in the conversation is simply to type a phrase at a prompt:

> patient(S):-
>> write(':   '),
>> read_in(S).

The read_in predicate needs further specification; its purpose is to convert the "patient's" input, which is simply a string of characters including spaces and punctuation, into a list of words. A definition of the predicates to achieve this can be found in Clocksin and Mellish (1984, p. 104).

The doctor's responses make repeated use of a simple predicate which separates a list into head and tail:

> headword([Head|Tail],Head,Tail).

If the patient answers "No" or "Yes" to the questions, the doctor asks for more information:

> doctor(S):-
>> headword(S,'no',_),
>> write('Tell me more.'),nl,!.

> doctor(S):-
>> headword(S,'yes',_),
>> write('ah.. Tell me more.'),nl,!.

If the patient's response contains the word "hate", the doctor asks for clarification. This rule makes use of the member predicate described above.

> doctor(S):-
>> member(hate,S),
>> write('Why do you hate me?'),nl,!.

Finally, if none of the above rules applies, the doctor responds by converting the patient's response into a question:

```
doctor(S):-
        respond(S),
        write('?'),nl.
```

The next two rules operate by substituting words which appear in the "translate" database for words as they appear in the input sentence and have the effect of transforming the input sentence into an interrogative. Words not in the translate database are passed over simply to be replicated in the response. For example, an input sentence such as "I am unhappy" would be transformed into "you are unhappy?".

```
respond(S):-
        headword(S,Head,Tail),
        translate(Head,Translation),
        write(Translation),write(' '),
        respond(Tail).

respond(S):-
        headword(S,Head,Tail),
        write(Head),write(' '),
        respond(Tail).

translate(i,you).
translate(you,'I').
translate(you,me).
translate(your,my).
translate(me,you).
translate(my,your).
translate(am,are).
translate(are,am).
```

The ELIZA program as it stands may seem to have little relevance to the language teacher. From the communicative point of view, this approach to language processing has at least two drawbacks: firstly, the computer is unable to interact with the "client" and cannot therefore take an interest in or learn anything from or about him/her. Secondly, the program knows nothing about language: if the client spouts gibberish, the program will simply regurgitate gibberish. If the client says nothing the program will cheerfully resort to its set of stock phrases and repeat them tirelessly. There are some circumstances, however, where this approach to language processing might be taken advantage of. The essential technique of the program is that of keyword analysis: the program scans input and responds on the basis of "trigger" phrases. Such a technique could be appropriate for scanning and checking answers to a comprehension exercise, for example, where a database of questions, acceptable answers and suitable computer responses (reinforcement, corrections, explanations) is linked to a text for comprehension. It is doubtful, however, that the programming effort required to get the computer to allow partially correct answers but respond with appropriate messages to incorrect input could justify the results.

Whether computers can be made to learn about learners and to understand about situations in which language is used is a problem we will return to towards the end of this chapter when we discuss artificial intelligence. But before addressing that issue, we should address the slightly easier question: can the computer be taught anything about language?

Schank (Schank, 1984) observes that "the real problem with today's computers is that they don't understand us when we use language the way we are used to", and linguists delight in constructing phrases of the type "flying planes made her duck" to demonstrate the ambiguity of natural language and hence the impossibility of computers ever understanding humans, whilst AI experts lament that no computer should be expected to accept sentences which would not be tolerated, let alone generated, by any human being other than a transformational grammarian. Nevertheless, we also know that language is not purely arbitrary; it is to a large extent a rule-based activity and knowledge about language may be formulated as rules of grammar. Such rules may be expressed as Prolog rules and these rules can be used descriptively (as an explicit definition of what is an acceptable utterance) or prescriptively (as in parsing). It is at least worth asking the question, therefore, whether the definition of natural languages as Prolog facts and rules has any application to language teaching and learning.

Parsing

Linguistic objects are structured objects, and understanding the meaning of a sentence depends on the ability of the speaker to recover the structure of the utterance, even though such an ability is often unconscious. A parser is a computational device for inferring structure from grammatical strings of words. A grammar and a parser are therefore two separate things: a grammar is an abstract definition of a set of well-formed structured objects, whereas a parser is an algorithm - a set of instructions - for arriving at such objects. For a description of parsing techniques the reader is referred to Gazdar and Mellish (1989). What follows assumes a definite clause grammar (DCG) and top-down parsing.

A simple Prolog grammar for declarative sentences in English might take the following form:

```
sentence(Inphrase,Outphrase):-
      nphrase(Inphrase,Temp),
      vphrase(Temp,Outphrase).
```

In other words, the input list (Inphrase) is a valid sentence if it has a noun phrase at the front and if what follows (Temp) is a verb phrase. If this succeeds, Outphrase will be an empty list; in other words, if a sentence is to be parsed successfully, all the words must be accounted for and there must be none left over. Such that, for example:

```
sentence([the,boy,ate,the,apple],[]).
```

would be true, but

```
sentence([the,boy,ate,the],[]).
```

would not.

Subsequent rules would define the acceptable components of noun phrases and verb phrases. A noun phrase is defined as consisting of an article followed by a noun expression:

```
nphrase([Art|Nounexp],Temp):-
      art(Art),
      noun_exp(Nounexp,Temp).
```

The next rule defines a verb phrase as consisting of a verb followed by a noun phrase:

```
vphrase([Verb|Nounphrase],Temp):-
      verb(Verb),
      nphrase(Nounphrase,Temp).
```

The next rule defines a verb phrase as containing only a verb:

```
vphrase([Verb|Temp],Temp):-
      verb(Verb).
```

A noun expression may contain only a noun:

```
noun_exp([Noun|Temp],Temp):-
      noun(Noun).
```

or it may contain an adjective followed by a noun:

```
noun_exp([Adj,Noun|Temp],Temp):-
      adj(Adj),
      noun(Noun).
```

The vocabulary might contain the following words:

```
art(a).
art(the).
noun(boy).
noun(ball).
noun(apple).
verb(kicked).
verb(ate).
adj(round).
adj(red).
```

Using the above facts and rules we could establish that "the boy ate the red apple" is a valid sentence with the query:

```
sentence([the,boy,ate,the,red,apple],[]).
```

But we can also use the rules as a sentence generator. The query

```
sentence(X,[]).
```

will generate all legal (and some slightly illegal) sentences from the defined syntax and vocabulary.

```
X = [a,boy,kicked,a,boy].
X = [a,boy,kicked,a,ball].
X = [a,boy,kicked,a,apple].
X = [a,boy,kicked,a,round,boy].
...
X = [the,red,apple,ate].
```

In the teaching of linguistics or machine translation, there are many possibilities for the development of this grammar: adding new parts of speech (prepositions, adverbs); allowing multiple, but not repeated adjectives to qualify a single noun; number checking between subject and verb; adding new constructions, such as relative clauses, and so on. The next step might be to construct a similar grammar for the foreign language (with new problems such as gender and case checking, word order, etc). Linking two such grammars together, and taking advantage of Prolog's power to generate sentences, it is possible to construct a basic machine translation system (see Crookes, 1988, pp 109-163 for a translator between French and English).

It may be argued that such activities sensitise students to the issues of grammar, and make explicit the student's knowledge about grammar, which is often passive and unsystematic. This in turn makes their learning more efficient. For students, and potential users, of machine translation, the exploration of rule-based systems lays bare the limitations of such systems and may induce the users to be more tolerant of the system's limitations and faults, and more realistic in their expectations.

Syntax checkers

Many of the techniques described above have been applied to the problem of checking syntax. The assumption behind such programs seems to be that grammar has to be learned; that grammar has not become easier to learn since the communicative revolution; and that grammatical competence must often be attained before real communication is possible (Kecskés, 1988). In systems designed for checking syntax, a sentence typed by a user will be analyzed, comments will be offered on syntactic errors, or further information will be requested of the user if the system encounters unforeseen problems (such as unknown lexical items). The main benefit of such systems is seen to be that "the computer normally provides immediate, individual, uncritical and unambiguous feedback about some aspect of language performance" (Galletly et al., 1989, p. 82); the basic premise of these authors is that human views on the correctness of utterances are "often ill-informed, evasive, contradictory or even wrong" (idem). This betrays an oddly mechanistic approach to grammatical problems and seems to deny the complexity of language production. The authors are at least cautious in their claims for their system, stating no more than that it "posed real and interesting problems" (for the student who did the work) and "generated a great deal of cooperation between the departments (computing and humanities) involved".

The problem with syntax checkers as described by Galletly et al., especially where they operate at the sentence level and focus on only one or two grammatical features (in their case, negation and pronoun word order in French), is that they inevitably abstract the language from the context within which it is used. It may be argued that such programs have a function in remedial correction of specific deficiencies, and hence conform to a structural-behaviourist mode of language tuition. A more communicative approach to the problem (if the problem is seen as the improvement of the ability of a student to handle a particular construct) might be to use the computer to conduct a systematic search of a large corpus of text for examples of the construction causing problems. This might be particularly rewarding where context is more important, as with the handling of pronouns. If, on the other hand, the problem is seen as one of improving the overall productive grammatical competence of the student, the focus should be on the document (rather than the sentence) and on a wider range of language issues, including problems of lexis and style as well as syntax. For this latter operation, style checkers are becoming available, and are likely to prove a more useful classroom tool for the communicative language teacher (see the chapter on word processing for further discussion).

Artificial intelligence

Artificial intelligence is that branch of computer science which investigates the possibility of designing machines which exhibit behaviour normally thought to require intelligence if performed by human beings. Applied to language teaching, AI attempts to overcome the inflexibility and non-adaptiveness of traditional CALL software by proposing and maintaining a computer model of the learner as s/he interacts with the knowledge domain. In achieving this, Yazdani suggests (Yazdani, 1989) that there are three problems to be overcome: firstly, whether to use general purpose AI shells or to develop customised systems; secondly, whether a teacher with limited computing skills can be expected to produce a shell for a new language; and thirdly, how to encode teaching skills into the system. Moreover, he states, "as we start to test our system with potential users, we shall need to address the broader pedagogical issues in the use of this new technology" (p. 102).

This seems to be addressing the problems in the wrong order. It implies that the technology is neutral and that technological solutions can be identified independently of the classroom and the teaching methodology. Whereas Wyatt (Wyatt, 1984, p. 10) has argued forcefully that "the computer is a medium that reveals the methodological assumptions of its authors with unusual clarity". What needs to be done is to address the pedagogical and methodological issues first, before addressing problems of system design. It is far from clear, for example, that AI techniques can be adapted easily to the vast domain of human language. AI techniques have indeed been used with some success in the design of expert systems but it is in the nature of expert systems that they address limited domains of human endeavour wherein a body of conscious knowledge can be identified, elicited and systematically taught (and this is no trivial matter even in narrowly defined domains). Natural languages do not fit this model, since the body of knowledge required to achieve the status of fluent speaker of a foreign language defies precise description and hence expert tutoring systems with any degree of semantic, pragmatic or discourse sophistication will be a long time coming. Alan Hirvela (Hirvela, 1988) sparked a heated exchange in *System* with his observation that:

> the learner must always shape his responses to the *computer's* demands in such a way that they are comprehensible within the computer's woefully limited linguistic boundaries. It is the learner who is attempting to acquire a language, but it is the computer's language that governs the relationship. Learners must *always* operate according to rules set by the *computer's* limitations. (p 307)

Whilst one may dispute Hirvela's argumentation, experience with current applications of AI to language teaching and learning indicates that his conclusion is not very wide of the mark. However, this is not to argue (as Hirvela does) that work in this area should to be abandoned, and the computer banished from the language teaching classroom until all its harmful effects can be identified and neutralised. Rather we should accept Nyns' answer to his own question (Nyns, 1989): "Is intelligent computer-assisted language learning (ICALL) possible?". If this means: is it possible to develop ICALL systems by applying AI techniques, the answer is no. If, on the other hand, the question means: is it possible for teachers and students to use CALL systems intelligently, the answer is yes.

Conclusion

In rejecting the NLP and AI approaches to language teaching and learning, it must also be recognised that, although learning (to use Krashen's terms) does not necessarily lead to acquisition, and knowledge of rules does not necessarily lead to increased competence, nevertheless, speech is at least in part a rule-governed process; communication does not occur as the result of the random generation of words. There is evidence to show that when adult learners learn rules, especially those which highlight the discrepancies between the rules of the native and target languages, the time taken to achieve proficiency in the target language can be greatly reduced. Such assumptions, if they are insufficient to justify the widespread use of NLP and AI techniques in the ordinary language teaching situation, do at least permit the continuation of research and the limited application of such techniques in carefully controlled circumstances.

Bibliography

Clocksin, W. F. & Mellish, C. S. (1984) *Programming in Prolog*, Springer-Verlag.

Cook, V. J. & Fass, D. (1986) Natural language processing by computer and language teaching, *System*, 14,2.

Crookes, D. (1988) *Introduction to Programming in Prolog*, Prentice Hall.

Fox, J. (Project Director) *et al.*, (1990) *Educational Technology in Modern Language Learning*, a report for the Training Agency by the University of East Anglia and the Bell Educational Trust.

Galletly, J. E. & Butcher, C. W. with J Lim How, (1989) Towards an intelligent syntax checker. In Cameron, K. *Computer Assisted Language Learning*, Intellect Books.

Gazdar, G. & Mellish, C. S. (1989) *Natural Language Processing in PROLOG*, Addison Wesley.

Hamilton, A. G. (1989) *The Professional Programmer's Guide to Prolog*, Pitman.

Hirvela, A. (1988) Marshall McLuhan and the case against CAI, *System*, 16,3.

Imlah, W. G. & du Boulay, J. B. H. (1985) Robust natural language parsing in computer-assisted language instruction, *System*, 13,2.

Kecskes, I. (1988) Computer programs to develop both accuracy and fluency, *System*, 16,1.

Lehnert, W. G. & Wringle, M. H. (1982) *Strategies for Natural Language Processing*, Lawrence Erlbaum.

Nyns, R. R. (1989) Is intelligent computer-assisted language learning possible? *System*, 17,1.

Roszak, T. (1986) *The Cult of Information*, Paladin.

Schank, R. C. (1984) *The Cognitive Computer*, Addison-Wesley.

Weizenbaum, J. (1976) *Computer Power and Human Reason: from judgement to calculation*, Penguin.

Wyatt, D. H. (1984) *Computers and ESL*, Harcourt Brace Jovanovich.

Yazdani, M. (1989) Language tutoring with Prolog. In Cameron, K. *Computer Assisted Language Learning*, Intellect Books.

7 INTERACTIVE MULTIMEDIA

James A. Coleman

The phrase "interactive videodisc" was still unfamiliar to many when, in 1987, I edited a collection of papers under the title *The Interactive Videodisc in Language Teaching*. Today, the very phrase "interactive videodisc" is obsolescent, replaced by the broader expression that heads this chapter. Such is the pace of development and technological change. Nonetheless, "interactive video" has, in the interim, acquired a degree of currency both as a term and as a concept. It is also a convenient starting point, since it identifies the key component in interactive multimedia for language teaching, namely the video component.

Why video?
In the past, some computer-literate linguists have thought of interactive video as CALL with a few pictures added. Few people these days would be likely to share such a definition. Video has imposed itself as the *sine qua non* of communicative language teaching, especially at intermediate and advanced levels. However, to evaluate the current and potential role of video-based interactive multimedia, it is essential first of all to recall just why video is the cornerstone of new teaching and learning methodologies.

"Language," said the American linguist Leonard Bloomfield, "is basically speech." The primacy of the spoken language is no longer challenged outside the most traditionalist university departments. In evolutionary terms, speech pre-dates writing by perhaps a million years, and the adjacency within the brain of language processing and speech organ control demonstrates how we are fundamentally oral-aural creatures, rather than reading-writing ones.   Most languages have never existed in a written form.   In all first language acquisition, the understanding and production of speech precede those of written texts. People talk far more than they write, and the importance of mastery of the spoken language as the primary objective among learners is confirmed time and again by surveys and needs analyses.   Only the survival of Latin-based teaching methodologies, and the confusion of language learning with literary prestige have obscured until recently the primary necessity of acquiring the spoken language rather than the written.

Video is to the spoken language what the book (or, more recently, the newspaper or magazine) is to the written language.   It gives permanency to what is usually characterised by its ephemerality: speech.   It provides a corpus for analysis, a model for imitation, a topic stimulus, a comprehension task.

Video is familiar and non-threatening to today's learners, who choose to spend on average more than three hours a day in front of the television screen.   Yet in the classroom it remains motivating, whether because of its novelty in an unfamiliar setting, or because of the variety it offers.   And indeed, no other medium can deliver a remotely comparable range of topics, settings, speakers, accents and locations.   The audio laboratory is a poor second best in providing the rich diversity of linguistic input the language learner needs.   Mere audio input falls down too on the scale of realism (radio programmes and phone calls excepted), and on anxiety levels: any class straw poll will reveal a number of learners who hate using the telephone even in English, and who systematically boycott audio lab classes.   Anxiety is well documented as an obstacle to language acquisition, and it is no wonder that an absence of visual information, especially eye contact, should make people uneasy, given that between fifty and eighty per cent of all human communication is non-verbal.

Video moderates this anxiety, and in so doing also offers a maximum of clues to comprehension.   The physical setting, the speaker's or speakers' identity (age, gender, socio-cultural markers such as clothes), paralinguistic features (including gesture, posture and facial expression), and last but not least visible lip movements, all help the learner to decode the verbal message.   This means that more challenging material can be used without departing from Krashen's principle of comprehensible input.   The sight of native speakers in context can also contribute significantly to the socio-cultural understanding which is increasingly seen as an indispensable adjunct to the more narrowly linguistic skills (grammatical, sociolinguistic, discourse, interactional and strategic) which together comprise communicative competence.

A further feature of video which makes it ideal for interactive use with computers is its controllability. Native speakers, however willing, cannot repeat a phrase without variation in its utterance. The same sentence on video can be repeated as often as is necessary for comprehension or perfect imitation, or can be broken up for analysis.

Research into language acquisition has redefined the role of the teacher, and once again video is well placed to step into the breach. To learn a foreign language is, after all, a unique undertaking: it is not just a matter of learning a corpus of knowledge (like some aspects of chemistry or civil law); nor is it just a question of learning new physical skills and practising them until they become intuitive (like playing tennis or the oboe). It is both of these and more: it is the voluntary acceptance of a profound and permanent change to the learner's psychological and physiological make-up (Fox, 1990). It is logical, then, to focus on the needs, desires and abilities of the individual learner, to concentrate in class on learner-centred activities, and to relegate to Oxbridge dustbins the notion of the language teacher as the fount of all knowledge expatiating *ex cathedra* to a group of empty vessels. The new teacher's role as animateur, as learning organiser and facilitator, as reference or referee is certainly no easier, but it means that the focus of the learner's attention is, quite rightly, elsewhere.

Methodologists agree that successful learning takes place where there is extensive, meaningful exposure to the target language, and intensive interaction in or with the target language. Such interaction may be social, or it may, in the physical absence of a native speaker, be psychological - there are innumerable examples of learners achieving success without contact with the target population, and the whole concept of self-access or distance-learning facilities rests on the validity of the hypothesis that psychological interaction with a foreign language helps acquisition. Such interaction brings us again to motivation and thus to video, with its topicality, its movement, its immediacy, and all the other qualities that have now made television viewing more important - at least in terms of time spent - than a child's days at school or an adult's entire lifetime of work.

This introductory discussion of video and of its role within teaching methodology, although it may appear tangential to a book on computer-assisted language learning, is essential to a comprehension of multimedia in language training. Technical aids must never be used in a methodological vacuum, and technology must not be allowed - as has sometimes been the case with both language labs and CALL - to dictate the shape of materials, when the learner's real interest may lie elsewhere.

Additionally, an understanding of those features that make video an exciting teaching medium is a prerequisite for evaluation of existing approaches to interactive use of video.

One final preliminary is also required: a brief review of the ways video can be used on its own. An appreciation of its versatility will help enable the reader to judge the quality of existing interactive multimedia packages.

Non-interactive video applications

There is of course no single method for exploiting video in the language classroom. A spoken text can be used in as many different ways as a written text, if not more. Practitioners occupy a continuum. At one end are those who perceive video as a coloured-in text, and whose first act is to strip the visuals and issue sound-only copies to students. At the other end can be found those who see the specificity of video as a sequence of moving images. The first act of this latter group is to strip the audio track and play the video with the sound off.

Both are valid techniques, and so are the many intermediate strategies. For linguistic analysis and as a model for imitation, a video-taped spoken text may be treated in the same way as a written text. But widespread exercises such as prediction or video split (in which half the class watch without sound, the other half listen without picture, then pairs reconstitute the original through discussion in the target language) are so successful because they exploit the unique features of the tool while adding the lucidity which enhances participation, involvement, rich psychological interaction, and language acquisition. Nor can it be too often stressed that purposeful viewing, where learners have a pre-defined task to accomplish in watching a video, is infinitely more effective than passive viewing, or decontextualised listen-and-repeat drills.

The most obvious applications for video are as an input for aural comprehension, and as a model for imitation. In the first instance, the video text could be replaced by a written passage or an audio recording, but the loss of realism could be considerable. Most encounters in a foreign country are verbal, and understanding what is said to you is the primary skill to be mastered. Responding appropriately is the second, and there is no doubt that model dialogues can help. By repeatedly imitating a phrase spoken on video by a native speaker, a learner can acquire the correct structure, lexis and intonation, and can soon produce the phrase fluently (i.e. without hesitations). The learning is efficient because relatively error-free, and even if one has doubts about the extreme and excessive application of Skinnerian behaviourism, the combination of short-term memory and repetition can certainly lodge the phrases in the long-term memory. Many learners also enjoy drilling because they feel, rightly or wrongly, that it is doing them good.

A further aspect of video, more or less present according to the producer's intentions, is the socio-cultural information - the physical sights and sounds of the country, its towns and its people. Their houses, their shops, their food, their manners and greetings, how they buy a drink in a café - video can often help reduce in advance the foreign-ness of, say, Spain or Japan, so that arriving and living there is less of a shock. This socio-cultural competence, an inseparable component, as we have noted, of global communicative competence, means that the learner is more at ease in an unfamiliar environment; by diminishing stress, it inevitably enhances linguistic performance, and is therefore not to be despised. No tool can convey the necessary input for socio-cultural competence as efficiently as video.

While aural comprehension, phrase repetition and socio-cultural input are three obvious uses of video, it should not be assumed that the medium's usefulness stops there. Indeed, these exercises by themselves provide a very poor diet, far removed from the rich interaction in and with the language that is, as we have seen, a prerequisite for effective language acquisition.

Most teachers will therefore consider these activities to be merely the first stage of exploiting a video extract. The succeeding activities will normally concentrate on the video text as, firstly, a linguistic quarry, and, secondly, a topic or imaginative stimulus.

In other words, the teacher will often draw from the language of the video text, be it authentic or scripted, a selection of structures, lexical items, or grammatical (i.e. syntactic, morphological, phonological, semantic or pragmatic) points for elaboration, extension and practice; and will use the ideas discussed or the images portrayed in the video as the departure point for further work in the shape of role plays, debates, discussions and projects. In most cases, naturally, the two go hand in hand: student language production on the particular topic will be expected to contain (and thus reinforce) the vocabulary and structures studied.

The relevance of this point for interactive multimedia is that the analytical stage of text exploitation is a collaborative task, where the teacher becomes more of a prompter, helping and encouraging learners to locate appropriate samples of language, and thus helping them also to achieve one target that is common to all undertakings in distance, open or self-access learning: knowing how to learn. There is hardly a course at higher education level - and increasingly at school level - that does not see it as an asset, if not a fundamental necessity, for the learner to become aware of the processes of learning a foreign language and of how s/he can actively improve her/his own language acquisition.

Such collaborative teacher-student activities, then, are a crucial stage in video exploitation. But they pose a considerable problem for programmers, for the very reason that student contributions are unpredictable, and that teacher responses need to be infinitely flexible.

An area of still greater difficulty for interactive multimedia programs designed for untutored mode is where the picture matters more than the language, when the video is selected primarily or exclusively for its inherent interest to the predominantly vision-oriented species that *Homo sapiens* is. There is nothing new in using visuals as stimulus for language work, but there are two distinct approaches: one triggers the memory, the other triggers the imagination.

When I learnt Welsh as a primary pupil in the 1950s, much of the lexical acquisition was stimulated by wall-charts which I can visualise even now. Showing pictures or flash-cards to stimulate target-language recall without mother-tongue interference is standard practice - witness for example the primary French course developed for Hampshire schools where a card bearing three stick people and a blob with an eye and a tail translates as "J'ai (Tu as, Il a, etc.) deux soeurs, un frère et un poisson".

This strategy, whereby visuals stimulate recall of predominantly lexical items, is extensively exploited by currently available interactive products. What they do not attempt, since the presence of a tutor or animateur seems once again to be crucial, is the showing of pictures to stimulate imaginative use of the target language. Most readers will remember the O-grade or O-level test where a six-box strip cartoon illustrated the successive stages of a story (inevitably, for some obscure reason, an accident while camping!) which the pupil's task was then to turn into spoken or written narrative.

More productive still for spontaneous generation of language is the open-ended activity in which a number of suggestive and perhaps exotic images - a night-time rendezvous, a sealed parcel, a ticket to Bangkok - must be combined into a coherent and cohesive story, usually by students working in pairs. Interactive video, if used initially in sound-off mode, can provide the similar activity in which students predict the dialogue or commentary that accompanies a video sequence, and then - with attention and motivation enhanced by expectation (and perhaps a competitive element) - check their version against the real one. The inescapable problem is that such an exercise, when controlled by computer, is a closed one. The classroom alternative, like the real world, is designed to be open, and to cope with all the diverse but equally valid responses to a stimulus.

Future videodiscs might do well to devote a few spare still frames to imaginative visual stimuli of this sort. Some research has suggested that learners do enjoy talking to computers: the absence of the intimidating teacher monitoring learner errors apparently relieves inhibitions. But there must be some doubt as to the value of generating spoken language whose accuracy and appropriacy will never be monitored, especially where the workstation activities are designed for a single learner without a partner.

From this overview of how video is used in the language classroom, then, we may expect to find that the first available videodiscs, particularly those designed for the commercial market, will have played safe and concentrated on those activities - comprehension, repetition, prediction and verification - which are low-risk, are most likely to provide error-free learning, but are least likely to generate the spontaneous, open language which is the mark of true acquisition.

Interactivity

Having opened this chapter's appraisal of interactive video with a consideration of video in isolation, we must now also define "interactive" in this context. "Interactive video" is sometimes heard in the sense of two-way simultaneous transmission of television pictures. Such interaction - the "videophone" of so many futuristic films of the past - is now a reality, with DCE Video-conferencing, albeit an expensive one for training purposes. No doubt live video-conferencing will have its uses in language learning, but it falls outside the scope of the present study, though it may help us define our terms.

True interactivity implies a dialogue in which both sides of a two-way exchange adapt their behaviour in the light of the other's response. For this reason, linear videotape can never be fully interactive: even if the software permits branching, the video bites remain the same - as, for example, in the Longman *Art of Negotiating* disc, in which a training film featuring a younger John Alderton and Penelope Keith has simply been separated into segments by the insertion of a few multiple choice questions (MCQs). The American IV market is full of repackaged films which have equally little interactivity. It is arguable that MCQs themselves are not very interactive, unless feedback is more informative than simply right/wrong. Branching, structured via matching of open-ended learner input to predicted responses, allows more sophisticated interactivity. Programmed learning, in any case wholly ill-suited to language acquisition, is hardly interactive at all.

The Nebraska scale of interactivity was originally designed to apply to hardware, but is now used also for courseware. Level 0 is only ON/OFF; Level 1 has the control features of a good domestic VCR (remote control, freeze frame, forward and backward motion at, above or below normal speed, including frame-by-frame) together with random access to specific frames; Level 2 describes players with an on-board microprocessor allowing real interactivity via branching based on MCQs or matching. Level 3 assumes computing hardware which controls the most complex of interactive routines and generates numerous text and graphics screens of high quality. Apart from resource discs at level 1 (iconography, archives, museum catalogues), most new videodiscs are at level 3 or beyond.

Interactive multimedia hardware
The interactive multimedia workstation has four essential components:
- a screen or screens to display video and computer-generated information;
- a player to transfer video pictures and sound from tape or disc to screen;
- a computer to implement the program on hard or floppy disc and transfer computer-generated text and/or graphics to the screen;
- an input device allowing the user to determine the pace and route followed by the program.

A schematic representation of the relationship between the workstation components and the user would show a circle with information flowing from user to computer to screen to user, and an additional route from computer to screen via the video player.

The screen
Some interactive video packages call for twin screens, one each for the video and computer output. This is rare, except where a text overlay would be distracting or where a great deal of computer information is needed on screen, for example in the BBC's Action television training discs.

The screen is not the only form of return communication from the workstation to the user. Apart from audio tracks, which may match or supplement the on-screen data, much interactive multimedia courseware allows attachment of a printer, which can provide hard copy of screen information which the user wishes to retain, and/or a record of the user's performance and the route and pace s/he chose to follow.

The video player
A rapid description of how video works will help understanding of what follows. The camera gives an impression of continuous unbroken movement by capturing a sequence of still images and projecting them so rapidly that the human eye

and brain cannot perceive the change from one to the next. The separate images, called frames, succeed each other at a rate of 25 (PAL or SECAM), 30 (NTSC) or 24 (film) frames per second. PAL, SECAM and NTSC are different ways of separating video into its components (essentially chrominance, luminance, sound, and data or teletext) and laying them down as electronic signals on magnetic tape. PAL is the standard in the UK, Germany and most of Europe, Africa and South America; SECAM in France and (thanks to a visit by De Gaulle shortly after he had taken France down the non-communautaire SECAM path) the Soviet Union; NTSC (a technically inferior standard, jocularly known as Never Twice the Same Colour) in North America.

Videotape and videodisc both have a place in interactive multimedia for language training. The choice will depend on the user's objectives and budget, but in practice institutional or in-house production means tape, while professional or commercial production mean disc. Videotape is cheap, widely available, and easily copied; users can record their own material, and re-record time and again on the same tape. But videotape stretches in use, so that frame-accurate programming is out of the question. It also loses quality when copied, and wears badly. Older video tape players tend to jiggle on freeze-frame.

In use, videotape has two major drawbacks - its slowness and its linearity. As all users know, "fast forward" is at best a relative term, at worst a dreadful euphemism. To go from one point on the tape to another, the heads must disengage, the motor must get up to speed then brake, and the heads must re-engage - a lengthy process. And the only way to get from A to Z is to go through the whole alphabet, whereas an interactive videodisc offers near-instantaneous random access.

An analogy with books may help visualise the problem. We may read page 6, then immediately afterwards turn to page 300, read a paragraph, and go back to page 7 to pick up where we left off. Imagine having to flick through every intervening page, and the drawback of a linear medium is clear. Both the slowness and the linearity can be minimised by using the computer to generate a task which will occupy the user while the VCR winds laboriously on, or by structuring the tape so that branches in the program trigger adjacent tape segments. This remains nonetheless one area where videodisc has the advantage.

The disc has other assets besides rapid random access; they include long life with minimal deterioration and virtually error-free reproduction. Today's industry standard data storage medium is the 30cm (12") LaserVision disc, introduced in 1984, which saw off several alternative formats in the 1980s. It looks like a silvered LP, but its recorded information is decoded differently.

Optical discs, like the old LPs, have a continuous spiral track and rotate at a fixed speed. Whilst the record-player stylus used to read a series of pits of different shapes, a laser beam now reads different patterns of light reflected from the shiny surface. For this reason, there is no contact between the disc (which is additionally protected by a transparent layer of plastic) and the reader. This means that wear is negligible, picture quality excellent, and freeze-frame totally stable. The computer can go to any one of the 54,000 frames per side and start playing with a pause of two or three seconds at most, and usually far less. As a result, a branching program appears seamless to the user (whose attention has no time to wander), and recap of a sentence or phrase is easily achieved.

A videodisc is not re-recordable: as with the LP, the material it holds is fixed when it is pressed. Cost is another drawback. To master a videodisc will cost several thousand pounds - although compared with the often six-figure cost of planning, shooting and editing half an hour's professional video this cost is relatively unimportant. A machine for making one's own discs (a WORM facility - Write Once Read Many) is available for under £20,000, but the disc quality makes it suitable only for prototyping, not mass-production.

The British IV (interactive video) industry - hardware manufacturers, courseware developers and users - has defined the basic specification of a LaserVision workstation: an IBM AT-compatible PC, running MS-DOS version 3.0 or later, with 640K RAM, minimum 20Mb hard disk, floppy drive, RS232 port, serial port, and at least one each 8-bit and 16-bit slots, together with a PAL LaserVision player with RS232 connection. The monitor should have 640x200 resolution, EGA card, and specific genlock board (to synchronise signals from the computer and the video player: otherwise they scramble each other). It can be purchased as a single package (e.g. the Sony View workstation); portable hardware (e.g. the Centaur G) is also available.

Interactive videotape
While this chapter concentrates on videodisc, it should not be assumed that interactive videotape does not have its uses. A £3000 disc and £4000 workstation are an unjustifiable investment if one's objective is simply to get more out of the cheap, topical and inexhaustible supply of authentic recordings from satellite television. There are several software options (such as TELSOFT from Brighton Polytechnic, Autotutor developed at Trinity College Dublin, or TOPCLASS from Format pc), costing from £200 upwards, which allow teachers to add interactivity to pre-existing videotape. At Brighton Polytechnic, for example, among many other activities, the evening's television news in French and German can be recorded off-air and processed to provide a lively alternative to the standard Quintilian comprehension grid.

A more developed procedure, for tutored classroom use at Wolver-hampton Polytechnic, is described by Goodison (1990). Purpose-made videos (business role-plays, lectures on socio-economic themes) are prepared in sections with various forms of learner help added mainly through subtitles. The programmed interactivity does away with all the problems of classroom management associated with video use, and alternative software allows a single piece of video to be used with learner groups of varying levels of competence. Although restricted to listening comprehension and to linear video, such approaches clearly demonstrate that the future for interactive video is not just in the one-to-one seclusion of the training booth, but in the classroom as a stimulus for solutions negotiated by the participants in the target language. This is a quite crucial lesson.

Input devices
Nonetheless, all courseware commercially available in the UK at the time of writing (February 1991) is on LaserVision discs, and to these we return. In the context of the present book, it is unnecessary to describe a computer, but the question of the input device - of how the user communicates with the workstation and therefore achieves interactivity - does merit some consideration.

There are many ways for the user to communicate responses to the computer. Most familiar is the keyboard itself: arrows can move a cursor around the screen until a selection is made by pressing "Enter" or "Return". An attached mouse, trackerball or joystick will offer a faster way of relocating the cursor and making one's choice with the click of a button. The alpha-numeric keys give either single-key responses - a figure 0-9 for multiple-choice, a letter Y or N or H for "Yes" or "No" or "Help", a function key F1 to F10 for preset commands - or fully typed words.

With today's emphasis on the spoken language, designers may be loath to give prominence to written input, and there is also a danger that learners unfamiliar with the keyboard will be distracted from the screen and the language task by the typing itself. The latter problem is temporary: no-one leaving school after 1995 will be without basic keyboarding skills.

There are, however, further difficulties with keyboard entry. Authoring software allows the programmer to allow "fuzzy matching", for example to accept Wahrheid where Wahrheit is expected. It can also provide branched responses, treating, for example, a gender error in a different way to an agreement error or a spelling mistake. But such discrimination can slow a program down and detract from its interest, and can be time-consuming and problematic to prepare. Should "le fakirs", for instance, be treated as an agreement error, a spelling mistake, or a slip of the finger?

For all these reasons, designers of interactive video programs have preferred simpler forms of user input. To those already mentioned should be added the barcode reader (a feature of many existing non-language packages, the codes being incorporated in the accompanying booklet), the light-pen and the touch-sensitive screen. Ideal for public locations since it offers no moving parts to be stolen or vandalised, the last does have two minor drawbacks: the user must regularly (a) pull it back to the front of the table, and (b) remove the smeary accumulation of greasy fingermarks.

A final alternative is to design a simplified keypad with a limited number of choices. This solution is well matched to a program structured by multiple choices, and has been adopted for the CD-I Japanese language disc.

Interactive audio
Before leaving this overview of today's systems, and despite previous comments on the indispensability of visual information, we must consider interactive audio, a medium in which at least one major UK publisher is shortly to publish language-teaching materials. Tandberg has for several years produced a cassette player which responds to computerised instructions. But audio tape suffers the same drawbacks as videotape - linearity, slow response, rapid degradation, poor copying, and stretching. More attractive is a voice card, a slot-in component for personal computers which digitises sound for storage, manipulation (e.g. phoneme isolation) and reproduction. With appropriate authoring software, there is scope for updating traditional lab exercises including drills, transcription and text reconstruction, though it must be hoped that new technology will not support outdated methodology: the artificiality and inauthenticity of most audio-only exercises is not easily overcome. However, storing audio on Compact Disc, with its more than 550 Megabytes of memory (allowing over three hours of high-quality, rapid-access 32-bit digitised sound) is an attractive option; an authoring package such as Apple's Voyager CD Audio Stack will help the teacher make use of appropriate CDs.

Authoring systems
Authoring systems allow non-programmers to write programs, and save time for professionals. They vary in power, sophistication and the level of expertise required to operate them. TenCORE is the industry standard for interactive multimedia authoring; TAKE5 is an integrated package including hardware and authoring software; PC Opensoft is cheap and allows users without extensive knowledge of programming to create or adapt videodisc programs. There are many others.

The next generation of hardware
What feature do computers share with the Hanson Trust and with Professor Quatermass's "Thing in Westminster Abbey" in the sci-fi classic? The answer is that all have a capacity to absorb previously alien forms of activity. Computers began with numbers, then moved to text, to graphics, to still pictures, and now to moving pictures. At every stage, sceptics said it would never catch on. Today, the video is controlled by computer but delivered by an external source. In the very near future, it will become routine for the computer itself to store, manipulate and deliver pictures.

The LaserVision disc already appears to be obsolescent. Despite the release of several feature films and a number of 'popular' discs with a degree of interactivity, such as the BBC's *Guide to Garden Birds*, the LaserVision format failed to establish itself as a domestic format outside Japan, and discs and players were soon remaindered. A different form of optical storage launched in 1982 did, however, conquer the domestic market by offering up to 72 minutes of top quality sound: CD-DA (Digital Audio). In 1989, 114 million audio Compact Discs were sold in Japan, 207 million in the USA, and 51 million CDs with a million players in the UK.

Whereas LaserVision is an analogue storage system, CD is digital. Put simply, an analogue signal records actual features - like a photograph of a hill; the digitising process measures the dimensions of the hill and records them in binary form as bits and bytes. This is why digital information is stable and manipulable where an analogue signal can suffer deterioration and is hard to handle. Digitised video can be resized, duplicated into adjacent on-screen windows, modified in several productive ways (hence the interest aroused by Video Logic's DVA 4000 card which digitises analogue video). CD technology also has the significant asset of adhering to a single worldwide standard.

CD-ROM (Compact Disc Read-Only Memory) stores large quantities of data (text, graphics or software) rather than digitised music. Its capacity of over 550 Mb gives the equivalent of nearly a quarter of a million A4 pages of text. Its drawback is that the individual user cannot modify the contents.

CD-ROM XA (Extended Architecture) adds a dimension to CD-ROM, by allowing limited videographics animation and an audio track which can be synchronous with on-screen text. Four CD-ROM XA discs for adult literacy training are already being developed.

CD-I (Compact Disc Interactive) is, however, potentially the most exciting CD-based delivery system. Its US launch as a consumer product is scheduled for 1991, the European launch for 1992. It can use its storage capacity for 600Mb of data or 72 minutes of hifi-quality stereo music or sixteen hours of "speech quality" (poor mono) sound or 6000 high quality digitised compressed video images - or any combination of these. The difficulty with digitised video, for CD-I as for DVI (see below), is that each full-screen image occupies some 0.5 to 1Mb of memory: a whole CD would thus be filled by less than a minute of video. Additionally, current technology can retrieve and display information no faster than 150Kb per second: the one minute of video would take more than two hours to play! To resolve this problem, data is compressed for storage and decompressed for playback.

CD-I, a Philips initiative supported by Sony and Matsushita among others, achieves compression by combining two strategies: "sampling" (i.e. selecting a small proportion of) the pixels or tiny dots that make up each frame; and using only one quarter of the screen area so that the extent to which picture quality has suffered is less noticeable. At present, the deterioration remains clearly visible in a grainy, jerky picture. Image size need not be a problem: it may well prove more effective to limit the video component to part of the screen, retaining the rest for titles, supporting text, graphics, route indicators, learning style options, location maps or help menus. Nonetheless, the stated objective of Full Screen Full Motion (FSFM) video has yet to be publicly demonstrated.

CDTV is a clever, if misleading, acronym, since the CD no longer stands for compact disc; Commodore Dynamic Total Vision (sic!) will nonetheless use the 12cm CD-ROM format, boxed with an Amiga 500 computer for £699. Targeted firmly at the domestic edutainment market, CDTV is designed to do to CD-I exactly what SKY television did to BSB: to be first on the market and thereby establish such a large user base that later arrivals, even if more technologically sophisticated, cannot get a foothold. Originally scheduled for worldwide launch in November 1990, CDTV should now be with us very soon, accompanied by more than a hundred education, reference and leisure packages, including cookery, an atlas and the Bible (promoters of both formats are assiduously wooing software publishers). Building on domestic viewers' habits, CDTV will come with a remote handset with a four-arrow pressure pad cursor control. It too promises FSFM video eventually, and is incompatible with CD-I, whose moderate picture quality it shares. A pilot scheme with Derbyshire County Council to teach Japanese to schoolchildren using CDTV may not be unrelated to Toyota's siting a £700m car plant in the county.

Where CD-I and CDTV are targeted principally at the home market, DVI (Digital Video Interactive, developed initially by RCA and now backed by Intel, IBM, Microsoft and Olivetti with UK marketing from Thorn EMI) is designed for professional use. Unlike CD technology, it is not hardware-specific and will run on any PC with the appropriate chipset (currently on two boards), regardless of operating system. It thus appears more flexible and future-proof, and will support a range of functions including desktop video editing. Since DVI supports video input from a camera, it will be possible for the learner to put her/his own efforts on screen alongside the tutor model and make a visual comparison of, for example, lip-rounding, sign-language - or meaningful culture-specific gestures! IBM's vision of the future of personal computing as a multimedia environment is also evidenced by its recently launched Audio Visual Connection (high quality sound and still pictures) and M-Motion video adapter (quality sound and stills with analogue video). DVI adopts a different compression-decompression strategy from CD-I. After the initial frame, it records, like a Walt Disney animator, only the relatively few changes between one frame and the next, rather than the majority of the picture which remains static. Quality is not yet to FSFM standard. Neither CD-I nor DVI will allow the random access to individual frames that analogue video supports.

The future of these competing technologies is a matter of guesswork: smart money yesterday was on CD-I for domestic use, DVI for professional applications, with LaserVision continuing to hold a place in education and training. The recession and Philips' financial problems may alter that prediction.

Interactive multimedia applications

Interactive multimedia is currently serving four purposes: information, marketing, education and training, with the last accounting for 70% of applications in the UK, which is ahead of the rest of Europe but behind the USA. The cost of freeing up staff, of transporting them, of lodging and feeding them, and of engaging trainers has led corporate personnel departments to embrace a technology that gives limitless training for a one-off investment. Situated at the workplace, the workstation is available 24 hours a day. Within a large multinational, the costs of originating a bespoke disc are small if it is used, with different language voice-overs, in every company site in the world. Controlled experiments have shown IV can release up to 60% of a trainer's time.

Trainers have identified factors which enhance adult learning. One formula states that trainees retain 25% of what they hear, 45% of what they see, and 70% of what they see, hear and do. Another source suggests we remember 10% of what we read, 20% of what we hear, 30% of what we see, 50% of what we see and hear, 80% of what we say, and 90% of what we say and do at the same time. (Academic experience may be different!) Be that as it may, adults generally learn best
- in their own surroundings
- at their own pace
- with local peer group pressure

- without interruption
- with clear objectives
- in the absence of error and "unlearning"
- with frequent self-testing and reinforcement
- when they believe in the training method
- through creative activity not rote learning
- drawing on their own experience.

With the possible exception of the last two, interactive multimedia meets all the criteria. Learners can study in private, when it suits them, without needing to travel. They work at their own pace, and via a personalised route which is remembered from one training session to the next. Small wonder that companies have consistently reported significant gains not only in cost-effectiveness, but also in time and in efficacy.

Jaguar, Renault and B & Q all use interactive multimedia to train sales staff. Hard skills (technical manuals, operating and maintenance procedures) are exemplified by the interactive multimedia package on diagnosing and dealing with failure of the French PTT's automatic letter-sorter, or British Rail's Super Service disc for carriage cleaners. Soft skills (human interaction, telephoning, delegating, interviewing, etc.) are covered by several generic discs, as well as by in-house productions for the Post Office, the Midland Bank, and the Alliance and Leicester. Simulations (escaping from a hotel fire, safety on oil platforms, Shell sales rep training) and surrogate travel are a further variety of training discs. POS/POI (Point of Sale, Point of Information) applications include Rover cars, Ladbrokes betting shops, Curry's cooker catalogue, the Bremen public transport system, BBC's Lasercast (details of 10,000 actors with photos and updatable CVs), and the guides to the Bank of England and US National Gallery of Art. The durability of the medium has led to its adoption by the seven-day-opening Guinness World of Records in London. An example of interactive multimedia as a visual database is the Vatican Library's Codex Vat. Lat. 39, a thirteenth-century illuminated manuscript. In education, there are now over 400 school-level discs in the USA, an achievement the UK's Interactive Video in Schools (IVIS) initiative hoped to begin to emulate: there is interactive multimedia support for national curriculum maths and science (3 double-sided discs, and a workstation costing below £2000). My own favourite title is the award-winning Swedish disc *Butchering Pigs Economically*, which illustrates how interactive multimedia, by simulating real activities and real outcomes, can in some cases remove the necessity for experimenting on human or animal subjects. Applications already exist which harness to interactive multimedia the power of hypertext (e.g. ABC News Interactive's *Great Moments in the Twentieth Century*) and the digitised voice card (e.g. Coates Viyella marketing/training disc for Dorma products), but artificial intelligence is in its infancy, and the strategies adopted so far for intelligent tutoring systems are methodologically and theoretically primitive when applied to language acquisition.

Current language courseware

The first two UK experiments were both at secondary level. Siville was a DTI-funded project led by Shropshire LEA within the IVIS scheme, designed to run on a BBC and to teach French to school pupils up to age 14. 350 schools piloted the popular and successful package, which is not commercially available but may be borrowed. *Siville ou l'embarras du choix* takes the form of a surrogate walk through the cartoon streets of a French village. Designed for pupils working in groups of four, it first identifies as male or female the interlocutor who is thereafter *tutoye(e)*. Menus are presented both visually and aurally (good reinforcement), and allow users to choose the level difficulty of their task, which is to buy a certain number of objects from a certain number of shops with a limited amount of money (i.e. shopping, seeking and understanding directions). Once a shop is reached (perhaps with the aid of a flic), a still of its façade is shown, and the language exercise begins, with a real shopkeeper supplying his/her side of the dialogue. A ghost voice speaks the responses chosen by the user (more reinforcement). Elements of adventure games are the (initially unseen) street plan, the randomised reasons for purchase (souvenirs, a picnic, etc.) and *fermeture annuelle* of certain shops, and the money. While adopting the first-person camera approach of a number of IV discs, Siville is exceptional in assuming the constant presence of a trainer (teacher) to whom unprogrammed queries can be addressed (*"Je ne comprends pas la question > Demande au prof"*). The concise and eminently practical accompanying booklets show the value of thorough pilot-testing. While Siville is undoubtedly enjoyable, worthwhile and well executed, with a good game concept, appropriate language content and acceptable video quality, it is, as might be expected from a first generation package, limited in its scope. It adds pictures and speech, but conceptually marks no advance over standard CALL package design.

The North West Educational Computing Project, with some hardware and some financial support from IBM and four LEAs, explored new ground in creating French and German discs for schools (Coleman, 1987). The first stage exploited the BBC's old *Ensemble* material, dividing utterances into about seven syllables for student modelling, then giving an English cue for student recall, before moving, in the student's own time, to a "fruit machine" stage of random combinations of learnt sentence components. Source language (SL) and target language (TL) help are available, and the important underlying assumption is that authentically communicative use of the language, with concentration on content not form, is a subsequent activity led by the teacher.

The second stage of the project used semi-scripted scenes acted out by school pupils in France and Germany - a cost-cutting expedient which unfortunately diminishes the value of the whole package and undermines some excellent approach and programming work. The user can choose whether the presentation shall be paused or unpaused at the end of each utterance, with or without sound, with or without TL subtitles, with or without SL subtitles. The choice of topics and language is good, and an attempt was made in the activities offered to imitate best practice in video exploitation. Students may browse, guess who spoke, guess what was said, or silence one speaker and perform his/her role.

Two key members of the North West Educational Computing Project team, linguist Mike Picciotto and programmer Ian Robertson, moved gradually into the commercial arena as Vektor Limited, severing relations with Lancashire Polytechnic. With new partners BBC English and IBM UK, they produced the award-winning *The European Connection*, the first UK-originated videodisc for business English.

The European Connection marks at one and the same time a continuity of approach and a new departure. Many of the best features of the school discs are retained - indeed, the underlying approach is identical. *The European Connection* claims to offer more than 100 hours of language training for any post-school level of user competence. Originally priced at a prohibitive £10,000, it is now available in education for £1950, or £2950 with a front-end (translation of all computer-generated text) in any of twelve languages for lower level learners.

The two discs are menu-driven, and the nineteen sequential modules that make up the story are fully scripted. There is no video branching in *The European Connection*, since the user is not a participant in the drama, but rather an observer of the soap-style struggle for success. The dialogue is dense and well researched, stuffed with widely usable business jargon. Transcripts are supplied. The user may watch each of the scenes, which offer multiple perspectives on greetings, meetings and negotiations, in unpaused or paused mode - the latter for repeating each phrase, which can be instantly recapped *ad lib*. Precise TL transcripts and/or, in bilingual versions, SL equivalents can be selected, as can sound-off or video-off options, the former for prediction or to observe non-verbal behaviour, the latter to concentrate on the sounds. It is debatable how often users might choose to cut either, and the main menu, whose layout is a weak feature, could profitably be redesigned to bring in realistic default settings. Help routines and a set of booklets offer further support.

In addition to the drama, the course provides 18 video and 10 audio interviews with leading figures on aspects of European integration. The inclusion of authentic language with motivating content is to be applauded, though the price paid is that a few items (e.g. concerning the role of the ECU and of 1992) are becoming dated. There are also eleven audio-only telephone exercises (eight authentic, three scripted). The emphasis throughout is on English as an international business language, so it is appropriate to have a wide sociolectal and dialectal range, including Japanese, Dutch, German and Italian speakers of English, though this does not dilute the laudably non-sexist socio-cultural impact.

User input is via a single keystroke (there is no mouse or printout facility), and movement within the package is flexible, mostly well designed and quickly learnt, though a minor update could make some operations more economical. Users can call up profiles of the real or fictional characters, summaries of the dramatic or linguistic content of a chapter, or can refer to the pronouncing dictionary of selected key items by consulting the oddly-named "Role Model" or "Dictionary". The first provides phrases, the second single words. Each is pronounced to camera by both an English and an American speaker, providing instant repetition or comparison. A red or yellow dot in the subtitle shows whether an item is in the pronouncing dictionary. A facility to display TL subtitles word by word completes the extensive range of support for word and phrase memorisation through repetition.

With the voice card option, users can record and playback their own short utterances. Non-English versions allow spelling and number practice: press any key. An add-on functional option provides a video collage of functional exponents, as in the video component of Hodder's French course *En Fin de Compte.*

The pack contains no grammatical backup, no exercises, and no lexical or cultural explanations, and has been criticised as a language lab with pictures, in which students can only listen and repeat. Nor is there an obvious role for a teacher. However, though the course authors can offer substantial advice on how to exploit *The European Connection* in a tutored context, they are clear in their belief that the particular niche for IV is for initial independent work - "the intensive language acquisition and practice phase of language learning" and some structured exploitation. Their strategy is to use IV to make the more mechanical presentation-and-practice or comprehension-and-controlled-production phase of learning more attractive, and thereby free up some 50-60% of the language teacher's time to devote to genuinely communicative work. It is a philosophy that is hard to disagree with, and it underlies a range of courseware that is building bit by bit into an extensive system.

Vektor has published French and German versions (*La Connection Française* and *Die Deutsche Verbindung*), and filming has been completed for the Spanish version.   The French version suffers from the same wooden acting that sometimes afflicts the English disc, but otherwise has all of its merits.   *The Meetings Connection* and *The Personal Connection* will extend the range of English-language discs.

The very first UK commercial language videodisc was the *Expodisc* for business Spanish, produced by Paul Bangs, then of Buckinghamshire College of Higher Education, and Sally Staddon of Ealing College.   It became one of the six DTI IVIFE (Interactive Video in Further Education) projects, though some funding was obtained elsewhere and, regrettably, unlike other IVIFE projects, an evaluation was not built in.

Expodisc is a simulation, using the subjective camera: it sees what you see, people talk to it as they would to you.   You are an assistant export manager developing a market in Spain for a new product.   As with *The European Connection*, a single storyline is broken up into stand-alone modules: preparation, identifying and contacting the target company, visiting Spain (hotel and bar scenes), meetings to clinch the deal, etc.   The filming is a strong point: very professional in scripting, acting and realisation, with a redolent sense of Spanish location and culture.

Role plays based on simulations are a staple of IV training packages, and are well suited to acquiring language.   The thrill of reality may be absent, but so is the embarrassment.   Without the threat of real consequences, the learner can take risks - exactly what is needed to develop fluency and a truly generative grammar, and to extend the learner's language resource.

Aimed at beginner to intermediate level, *Expodisc* retains features of the adventure game: real choices with video branching, a briefcase into which, if you were wise, you packed all the briefing documents before leaving Britain, and an outcome that depends on your performance.   There is a (rather remotely) linked textbook, valuable in itself, and extra audio material on the second audio channel.   It currently sells at £1350.

The menu offers a recap, SL and/or TL subtitles, and help on language or business practice.   Here it differs considerably from *The European Connection*, offering an immense store of back-up explanations on everything from *ser/estar* to export documentation.   There are in all 1600 text screens containing 85,000 words, and some have criticised *Expodisc* for putting on screen too much text that could just as well be on a more comfortably readable printed page.   This is to ignore the fact that, as with hypertext buttons, the user calls up only what s/he needs, when s/he needs it. A more pertinent criticism is the quantity of English - but again, how else to present complex data to someone with severely limited Spanish? The screen presentation lacks design, and there is no unscripted, authentic language, but overall *Expodisc* blends a traditional approach (explicit grammar, drills) with a communicative one (contextualised structures within extensive, real, meaningful interaction). The thorough attention to and working out of detail, and a recognition of the limitations of the medium for spoken interactions, mean that a fundamentally simple idea has led to an impressively useful language learning tool.

Interactive Information Systems, with their French partner Interaxis, market a series of soft-skills IV discs for business. Because sophisticated UK courseware design is so good, European versions are being modelled precisely on the British originals, so that *Leading Your Team* becomes *Animez votre Equipe* and *Making the Telephone Work for You* is *Le Téléphone à votre Service*. Although not designed for language teaching, a number of HE and some secondary institutions are already using them for open access or short courses. Instantly memorable icons on a well designed screen take you through four *Equipe* and three *Téléphone* discs, each designed for a couple of hours' work.

Each disc is divided into modules, but with recurring characters and a coherent overall story. Accompanying leaflets summarise the target audience and objectives, and an *aide-mémoire* helps learners recall the skills learnt. The scripting and filming are first class, with a wealth of realism and humour, and the transition to France (or Holland or Germany) is totally convincing. There is good but sparing use of graphics, and revision and self-testing where appropriate. MCQs or "Interrupt when..." give a variety of structure, and feedback by video branching is ingenious: after the user has watched a scene and chosen a course of action, the scene is replayed with your interlocutor's often sarcastic response as a *monologue intérieur* voice-over.

The discs would provide an excellent route for integrating business skills into language learning, in that the language acquisition is indirect. Separate exercises would need to be developed, and the disc would need to be reserved for advanced learners, since there are no concessions in speed, clarity or register. On the other hand, the speaker is nearly always clearly visible on screen, and there is a wealth of body-language - the natural, deliberate focus for training in interpersonal skills. Both disc sets are valuable and entertaining in themselves, even if the language content is too advanced for most British telephonists.

Interaxis' own *You're in Business* is equally sophisticated and impressive, with good screen layout and realisation, but this disc is designed for learning a language: American English. Charlie Simpson leads the user through various activities, including introducing himself and telephoning, during which the user can replay, pause, recap, fast forward or skip. Each video section has back-up in the form of a study centre, an exercise centre, and a quiz; a dictionary is also available, so that the user is kept entertained by a variety of activities, is never far from appropriate help, and is never lost, thanks to a system of highlighting locations already visited. Much productive use is made of audio, for example for intonation practice, where the user taps, then hums, then sings the pattern before adding an accent or mood ("He's Texan", "She's upset", "She has a confident, laughing style"). The program is occasionally weird, and is throughout heavily didactic in the American manner, but full of fun and good ideas.

A pre-production pilot of the first CD-I language disc was revealed in October 1990. Commissioned by the Training Agency, it provides basic business Japanese for English speakers, and the structure and approach, supplied by Vektor, follows the same methodology as their LaserVision discs described above. The other partner is New Media, who are very experienced producers of IV and contributed to the very promising but ill-fated Eurocentres English disc, *Getting the Message/Danger Mission.* Japanese Language Training won a British Interactive Multimedia Association award for innovation. This, the UK's first generic training application on CD-I, has a modular structure with scenes in the restaurant, the inn, the bank and the department store and sections on greetings, phoning and visiting. The video in the pilot version covers only 20 per cent of screen area, but users are close so this poses no problem - indeed, it allows all control options to be constantly on screen. Limiting the video to 15 frames per second does, however, make it jerky. Choices, communicated by a remote control keypad with thumb-operated joystick (cf. the CDTV approach above), lead you through the course map (main menu), a very clear tutorial, and the introductory overview, and then to familiar Vektor features such as paused or unpaused listening and gapped dialogue.

Maxwell Communications and Philips, with their language subsidiaries (Berlitz and Philips Language Learning Systems) are promising a series of courses on CD-I for the end of 1991.

Evaluation

In evaluating new packages as they appear, we should be looking for real interactivity and individualisation, a high degree of user-centredness (pace and route control by the user not the program creator), a wide range of activities which are as communicative as possible, and a professional standard for scripting, acting, sound and pictures. Compared with classroom teaching, good interactive multimedia language courseware will bring all the benefits of a successful CALL package, and then some:

- learner autonomy
- immediate, interactive response
- enhanced interaction between user and TL content
- intensive TL work
- more personalised attention than a busy classroom teacher can offer
- unpredictability
- consistency
- elimination of the chronically ineffective or temporarily hung-over trainer
- handy reference sources (grammar, lexis, culture of target country)
- elimination of "lowest common denominator" response to uneven competence levels, which can sabotage classwork
- real task-based activities with real outcomes
- striking audiovisual content that, through learner motivation, disguises the necessary drudgery
- self-assessment, evaluation and feedback.

Future courseware trends

Currently available offerings are essentially for the individual learner in stand-alone, self-access situations. There is little role for a tutor, nor for the imaginative exercises evoked at the beginning of the chapter. There remains an element of the "repeat-after-me" school of language learning, and some courseware is closely modelled on other training packs, where there is a single desired behavioural outcome - not the case in language use.

I see future products as more diversified, with some for the advanced learner and the trainee teacher. A single disc will serve learners at many levels, just as a current gardening disc has 15 workbooks each at a different level. Designers' and learners' imagination will be given freer rein - it would be ironic to put so many state-of-the-art communications tools into students' hands and then forbid them to be creative.

Producers will sacrifice one minute's video for 1500 stills which, randomised, will serve as a stimulus for story-telling, as decor and character-isation for role plays, as diagrams, maps and clues for murder mysteries. Stills will provide the differentiated input so necessary for communication across an information gap but hard and expensive to achieve with video.

Other authors will transfer to interactive multimedia the text maze concept, currently exemplified in print by Edwards and Bérube's odd but endearing bilingual *Découvrez ... who stole Granny* and as software by Osman Durrani's *Schattenburg*. Such an approach is built around branching structures, and can be highly motivating through imaginative interaction with the adventure story and its population of goodies, baddies, weirdies, witches, goblins and dragons. It would transfer wonderfully to interactive multimedia, with visual, aural and written information sources complementing each other.

Eventually, digitised video will become banal, storage infinite, authoring less burdensome. And the specialised workstation will have gone: all the facilities will be bundled into the humdrum desktop PC. And we still won't have achieved acceptable voice recognition and synthesis.

Research

As in so many aspects of language learning, there is little empirical evidence of the effectiveness of particular interactive multimedia techniques, since variables are so difficult - some would claim impossible - to control. The 1986 thesis by Catherine Watts noted substantially enhanced motivation, satisfaction and language acquisition, but there is a clear need for more investment in research and evaluation. Do students really enjoy talking to computers? Is it true, as more recent findings suggest, that small groups gathered round a terminal do not interact enthusiastically in TL but grunt in TL or lapse into SL?

In looking at learning package design, we need more data on the distinct contribution of different types of video and audio input (authentic, semi-scripted, scripted, off-air, stills, spoken dictionary), on strategies of and criteria for image selection, on the interaction of visual and aural perception. We need to know how best to adapt to individual learning styles, and to implement learner tasks combining high relevance, authenticity and motivation. We must establish how best to incorporate cyclical reinforcement, arcade game strategies and excitement, and unpredictable authentic materials such as current sales figures or today's press reports. Comparative studies should be undertaken on alternative branching triggers (MCQs versus fuzzy matching) and on different forms of user help (SL translation, TL transcript, caption or voice-over, keywords or full text, simplified or slower or clearer alternative soundtrack, etc.). We should discover which user input device is least distracting (and why), and which screen presentation of multiple simultaneous information sources is most effective (and why). We should ascertain whether different interactive multimedia learning modes (self-access, pairs, small groups, tutored or untutored) have different outcomes. Finally, research should establish how best to evaluate motivation, retention and retrieval in a language learning context, and compare interactive multimedia packages with each other and with other training methods.

Conclusion

Interactive multimedia for language teaching is in its second generation. It is already impressive, but future generations of applications will almost certainly look very different, both in delivery system and in approach. CALL programs without a video component may, in my view, expect a shortish shelf-life.

No technology will ever make trainers obsolete, especially in the language field. The quality of the learner's experience must depend more on the trainer's approach and skill than on the tools at the trainer's disposition. Good tools can enhance good practice: they cannot eliminate bad practice. Nonetheless, interactive multimedia has features that even the most professional trainer is unable to match. If investment is forthcoming, it will become the key support technology in language teaching and learning.

Bibliography

Ayre, J. (1990) *A Beginner's Guide to Multimedia*, NIVC.
Bayard-White, C. (1990) *Multimedia Notes*, Chrysalis Interactive Services.
Coleman, J. A. (ed.) (1987) *The Interactive Videodisc in Language Teaching*, Dundee.
Fox, J. (*et al.*) (1990) *Educational Technology in Modern Language Learning*, Training Agency Report.
Goodison, T. (1990) Interactive video, *Language Learning Journal*, **September**.
Watts, C. (1986) *The Use of Interactive Video in Language Learning*, unpublished MPhil dissertation, Brighton Polytechnic.

8 DATABASE

William Brierley

Database is a particularly difficult concept to define unambiguously. The *Penguin Dictionary of Microprocessors*, for example, gives two definitions:

- A file of data structured to allow a number of applications to access the data and update it without dictating or constraining the overall file design or content.
- Any file which might sound more important if called a database.

To be slightly more charitable, some use the word to refer simply to a large amount of factual information (the more the better), probably loosely organised (if organised at all), and often in a single file or on a single disc. Others use the concept to refer to a complex but organised set of related files, with highly articulated methods for search, retrieval and display of information. In any case, it is certainly true that "database" is a much over-used word. This chapter proposes briefly to examine both types of database, and suggest ways in which they might be used by language teachers.

But first a word about the technology. Given that databases tend to be large, disk storage capacity and speed of retrieval both become more important factors. Many large databases are only available on CD-ROM (compact disk, read-only memory). Computer CDs are produced in the same way as hi-fi CDs, using optical laser storage techniques. A laser is used to store digital data as microscopic 'pits' on concentric tracks and the data is then read by photo-electric sensors which do not make active contact with the storage medium. CDs provide robustness, ease of handling and greatly enhanced storage capacity: a standard CD-ROM holds the equivalent of 250,000 A4 pages of text. Unfortunately (or fortunately) CDs cannot be erased in the same way as magnetic disks and cannot be written to - though advances in this technology are being made. CD-ROMs also need special players and interfaces, which add to the costs of the equipment. Some databases, especially those combining text with other forms of data representation (especially pictures), are stored on videodisc.

Factual databases
Contemporary and historical "area studies" databases
Increasing numbers of CD-ROMs are available which offer relatively unstructured, but nevertheless massive, sources of information. National newspapers are now becoming available, with a whole year's issues on a single disk. For example, in the UK, *The Times* and *Sunday Times*, *The Guardian* and *The Independent* are all available. Most offer search facilities (search headlines or text for keywords), facsimiles of front pages for screen display, and off-prints of articles to ASCII file for subsequent printing.

The possibilities for integration into language and area studies teaching here are almost endless, but an obvious one is for students to search the disk for articles on a particular topic in advance of a discussion or essay writing class and to prepare a summary of the articles (a multiple file, cut and paste exercise) for distribution to the rest of the class. The same resource would also be invaluable to teachers of contemporary affairs who, one suspects, spend a great deal of time scanning newspapers for articles on interesting topics and cutting them out with scissors.

The newspaper CD-ROMs are published year by year. For an historical perspective, though, selective databases are also available. Some may also contain a wider range of media than just text. *L'Histoire au Jour le Jour*, for example, is a multi-media CD-ROM which contains records of world events over the last forty years, as published by *Le Monde*, in a variety of different formats, including maps, pictures, portraits and sound, enabling the user to hear the speeches of world leaders in their original language.

Le Monde en Chiffres by contrast deals with economic statistics from *The Economist* over the last eighteen years. Data from this package (available in either English or French) can be downloaded directly into spreadsheets, and is of obvious relevance to courses combining language study with economics or business.

For students of French language and literature, there is the *1000 Ans de Littérature* CD-ROM, which contains 800 works dating from the end of the ninth to the end of the nineteenth centuries from over 280 authors. *Textes et Contextes* is another French literature database, this time with 6000 extracts from 1500 authors.

For the historian, the French Revolution has spawned several exciting developments. *Révolutions!* covers the whole period on CD-ROM. The data is accessible via a day-to-day agenda or a dictionary of events and biographies. It also contains musical illustrations and reproductions of famous paintings of the period. *Images of the French Revolution* is a videodisc containing 38,000 images taken principally from the Department of Engravings of the French Bibliothèque Nationale.

Also available on videodisc (and under certain conditions free of charge from the publisher, the Fondazione Giovanni Agnelli) is the spectacular *De Italia* encyclopedia of Italian civilisation. It contains 20,000 photographs and 15,000 texts (unfortunately for the language teacher, in English) and tables on every aspect of Italian life, including art, history, literature, architecture, geography, economics, politics, technology, and everyday life.

Materials databases

Databases are being established, largely as the result of cooperation among language teachers, of language teaching materials. The *Datenbank Deutsch als Fachsprache* and the *Vernetzeter Lehrmaterialsteinbruch* are disc-based databases of teaching materials for German which contain texts classified according to subject, grammar content, type of text and classroom activity. The *French Resources Project* (published by La Sainte Union FE College, Southampton) is a similar database with articles from the French weekly press.

Language databases and dictionaries

Zyzomys is an encyclopedia of the French language on CD-ROM, containing 400,000 terms, including 72,000 headwords. It also has a world atlas and includes pictures and sound. More traditional (text) dictionaries are also increasingly available. Collins, for example, supply on-line dictionaries for English, French, German, Italian and Spanish. Harraps have put eighteen dictionaries onto one CD-ROM. From a word processor, it is possible to consult any of the dictionaries (Danish, Dutch, English, Finnish, French, German, Italian, Japanese, Norwegian, Spanish, or Swedish), check definitions, and paste translations directly from the dictionary into the word processor document.

Videodiscs and access to external databases via electronic mail are the subject of other chapters of this book, so I propose now to focus on the type of database that might be used in a business application, to demonstrate possible applications to the language teacher.

Business databases
Databases are powerful tools for the storage, retrieval and manipulation of data. They clearly have relevance and value in language work, and their use is one of many IT applications to have been recommended for the National Curriculum. Even where the database does not contribute directly to language acquisition, the additional skills of data manipulation are useful skills for students to develop.

Fox (1990) outlines some exercises, where the student listens to information on tape, answers questions, then checks the answers against information stored in a database. The sample database (*French Database*) contains information on the town of Orthez in the Pyrenees. NCET's *Modern Languages Find* can be used in the same way.

These databases do not, however, reflect the way "real" databases are used in the real world. So, if databases are indeed to be used as real-world tools, real-world applications will need to be developed. If the focus of the language teaching programme is business, then a database could make a useful contribution to the simulation of an office environment. I propose, therefore, to describe such a simulation.

Long before beginning to set up and use their database, students must be sensitised to the issues of data organisation and information flows through a typical business organisation. This can be dealt with in abstract terms, but becomes more meaningful if a type of organisation can be specified: an agent distributing goods from a number of suppliers to a number of customers, for example. It then becomes clear that the organisation holds and processes different types of information: about customers, manufacturers, orders, and stock, for example. Such information cannot, however, be held in completely separate files, since it will be necessary, for example, to relate information about a customer's address with a filled order (so that it can be delivered). Similarly, it will soon become obvious that if all the information is held in a single file, it will quickly become full of redundant or unnecessary information.

The purpose of this activity is to reveal the basic principles of databases:
- data should be input once only;
- redundant data should be eliminated;
- data should be easily retrievable;
- files should be easy to maintain;

■   files should be expandable.
Further issues might also be addressed:
■   how to maintain security of data;
■   what backup, restart or recovery procedures might be necessary;
■   how might data be output for different purposes (reports, letters, etc).
"Database" now corresponds to a much narrower definition:

> A non-redundant collection of all data serving one or more defined business applications, that data being structurally linked to and permitting access to all other data in that collection for which a natural or logical business relationship has been defined to exist, however complex (F. Johnson, in Anderson, 1974).

It will now be possible to set up the database as a series of connected (related) tables, each table containing data about one aspect of the company's activities. The example below shows a possible arrangement to store information about customers, their orders and the individual items on each order. Table names are shown in **bold**, and the data fields used to relate the tables together are shown in *italic*.

customer	orders	items	stock	manufact
		item_num		
	order_num	*order_num*		
	order_date	*stock_num*	*stock_num*	
customer_no	*customer_no*	*manu_code*	*manu_code*	*manu_code*
title	deliv_inst	quantity	description	manu_name
fname	purchase_no	total_price	unit_price	
lname	deliv_date		unit_descr	
address1	paid_date			
address2				
town				
postcode				
phone				

Having established the database, it now becomes possible to make use of it in the simulation of business activities. The class can be asked to compose standard letters, such as confirmation of orders, focusing on culture-specific differences in composition and layout. A more ambitious exercise might involve the class in a survey of its fictional customers concerning their views of the future trends in the market. Each member of the class could then reply on behalf of a customer, and the responses could be collated and presented in the form of a report. Class members could also be required to respond to a variety of business letters: complaints, enquiries about specific orders, requests for information. These exercises can be enhanced by the use of other computer tools such as *LinguaWrite* which contains a database of 1800 commonly-used business phrases. *LinguaWrite* is available for English, French, German, Italian and Spanish.

Conclusion

Databases (of either type described above) are not easily assimilated into the language classroom. Factual databases are, of their nature, undiscriminating, and some care must be taken in the selection of data for exploration. Nevertheless, their sheer size and the relative ease of access give them enormous advantages over other forms of information storage and retrieval. Business databases are not easy to set up, and if they are to be effective in simulating the business environment it is likely that some programming skills will be required of both the teacher and the student. The pay off, though, may be seen in giving language students additional computing skills, which will prove useful in their future employment. Databases may yet come into their own, therefore, as an exciting and engaging way of linking language study with other aspects of the curriculum, such as business studies or area studies.

Bibliography

Anderson, R. G. (1974) *Data Processing and Management Information Systems*, Macdonald & Evans.

Chesters, G. & McNab, A. (1990) CD-ROMs and the language learner, *Recall*, 3.

Darby, J. (ed.) (1990) *The CTISS File*, 10 (theme issue: Exploiting CD-ROM Technology).

Fox, J. (*et al.*) (eds.) (1990) *Educational Technology in Modern Language Learning*, University of East Anglia and the Bell Trust.

9 ELECTRONIC COMMUNICATION

Raymond Gallery

Attention usually focuses on the use of the computer as a stand-alone device with due consideration given to the types of application and software available to the linguist. There is however great potential in connecting a micro-computer to other computers or hosts. The following chapter looks at the hardware and software requirements to achieve this and describes some of the services available that are likely to be of interest to the language teacher and learner.

In order to communicate with a remote host, in addition to a computer, the following equipment is required: a modem and communications software and terminal emulation.

A modem (MOdulator/DEModulator) converts the out-going digital computer signals into a form which enables them to be sent via the telephone network and translates the in-coming analogue signals back into digital. Modems operate at a variety of speeds measured in bits per second; the baud rate. The baud rates are often referred to by their V standards laid down by the CCITT (Consultative Committee on International Telephone and Telegraph.

V.21 300 baud
V.23 1200/75 baud
V.22 1200/1200 baud
V.22 bis 2400/2400 baud
V.29 9600 baud

The faster the modem, the faster the data can be moved between the PC and the host; this can significantly reduce the cost of accessing a remote system since the connect time can be kept to a minimum. Prices of modems have fallen over the years and one is looking typically at a cost of £100-150 for a 1200/1200 modem and £250-350 for a 2400/2400 modem. Some modems also support error correction which prevents data from being corrupted and increases transmission speeds. Some communications software also provides the error correction.

Modems can either be external or internal cards that fit inside the computer and occupy one of the expansion slots. The modem is connected to the computer's serial (RS232) port and to a British Telecom phone jack. The communications software "talks" to the modem by means of a set of instructions. The Hayes Microcomputer Products Inc. of America developed an instruction set know as the "AT" command set, and it has become a de facto standard. Modems that support the "AT" command set are known as "Hayes compatible" modems.

The communications software also emulates the behaviour of a computer terminal. With some of the services described further on the correct emulation is critical in determining whether foreign characters can be displayed or generated. Modems often come with 'bundled' communications software; in some cases special software is needed to access the host and is provided as part of the subscription. I propose now to describe a variety of systems to which linguists can connect and explore their potential in communicative language work, beginning with The Times Network Systems.

In 1985 The Times Network Systems (TTNS) launched an electronic mail (e-mail) system specifically designed for education. A second service was launched by Prestel Education and in January 1989 both services were combined and operate under the name Campus 2000. In the UK, Campus 2000 links the majority of Secondary Schools, most of the Higher/Further Education sector and a rapidly growing number of Primary Schools.

The software system used by Campus 2000 was produced by Dialcom, a company based in the United States but which is a wholly-owned subsidiary of British Telecom. Dialcom licenses its software to a number of Network Providers worldwide, one of whom is Telecom Gold. Electronic mail can be sent to other systems operating the Dialcom protocol. The countries which currently have mail systems compatible with Campus 2000 are:

Australia	Hong Kong	Netherlands	Canada	Israel	
New Zealand	Denmark	Italy	Puerto Rico	Eire	Japan
Singapore	Finland	Korea	Germany	Malta	USA

Communications initially covered pen-friends and language exchanges but have developed into adventure games, chain-story writing, genealogical studies and environmental comparisons.

In 1986 TTNS introduced a competition known as 'Newspaper Days'. On the 'Newspaper Day', participating schools are supplied via e-mail with the latest bulletins from a news agency. Pupils are released from their normal timetable in order to produce a newspaper which they must try to have ready for sale by the end of the school day. 'Newspaper days' now take place regularly in the spring and autumn of each year. The dates are announced well in advance by Campus 2000. Other projects organised by TTNS have tackled issues like national and European elections, support for the Third World and the bi-centenary celebrations in Australia.

In addition to electronic mail, Campus 2000 also provides access to databases and computer conferencing. Campus 2000 has produced an easy to use software package, called Campus Communicator, catering specifically for the needs of Campus 2000 users. Campus 2000 users need to take out a subscription to obtain an account number and password. Details of current tariffs can be obtained from Campus 2000, PO Box 7, 214 Grays Inn Road, London WC1X 8EZ. Access to Campus 2000 can be by direct dialling or via the Packet Switched Data Network (PSDN). Many of the services described in this chapter can only be used cost-effectively if the user has a subscription to the British PSDN. This was formerly known as Packet SwitchStream (PSS) but recently changed its name to Global Network Services (GNS). A subscription to GNS involves a one-off connection charge, a quarterly rental and a usage charge (currently £1.80 per hour). The subscriber connects to the data network via a local Packet Assembler/Disassembler (PAD), usually for the price of a local call. A subscription gives the user a Network User Identifier (NUI) and he/she then connects to the appropriate Network User Address (NUA). Connections can also be made overseas to countries in the International Packet SwitchStream (IPSS) network.

Campus 2000 is relatively easy to use since it adopts a "menu driven" approach which presents the user with a range of items to select from by number or mnemonic. The following examples are authentic 'recordings' of a Campus 2000 session. Throughout this chapter examples of terminal sessions are shown in **bold**.

Having successfully logged-in by giving an ID and password, the user is presented with the Main Menu:

```
****************
*CAMPUS  2000 *
*   Main Menu  *
****************
```

1 CAMPUS Electronic Mail   MAIL
2 Your own Local database   LOCAL
3 Searchable index to CAMPUS   CAT
4 Directory of users   ENQUIRE
5 CAMPUS Conferencing   CAUCUS2
6 CAMPUS Noticeboard   NOTICEBD
7 System INFO and help files   INFO
8 System prompt   QUIT
9 Leave CAMPUS GOLD   LOGOUT

Which option: 3

The Campus index enables the user to quickly locate the relevant sections:

```
********************************
*                              *
*The CAMPUS searchable index   *
*                              *
********************************
```

What are you searching for (Q to QUIT or H for HELP) :
MODERN LANGUAGES

1 CAMPUS Modern Languages Database (MODLANG)
2 CAMPUS Secondary Database (SECOND)

Which would you like to see (Q to QUIT or H for HELP) : 1

Most of the information of interest to linguists is to be found in the Modern
Languages Database (MODLANG).

********** THE MODERN LANGUAGES DATABASE *************
*************** MNEMONIC: MODLANG ******************

CODE   OPTION

* 1   Authentic Foreign Texts including FRANTEL
* 2   New Publications
* 3   Newsbrief

* 4   CILT Services
* 5   Examinations and Assessment
* 6   International Travel and Links
* 7   Work Links
* 8   Organisations and Agencies
* 9   ** The Modlang Noticeboard **
* 10   Help Files - How to use this database
* 95   Profile Builder
* 96   Return to the Secondary Education Menu
* 97   Return to the Campus Searchable Index
* 98   Return to the CAMPUS Main Menu
  Q   Return to the System Prompt (at any point)

Enter a service code

Selecting service code 1 brings up a further sub-menu from which the appropriate selection is made:

********** AUTHENTIC FOREIGN TEXTS DATABASE **********
**************** MNEMONIC: <FOREIGN> *****************

        CODE   OPTION

* 1   FRANTEL Database - Online Version
* 2   FRANTEL - Teachers Notes and Worksheets
* 3   French Classroom Exercises and Adventure Game
* 4   Authentic French Text
* 5   French Archive Material - Please Search
* 6   French from Derbyshire - FELINE
* 7   Authentic German Text
* 8   German Archive Material - Please Search
* 9   German from Derbyshire - FELINE
* 10   Authentic Spanish Text
* 11   Spanish Archive Material - Please Search
* 12   FRANTEL - Downloadable Communitel Files
* 94   Help on Using the Database
* 95   Profile Builder
* 96   Return to the Modern Languages Database Menu
* 97   Return to the Campus Searchable Index
* 98   Return to the CAMPUS Main Menu
  Q   Return to the Systems Prompt (at any point)

Enter a service code

Option 7 from the Authentic Foreign Texts Database produces the following:

Read, Scan or Search
R
A N G E K U N D I G T
GATT-VERHANDLUNGEN KONNEN NACH EG-KOMPROMIS WIEDER STARTEN
INFORMATION SUPPLIED BY AFP - 7/11/90

    - DEUTSCHE UND FRANZOSISCHE BAUERN KRITISIEREN EG SCHARF
    - KIECHLE ERWARTET EG-BEITRAG FUR AUSGLEICHSMASNAHMEN (ZUSAMMENFASSUNG)

     GENF/BONN, 7.   OOVEMBER (AFP) - DIE SEIT EINEM AONAT BLOCKIERTEN VERHANDLUNGEN DER URUGUAY-RUNDE IM RAHMEN DES ALLGEMEINEN ZOLL- UND HANDELSABKOMMENS (GATT) KONNEN NACH DEM AM DIENSTAG ABEND VERABSCHIEDETEN EG-KOMPROMIS UBER DIE AGRARSUBVENTIONEN WIEDER AUFGENOMMEN WERDEN. DENNOCH WAR AM AITTWOCH IN GENFER GATT-KREISEN DEUTLICHE SKEPSIS UBER EINEN MOGLICHEN VERHANDLUNGSERFOLG ZU VERSPUREN.   SIE HABE DEN GENAUEN EG-BESCHLUS NOCH NICHT GELESEN, DESHALB WERDE SIE ZUNACHST KEINE STELLUNG NEHMEN, SAGTE DIE US-HANDELSBEAUFTRAGTE CARLA HILLS IN GENF VOR IHREM ABFLUG NACH WASHINGTON.   UNTERDESSEN HABEN DIE DEUTSCHEN UND FRANZOSISCHEN

More?...(Yes or No) N

     As can be seen from the above, the authentic material originates from the French press agency, Agence France Presse (AFP). The problem of accents is tackled by using upper case letters only. In practice therefore one would need to import the text into a suitable word processor, convert from upper to lower case, edit in the accented characters and edit out any errors. Not a difficult task and one that could well be left to the learner, but it does involve an intermediate process before the learner is presented with truly authentic looking material.

     The Campus Noticeboard option from the Main Menu (option 6) also provides material originating from abroad as does Campus Conferencing (option 5):

Subject: Brevveksling p^Faa norsk.
From: YNP038   Posted: Thu 13-Dec-90 12:29   Sys 1

Er det noen der ute som kan skrive til oss p^Faa norsk ?
Vi er en barneskole i Norge som gjerne vil skrive med noen p^Faa norsk
(nynorsk). Skolen ligger p^Faa norvestkysten av Norge, ved byen ^FAalesund,
paa en

Continue to Next Item?

Item 4   01-MAY-90   22:34   Tony Leigh
Global Village

This item is to support schools involved in the Global Village Project.
More information on this project can be obtained from the Devon Local
Database under International Links.

4:3) Finland Putus   12-DEC-90   16:33
                            FINNISH CHRISTMAS EVE
Pohjoispuisto Senior Secondary School, Hyvinkaa, Finland

On the day before Crismas Eve we roast ham for about 12 hours. In the
morning when we have woken up we go out into the forest to look for a
Christmas tree.   When we has got back from the forest we take the tree
inside to melt. After it has melted we start to trim it. The day will pass
by making Christmas food. In the afternoon we visit the graveyard and take
candles to our relatives' graves. In the evening at about six o'clock we start
to eat Christmas dinner and after that the doorbell rings and Santa Claus
comes to visit us and distributes the gifts and then he goes to other homes.
For the rest of the evening we sing Christmas Carols and open the gift boxes.
We would be wery interesting to read about your Christmas traditions, whoever
and wherever you are.
Merry Christmas to all of you
Yours,

        Clearly the technology is being used to promote cultural exchanges and
a greater awareness of other countries' customs.   Computer conferencing in
general, with illustrations from other systems will be dealt with further on.

        The Modern Languages Database has been developed in close
cooperation with the Centre for Information on Language Teaching and
Research - CILT. The Modern Languages Database is now in two sections,

one comprising information provided by CILT, the other containing authentic French, German and Spanish text, for use in the classroom.

The majority of information contained in all sections of the Modern Languages Database is in 80 column text and is fully 'keyword' searchable. The exceptions are the new French viewdata database, FRANTEL, Spanish from Sandwell and the Derbyshire Feline database. Keyword searching provides an efficient and economical way of locating information; thus a search for Spanish teaching materials yields the following information:

UZ   460   UKX

GALAN, Pilar, RICHARDSON, J.   and TURNER, K.
A camping holiday in Spain.   London: ILEA Languages Centre, (1988).
File containing task sheets.   Cassette.   S160.
Search Terms: SPANISH LISTENING SPEAKING READING WRITING GCSE LEVEL3

UZ   460   UMD

RIPON LANGUAGE CENTRE
YORKFLAW assignments: Spanish.   Ripon: Ripon Language Centre, (1988?).   Topic books A, B, C, D, E, F.
Search Terms: SPANISH FLAW LEVEL 4 VOCATIONAL

Subscribers to the Campus 2000 Premium service can access the ECCTIS database (Educational Counselling and Credit Transfer Information Service), which provides information on courses and entry requirements, the NERIS database (National Educational Resource and Information Service), a catalogue of available teaching materials and PROFILE, a database which gives the text of articles published in English newspapers and magazines.

In summary, Campus 2000 provides inland and international electronic mail, computer conferencing and educational and specialist databases. However Campus 2000 is not the only way to send and receive electronic mail; a large number of universities, polytechnics and colleges are members of the United Kingdom academic network called JANET and the following section describes the use of the network to send and receive local, inland and international mail.

The method of sending mail to other machines in the JANET network is almost identical to that of sending mail to another user on your local system. All one needs to know is the recipient's unique computer identity. Mail can be written and sent directly from the computer's mail system or prepared using a text editor, stored in a file and then sent to the recipient.

The dramatic fall in the price of micro-computers has meant that it is increasingly likely that the device used to access a remote host is a micro-computer with suitable communications and emulation software. This means that material can be prepared locally using word processing software and transferred to the host computer when ready by means of a suitable file transfer protocol, Kermit for example. If this method is being used, the word processed document should be saved as an ASCII text file and, if it contains accented characters, sent to the host computer as a binary and not a text file. Failure to do this causes the accented characters to be lost during the transfer.

The following terminal session illustrates the reading, writing and sending of a piece of mail on a UNIX system. On logging onto the computer you are warned if there is mail:

```
You have mail.
rc_galle@gould2 [21] mail
Mail version 5.2 6/21/85.  Type ? for help.
"/usr/spool/mail/rc_galle": 12 messages
>    1 cshroot   Fri Nov  9 15:13   30/1176 "Central Systems Replacement"
     2 cshroot   Mon Nov 12 12:58   41/887 "Gould Replacement Forum Group"
     3 HUBERT.ULLIAC@fr.uhb Tue Nov 27 13:42   41/1417 "RE:"
     4 lm2_smit Tue Nov 27 16:44   11/488 "Ray,"
     5 sj_smith Tue Nov 27 16:45   26/931
     6 sj_smith Tue Nov 27 17:56   21/526
     7 wa_sincl Wed Nov 28 11:10   13/358 "contact with France"
     8 em_husse Thu Nov 29 13:26   19/409
     9 e_bennet Thu Nov 29 13:55   13/416 "Rolls-Royce trip"
    10 cshroot   Fri Nov 30 13:55   12/754 "Erasmus user names"
    11 cshroot   Mon Dec 10 16:31   20/558 "hhcp"
    12 cshroot   Tue Dec 11 08:58   34/587 "Gould Replacement"
&
```

Messages are read by typing in the message number at the mail system prompt &:

```
& 7
Message   7:
From wa_sincl Wed Nov 28 11:10:09 1990
Received: by gould1.XXX (5.54/5.17)
          id AA03176; Wed, 28 Nov 90 11:05:25 GMT
Date: Wed, 28 Nov 90 11:05:25 GMT
From: wa_sincl (sinclair)
Message-Id: <9011281105.AA03176@gould1.XXX>
```

To: 005, lml
Subject: contact with France
Status: RO

I have written to the French student in Rennes to make contact!

&

A reply to mail can be typed directly at the keyboard:

& reply
To: 005 lml wa_sincl
Subject: Re: contact with France

Thanks for writing to France.   Will you let me know if you get a reply?
EOT
&

The reply command is useful for entering short messages but offers very limited editing.   For longer documents which have been created using a text editor and saved in a file the procedure is slightly different.   The mail command is given at the system prompt followed by the name of the recipient and the name of the file containing the text of the message separated by <.

rc_galle@gould2 [21] mail wa_sincl < filename

Before illustrating the sending of mail to a user in France, it is perhaps appropriate to describe the JANET network briefly.   This material is adapted from the Janet Starter Pack produced on behalf of the Network Executive.

JANET stands for the Joint Academic NETwork which is a private packet switched computer network for academic and research activities within the UK.   It links over a hundred academic institutions, including all universities and polytechnics, several colleges of higher education and many research council establishments.   About a thousand computers are currently connected to the network.

The following network services are available between these computers:
Electronic Mail
File Transfer
Interactive Access
Remote Job Transfer

Each computer service on JANET has a unique name which is registered in the Name Registration Scheme (NRS) together with its associated numeric addresses for the network services that it supports. The name has a standard and an abbreviated form, for example:

UK.AC.SUSSEX.LIBRARY   standard name

UK.AC.SUSX.LIB   abbreviated name

The names of all computer services registered on JANET, with their descriptions and the network services they support, are listed on the JANET.NEWS information service.

To send mail to a person who uses another computer connected to JANET the following information is needed:

person: mailname or username of other person

site: name of their computer as registered in the NRS

usually given as: person@site

e.g. RC_GALLERY@uk.ac.brispoly.g2

Within JANET, user communities are organised into "domains". Firstly there is the domain of academic users in the UK. The domain name for this set of users is "uk.ac". Within this domain there may be sub-domains. In the example above, Sussex library is a sub-domain of uk.ac.sussex.

Mail Command Examples

The commands for dealing with mail depend on the specific computer and operating system. The examples below illustrate the mail commands for a UNIX and VAX/VMS environment.

UNIX

% mail person@site

e.g.

% mail RC_GALLERY@uk.ac.brispoly.g2

VAX/VMS

$ mail

MAIL> send

To: cbs%site::person

e.g.

To: cbs%uk.ac.brispoly.g2::RC_GALLERY

In addition to electronic mail, it is possible to connect to a remote computer over the network. In order to access a computer over the network the terminal must be connected to a PAD (Packet Assembler/Disassembler). The main commands for using a PAD are similar irrespective of the system being used:

PAD>   call site   connect to a computer

e.g.   call janet.news

PAD> help address   list the names or hosts recog-
                                            nised by the PAD

National services on JANET

Several nationally supported computing and information services can be accessed interactively over JANET, and no previous registration is required. Some support mail and file transfer as well.

- JANET.NEWS: Information service about JANET, maintained by the Network Executive on a computer at Rutherford.

Name	UK.AC.JANET.NEWS
Username	news

- NISS Bulletin Board: Information dissemination in the UK higher education computing community, provided by the National Information on Software and Services team at Bath University.

Name	UK.AC.NISS

- National Public Domain Software Archive: Archive of software for microcomputers and also the Kermit file transfer packages at Lancaster University.

Name	UK.AC.LANCASTER.PD-SOFTWARE

- Library Catalogues: There are currently over 50 library online public access catalogues (OPACs) that can be accessed over JANET. A brief description of each OPAC, with its name and network address, can be found on both the JANET.NEWS and the NISS information services.

JANET links to other networks

JANET is linked to many other networks, both in the UK and around the world, via gateways. The gateways support different network services: mail, file transfer, interactive access, and have different authorisation procedures and charges.

- EARN-RELAY: to European Academic Research Network and BITNET in USA
- NSFNET-RELAY: to Internet in USA
- SPAN-RELAY: to Space Physics Analysis Network
- UKC: to UNIX network, UKnet, EUnet and USENET
- PSS-GATE: to Packet SwitchStream and IPSS. Access to this network offers the ability to transfer files, jobs and mail between dissimilar machines as well as providing interactive terminal access from one machine to another.

As can be seen from the above, the PSDN (GNS) can be reached through the appropriate gateway. For example the Campus 2000 network could be accessed via a JANET gateway.

When mailing abroad the message is first sent into JANET and then on, via a gateway, into the European Academic Research Network (EARN) and forwarded to the user at the foreign site. Thus the mail system needs to have additional information relating to the recipient's identity, address and the appropriate gateway. The following message from the University of Rennes in France illustrates the point:

& 3
Message 3:
From HUBERT.ILLIAC@fr.uhb Tue Nov 27 13:42:42 1990
Received: from mhs.ac.uk by g2.brispoly.ac.uk; Tue, 27 Nov 90 13:42:25 GMT
X400-Received: by mta mhs-relay.ac.uk in /PRMD=uk.ac/ADMD= /C=gb/; Relayed;
           Tue, 27 Nov 1990 13:43:50 +0000
X400-Received: by /PRMD=reunir/ADMD=atlas/C=FR/; Relayed;
           Tue, 27 Nov 1990 13:46:57 +0000
X400-Received: by /PRMD=CICB/ADMD=ATLAS/C=FR/; Relayed;
           Tue, 27 Nov 1990 15:51:05 +0000
Date: Tue, 27 Nov 1990 13:43:50 +0000
X400-Originator: HUBERT.ILLIAC@fr.uhb
X 4 0 0 - M t s - I d e n t i f i e r :
[/PRMD=CICB/ADMD=ATLAS/C=FR/;75054172110991/2391@UHB]
X400-Content-Type: P2-1984 (2)
Content-Identifier: RE:
From: HUBERT.ILLIAC@fr.uhb
Message-Id: <"50154172110991/5729 X400*"@MHS>
To: LML005@uk.ac.bristol-poly.gould2
Subject: RE:
Status: RO

Bonjour,
Nom de compte de JPH : hugo@uhb.fr   (si ca ne marche pas c'est @uhb.cicb.fr)

Quelques noms de comptes etudiants :

                     ribeiro@uhb.fr
                     simeon@uhb.fr
                     marzin@uhb.fr
                     beaume@uhb.fr
                     janin@uhb.fr
                     ilias@uhb.fr
                     rebour@uhb.fr

Ces etudiants font deja de la messagerie avec Barcelone et/ou les USA.

A bientot,

Hubert ILLIAC

PS : Je previens JPH. N'hesite pas a me contacter si tu as des problemes.

&

     The long mail header at the start of the message shows clearly that the mail originated from Hubert Illiac at fr.uhb. This indicates that the message comes from France (fr) and that the address of the host is the Université de Haute Bretagne (uhb). As can also be seen the message went through several gateways (the relays in the mail header) before reaching its destination.

     Until fairly recently there was no internationally agreed standard for electronic mail. The new standard, which is usually known as X.400, has been ratified by the international standards organisations CCITT and ISO (International Standards Organisation). This standard is now being implemented by software producers and computer suppliers worldwide and will, eventually, enable the interchange of electronic mail between any mainframe or microcomputer system which has implemented this standard. The French host at the University of Rennes is on the new standard and one of the gateways outgoing mail has to go through converts from the JANET X.25 standard to X.400. Students corresponding with France route their mail through a gateway at Universiy College London. The mail command they use therefore has an extended address with the gateway in London being appended to the French address:

       rc_galle@gould2 [21] mail user%fr.uhb@uk.ac.ucl.cs < filename

Reading from right to left, the mail message is sent through the JANET network to "uk.ac.ucl.cs" in the UK domain, then crosses through a gateway into the French data network and is routed to the appropriate "user" at "fr.uhb" in the French domain. Note that each of the components in the address is seperated by boundary markers (% and @). The same conventions apply when sending mail to other destinations.

     Electronic mail to France (Rennes) and Spain (Barcelona) has been used sucessfully in the context of an ERASMUS Joint Study Programme to transfer academic and administrative material. The mail links are currently being used to encourage collaborative group work between students. Thus it may be that field work is undertaken by a group of French students on behalf of an English group and the results mailed back. In the area of technical translation, primary documents are sought out to enable students in the other country to create their own terminology banks. Electronic mail is being used by staff to maintain links with students on study placements abroad and by students to forge contacts before their departure. However electronic mail is essentially a means of one-to-one or one-to-many communication. Computer conferencing provides greater flexibility and structure to group communications.

A computer conference is best thought of as an electronic discussion table. Conference members are invited to discuss a given topic. The conference convenor or moderator usually opens discussion by placing a message 'on the table' for participants to read and comment on. The conference develops through an accumulation of replies or comments. Conference items or topics are visible to all participants but there is also a mail system which allows private communication between participants and the moderator. It is proposed to look briefly at two conferencing systems; Caucus 2 and Vaxnotes.

There is no single terminology to describe what goes on inside a computer conference. The terms used depend on the conferencing system being used. There follows below a brief extract from a session with the Caucus 2 system which is one of the options available from the Campus 2000 Main Menu (Option 5):

```
**** CAMPUS 2000 CONFERENCING ****
***** Mnemonic <CAUCUS2> *****
```

	CODE	OPTION
*	1	List of PUBLIC conferences
*	2	List of PRIVATE conferences
*	3	Join conferences menu
*	98	Return to the CAMPUS Gold main menu

Selecting option 1 produces a list of the public conferences that can be joined by anyone. There are also closed or private conferences.

CAUCUS2 - List of PUBLIC Conferences

The following Campus 2000 Public Conferences are open to all Campus users. We hope that you will join as many of them as possible and take an active part in the discussions:

ENVIRONMENT   Moderator: Justin Dillon   YNS020
A chance for participants to examine their attitudes and opinions on environmental issues.

JOLLY   Moderator: Tony Leigh   YMB080

A 'fun-filled outing' - an opportunity to open a door for friendly communication and cooperation into each others classrooms, nationally and internationally.

NEWSLINE   Moderator: John Dally   YPR008
A fast moving and dynamic conference to discuss topical issues from the week's news.

PHOENIX   Moderator: Ros Keep   YLS023
This conference explores the make up of society, its governing laws and conventions. Participants become one of a shipload of people on the Starship 'Phoenix' who have decided to start afresh on a new planet. Colonists will need to develop a new society and a Code of Conduct for living together in harmony.

STAFFROOM   Moderator: Dr Niki Davis   TCD016
An opportunity for teachers to exchange views, advice and problems. The topics will indicate general areas of concern to teachers and support staff in schools.

Selecting option 3 from the Campus 2000 Conferencing menu produces a further sub-menu from which the user makes his/her choice of topic.

**** CAMPUS 2000 CONFERENCING ****

Join which CAUCUS2 Conference ?

* 1   Environment
* 2   Staffroom
* 3   Newsline
* 4   Jolly
* 5   Phoenix2
* 6   Health
* 7   Treasure Hunt

If we look at the "Jolly" Conference we can see that it is broken down into 'Items'; each 'Item' has a series of 'Responses' associated with it, that can be added to by any of the participants. Alternatively the participants can create a new 'Item' if appropriate to accommodate a new theme or thread.

Caucus (TM) version 2.2/PR. Copyright (C) 1988 Camber-Roth.

- - - -WELCOME to JOLLY for the new school year - - - - - - -
Currently active items are:

    Item 1   :Conference Bulletin Board (updated 9/90)
    Item 3   :SOAPBOX.
    Item 4   :GLOBAL VILLAGE.
    Item 9   :HEROES. (PS26, New York)
    Item 11   :BRAVERY (Papa Stour P.S.)
    Item 12   :QUIZ.

SOAPBOX

Got a strong opinion about something?
Want to express your views?

Maybe it's a news item, something you've read or seen on TV.   Maybe its something you've studied or discussed in class.   Maybe it's something that has happened to you or something familiar that's now changed.

Air your views here - - - but please remember you'll encourage responses if you express yourself clearly , briefly and politely.

17 Discussion responses

As with electronic mail, responses to 'Items' or new 'Items' can be written on-line during the terminal session, or off-line and uploaded when ready. The great appeal of computer conferencing is that 'delegates' participate in their own time, at their own rate and from their own location.

I have dwelt at some length on the Campus 2000 system because it is readily accessible to those who already have a Campus 2000 subscription. Presently though, whilst Caucus 2 on Campus 2000 is used by overseas subscribers to promote links, it does not adequately resolve the issues of accented characters and a foreign language interface.   These issues are being addressed by a new network, the European Business and Languages Learning Network (ELNET), piloted by the Centre for Electronic Communications and Open Support Systems in Education (CECOMM) based at Southampton Institute of Higher Education.

ELNET uses the same conferencing system as Campus 2000, Caucus 2, but gives the participant the option of changing the language of the user interface.   Versions currently exist in French, German, Spanish and Italian.   But more importantly, perhaps, it has adopted the 8 bit International Standards Organisation (ISO)/American National Standards Institute(ANSI) character set and is consequently able to display a full range of accented characters, provided the appropriate terminal emulation is being used.   It is not generally realised that not all computers use the same character set.   Most linguists will be familiar with the IBM PC extended character (extended ASCII) set; unfortunately this is not the same as the ANSI set. Material prepared off-line on an IBM PC for uploading, therefore, either has to be translated from ASCII to ANSI or written using an ANSI word processor or text editor.

The terminal emulation packages used to record these sessions are Kermit (release 3) and WinQVT. Kermit provides the necessary DEC VT 320 terminal emulation and enables the IBM keyboard to be remapped to generate the all-important ANSI character set. WinQVT, as its name implies, runs under Microsoft Windows 3, supports DEC VT220 emulation and also enables the IBM keyboard to be remapped. It runs under Windows as a Windows accessory. Windows uses the ANSI character set. ELNET have also developed their own, easy to use, communications software. Links currently exist with a number of post-16 educational institutions in France and data is exchanged several times daily between the Paris and London ELNET hosts.

The terminal session below attempts to give the feel and flavour of an ELNET session. The ELNET host in London is The London Caucus (TLC). So that the accents can be displayed on an IBM compatible computer the terminal session has been converted from an ANSI to an ASCII file.

Welcome to The London Caucus (TLC) from X-ON Software Ltd

Caucus (TM) version 2.3/MV. Copyright (C) 1988 Camber-Roth.
          WELCOME TO / BIENVENUE A / HERZLICH WILLKOMMEN BEI

```
                    ***********
                    *  ADMIN  *
                    ***********
```

The Administration area of the European "virtual " College
La zone Administration du Collège "virtuel" européen
Dem Raum für die Verwaltung des europäischen "quasi-" College.

Charles Jennings is the Moderator / l'organisateur
     Please read ITEM 11 in this ADMIN area - It provides help
with the system changes which have taken place with ELNET

ITEM 12 tells you how to move around ELNET

PLEASE CHECK ELNET_TECHAID CONFERENCE FOR UPDATES AND TECHNICAL INFORMATION ABOUT THE NEW SYSTEM.

*****FRENCH USERS - PLEASE NOTE*****
ALL THE "WORKING" AREAS ARE NOW AVAILABLE IN FRANCE

AND NOW? (ME for menus, ? for help) français

By typing "français" at the Caucus prompt the user is able to change
the language in which the prompts appear from English to French or any of
the other foreign language versions.

ET ENSUITE? (? pour demander des renseignements)?
On vous offre de l'AIDE sur tous les aspects de l'opération de CAUCUS.A
tout moment, quand CAUCUS attend que vous tapiez quelque chose, vous
avez le droit de taper ? ou AIDE pour découvrir les options possibles.

Italian for example

E ADESSO? (Per informazioni, scrivi ?) ?
Il comando AIUTO puo' essere usato durante tutte le operazioni di
CAUCUS.
Quando CAUCUS ti chiede di inserire le tue istruzioni, puoi sempre
scrivere '?' o 'AIUTO' per sapere quali sono le tue possibilita'.

An 'Item' in one of the other conferences on The London Caucus
confirms support for accented characters:

Item 73   07-APR-90   8:53   John Coll
Does caucus support 8 bits chars (french accents for eg.)???

It certainly does. You need an ISO/ANSI/ECMA standard terminal emulation
to get all the characters. The DEC VT320 does just that. If you are using
a terminal emulator not built to correctly handle international characters (such
as many IBM PC emulators) you will get other (wrong) characters.

ELNET and Caucus 2 are not alone in supporting foreign characters.
The Vaxnotes computer conferencing system, running on a DEC Vax computer
has been used to animate a final year French area studies option at Bristol
Polytechnic on the 'Computerisation of Society' and student feedback has been
very positive. The use of computer conferencing reflects a desire on the part
on the option tutor to widen the scope of the option to allow students a much
freer choice in the range of themes covered within the option. It also seeks
to promote wider readership of the semi-specialised press and to develop skills
in the synthesising of written language.

Much of the material covering recent developments in computing can only be found in the relevant technical periodicals (in English or any of the students' foreign languages). Since these journals are not indexed, it is necessary for students to undertake the scanning of periodicals with a view to identifying references that can later be consulted, once it has been established that sufficient material is available to underpin a theme.

A computer conference provides a vehicle for students to work collaboratively, yet in their own free time. The periodical scanning is too much for students to undertake individually, so students work in groups of 3/4 and commit any relevant references to the relevant conference 'Topic'. Vaxnotes terminology differs from Caucus and 'Items' are referred to as 'Topics'. Once the scanning has been completed and the various bibliographies consulted, students 'negotiate' a conference theme or 'Topic' they would like to document. The relevant references are then summarised, in the foreign language, into a dedicated 'Topic'. All option members have sight of all the summaries and can contribute to the discussions. Any material summarised in the conference can be exported to a micro-computer for reworking into an option essay or revision notes.

The written summaries are roughly the equivalent of a conventional seminar paper. However they are visible and usable by all option members and do form the basis of subsequent essays. The summarising into written French from French sources or from other language sources (not all students do the same second language) has proved to be a valuable exercise in its own right. Where a summary demonstrates worrying linguistic weaknesses, the moderator is able to advise the student by private mail rather than in the full view of the other participants. Conference material can be added to year on year and outdated or unwanted information removed.

At present this option only runs locally, but there is no technical reason why students from other institutions, or in other countries, could not participate. This technology could allow schools to develop materials collaboratively, possibly in partnership with their local university, polytechnic or college.

The following list of 'Topics' from the Bristol Modern Languages Conference conveys the structure and content of the option.

Created: 4-JAN-1990 12:32   32 topics   Updated: 17-DEC-1990

Topic	Author	Date	Repl	Title
1	ZEUS::LML005	5-JAN-1990	1	But de cette conference
2	ATHENA::LML005	5-JAN-1990	1	Bibliographie et lectures

preliminaires

3	ATHENA::LML005	5-JAN-1990	0	references bibliotheque
4	ATHENA::LML005	5-JAN-1990	0	references microfiche
5	ATHENA::LML005	5-JAN-1990	0	references periodiques 88
6	ZEUS::LML005	9-JAN-1990	1	Mots clefs pour votre

depouillement

8	ZEUS::LML005	12-JAN-1990	1	Choix de themes a traiter
9	ZEUS::LML005	20-JAN-1990	15	Depouillement de periodiques
11	ATHENA::LML005	1-FEB-1990	8	Problems with Vaxnotes

The early 'Topics' contain bibliographic information, a thesaurus of search terms for their periodical scanning, some suggested option themes and an area to report any operational difficulties with the conferencing software. Once the scanning has been completed by the student groups, references are simply entered into the 'Topic' accompanied by a series of keywords or descriptors to facilitate later searching.

ROSEMOUNT ATTAQUE HONEYWELL, USINE, 14th JANVIER 1988, p.25, INDUSTRIE INFORMATIQUE

APPLE SIGNE UN ACCORD DE COOPERATION AVEC DEC, USINE, 14TH JANVIER 1988, p.28, INFORMATIQUE INDUSTRIE TECHNOLOGIE

CGI-EUREQUIP; LA STRATEGIE EPOUSE L'INFORMATIQUE, USINE, 14TH JANVIER 1988, p.43, INFORMATIQUE INDUSTRIE TECHNOLOGIE

IBM REDRESSE LA BARRE, USINE, 28TH JANVIER 1988, P.22 INDUSTRIE, TECHNOLOGIE

RESEAUX NUMERIQUES PRIVES: PREMIERE DANS LES TELECOMMUNI-CATIONS, USINE 28TH JANVIER 1988, P.42, RESEAUX TELECOMMUNI-CATIONS, INDUSTRIE

Students are then able to interrogate this periodical database and the other bibliographic sources to determine their option theme. Each of those themes, once approved, becomes a 'Topic'. The 'Topic' list below gives an idea of the themes chosen in the last two years. The number alongside the 'Topic' title indicates the number of 'Replies' or summaries that have been written

13	ZEUS::LML005	8-FEB-1990	8	Informatique et Formation
14	ZEUS::LML005	8-FEB-1990	13	Intelligence artificielle et robotique
15	ZEUS::LML005	8-FEB-1990	16	Systemes-experts

16	ZEUS::LML005	8-FEB-1990	1	La securite informatique
17	ZEUS::LML005	8-FEB-1990	14	La traduction automatique
27	OLYMPS::RC_GALLERY	31-OCT-1990	12	Le Teletravail
28	OLYMPS::RC_GALLERY	2-NOV-1990	6	Informatique et Libertes
30	OLYMPS::RC_GALLERY	2-NOV-1990	12	EAO
31	OLYMPS::RC_GALLERY	2-NOV-1990	1	CAO-CFAO

After the various readings have been summarised, the option meets around a real table to discuss the conference topics. Since all participants have had sight of all the summaries, the discussion is usually better informed than many conventional seminars. The technology of conferencing lends itself particularly well to certain types of academic activity:

■ collaborative course development
■ open learning;
■ modular and credit accumulation and transfer schemes;
■ support for part-time and access students;
■ developing and disseminating remedial materials;
■ keeping in touch.

Once one has the ability to establish a connection with another computer, there are a number of services of particular interest to linguists. This concluding section will look at three such services. The first is the French viewdata system, Minitel.

Accessing Minitel presents a number of problems. It requires special software to communicate with and emulate the characteristics of a Minitel terminal. Minitel pages are similar in appearance to Prestel, the British viewdata system, or more familiarly, Ceefax and Oracle teletext pages. The terminal emulation must be able handle text and viewdata 'chunky' graphics and provide the same functionality as the special keys on a Minitel terminal. Whilst shareware Minitel emulations are available, the most likely source is Aldoda International Limited in London who supply an emulation and communications package called Videotel.

Minitel can be accessed by direct dialing to France but, as can be appreciated, the cost of an international call is very high and a more economical method is to take out a subscription to Minitelnet. This network enables Minitel to be accessed via the Packet Switched Data Network (GNS) and considerably reduces the communications cost. Blocks of Minitelnet access time are also available from Aldoda.

With the emulation supplied by Aldoda, Minitel sessions can be 'recorded' and replayed off-line using the emulation software. A more useful alternative is to store the text of a Minitel page without its accompanying graphics, since the text can subsequently be imported into a word processor. The following extract from a Minitel session illustrates the point.

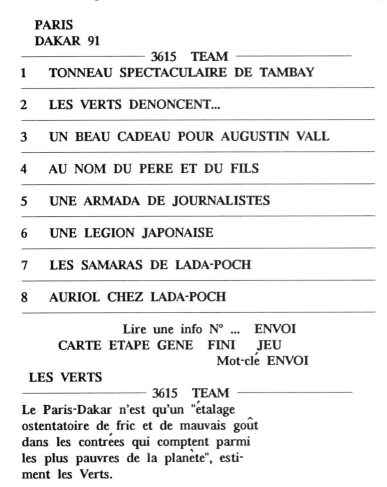

```
PARIS
DAKAR 91
───────────────── 3615   TEAM ─────────────
1    TONNEAU SPECTACULAIRE DE TAMBAY
─────────────────────────────────────────────
2    LES VERTS DENONCENT...
─────────────────────────────────────────────
3    UN BEAU CADEAU POUR AUGUSTIN VALL
─────────────────────────────────────────────
4    AU NOM DU PERE ET DU FILS
─────────────────────────────────────────────
5    UNE ARMADA DE JOURNALISTES
─────────────────────────────────────────────
6    UNE LEGION JAPONAISE
─────────────────────────────────────────────
7    LES SAMARAS DE LADA-POCH
─────────────────────────────────────────────
8    AURIOL CHEZ LADA-POCH
─────────────────────────────────────────────

                  Lire une info N° ...   ENVOI
         CARTE ETAPE GENE   FINI    JEU
                            Mot-clé ENVOI
LES VERTS
───────────────── 3615   TEAM ─────────────
Le Paris-Dakar n'est qu'un "étalage
ostentatoire de fric et de mauvais goût
dans les contrées qui comptent parmi
les plus pauvres de la planète", esti-
ment les Verts.
```

There are an estimated 10,000 information providers on Minitel and it can provide a valuable source of up-to-date information. It gives access to the electronic telephone directory, plane and train times, and hotel bookings can be made interactively. Many newspapers and magazines provide a Minitel service including "messageries" or chat lines and electronic mail. The extract above was taken from the daily newspaper "Libération". Minitel's greatest potential is probably as a source of up-to-the-minute, authentic actuality. From the Minitelnet opening menu users are given the option of searching for a service by theme which enables the appropriate information provider to be identified.

Whilst access to Minitelnet has to be bought, the European Commission Host Organisation (ECHO) in Luxembourg currently provides free access to a wide range of databases and databanks; the one likely to be of most interest is Eurodicautom, an online terminology databank. Access to the ECHO computer can again be by direct dialing or via the Packet Switched Data Network. Eurodicautom contains scientific and technical terms, contextual phrases and abbreviations in all of the official European Community languages (with the exception of Greek). The databank is clearly invaluable to practising or aspiring translators.

Having logged in to the ECHO computer, one selects Eurodicautom as the base one wishes to search and then specifies the source and target languages before entering the term for which one is seeking the translation.

```
%THIS IS ECHO; PLEASE ENTER YOUR CODE
%USERCODE USED LAST ON 18.12.90 AT 13:31
YOU ARE NOW ACCEPTED BY GRIPS VERSION 4.01
ENTER BASE COMMAND
base eu92
BASE COMMAND ACCEPTED FOR EU92;EURODICAUTOM;ED = 01.01.85 TO
15.02.90;TL = ENGL
ECHO NOW OFFERS THE EUROPEAN AUTOMATED DICTIONARY


     E U R O D I C A U T O M

PRESS L FOR TERMINOLOGY OR X FOR ABBREVIATION
*l
 TYPE CODE OF SOURCE LANGUAGE
 DE GERMAN          DA DANISH          EN ENGLISH          FR FRENCH

 IT ITALIAN      NL DUTCH          PT PORTUGUESE    ES SPANISH
*en
 TYPE CODE(S) OF TARGET LANGUAGE(S) WITH SINGLE SPACE
BETWEEN
 (FOR EXAMPLE: DE NL) OR A FOR ANY LANGUAGES
*fr de it
 SOURCE LANGUAGE      :EN
 TARGET LANGUAGE(S) :FR DE IT
 SUBJECT CODE        :
 PRESS Q
*Q
 TYPE YOUR QUESTION
*OUTPUT DEVICE
```

                                                    DOC =   1   PAGE =   1
  BE= BTL   TY= UTD76   NI= 0004230   DATE = 900507   CF= 4
       CM   AUL
  EN VE   output unit;output device
       DF   a device in a data processing system by which data may be received
  from the system
  FR VE   unite de sortie;dispositif de sortie
       NT   DF:EG
  DE VE   Ausgabeeinheit;Ausgabegeraet
       NT   DF:EG

       Another useful ECHO database is JUSletter which provides information
on European legislation.

Jusletter est une association qui rassemble et resume chaque semaine les
initiatives et decisions prises par la Communaute (Conseil, Commission, Court
de Justice, Parlement, Comite economique et social) dans le contexte et
l'evolution du droit communautaire.

Les informations sont classees sous les rubriques suivantes :

1.   Institutions communautaires
2.   Libre circulation des personnes
3.   Libre circulation des biens et des services
4.   Concurrence
5.   Securite sociale, conditions de vie et de travail
6.   Protection de la sante et securite
7.   Culture - education - formation professionnelle
8.   Environnement
9.   Protection des consommateurs
10. Droit de l'entreprise, fiscalite, monnaie
11. Divers

       A final service that has yielded some valuable teaching material is the
Systran machine translation system which can be accessed in Paris.   Again
special software is needed to dial into the computer, upload the text for
translation, and download the translated version.   Machine translated material
has been succesfully used with students following natural language processing and
critique of translation options.   The software and connect time are obtainable
from Groupe Gachot in Paris.

       In the preceding pages I have tried to outline ways in which the
computer can promote communication between users.   The advent of relatively

low-cost, powerful computers, offering multi-tasking, opens up exciting prospects for computing linguists.   Products like Microsoft Windows radically change the way in which we might use computers.   In addition to running word processing software, the learner could be concurrently searching a termbank, cutting and pasting information from a computer conference or composing and then sending a piece of electronic mail to an overseas correspondent asking for material.   It appears to me that communications is what makes computing a truly enabling technology.

10   HYPERMEDIA

Michael Harland

Peering through the mists of HyperFog
It is a sad fact regarding Hypertext and HyperMedia that the "Hype" already
built into the titles has so devalued their meaning that they can now mean
virtually anything to anybody - add "MultiMedia", and things get progressively
worse!   That being so, and despite it being 'bad style' to start off a chapter
on HyperMedia with what may appear to be a treatise on lexicography or
linguistics, I should first like to try and map out the various ways in which
these concepts have been approached and thus lead us to a more meaningful
discussion of their use and potential in language learning.

"Hyper-ness"
The problem would seem to revolve around what one understands by the prefix
"hyper-".   A look in the dictionary will tell us: "above, over or in excess".   In
the case of the term Hypertext, one might readily see that the idea of
structuring and understanding a document in a manner over and above the
normal sequential or linear nature of text ought therefore to be implied.   It
would appear, however, that a lot of people form an analogy with day-to-day
terms such as 'hypermarket' and 'hyperactive' and understand Hypertext to be
something huge or in excess of normal text.   Ironically this is what Ted Nelson,
the begetter of the term, seemingly meant by it: a massive body of texts all
interlinked with one another.   I personally never considered the Greek prefix
when I came to work with Hypertext and the main concept forged in my mind

has always been that of interlinking and interrelating textual information: the basic structure of Hypertext is that of "nodes" of information linked both in a hierarchical or non-hierarchical manner. In other words, they form a "tree" structure, but you can also jump across from "branch" to "branch"; there is also a visual difference with most flat-file databases, and even relational databases, in that when you access a piece of data you usually remain at the point where the data is found and continue further searches from there, hence the feeling of browsing and exploring.

I suspect that many other people have likewise formed an individual concept of Hypertext from the key features of whatever product they first used: the 'hot' buttoned links between words and phrases; the replacement of sections of text with alternative or explanatory text; the annotation of text with text windows popping up on top of the text; the illustration of text with linked graphics; or the ability to jump over from one interconnected text or application to another.

To tell the truth, one could just as easily have called Hypertext by any similar name such as InterText, SuperText, MultiText, Metatext or even 3D-Text. The latter (hinting at the three dimensional layering of some hypertexts and the ability to 'zoom' in and out) introduces a visual element which is the basis for even more 'fuzziness' surrounding the terms. The use of graphic items within text has been inherent right from the start of the new age of HyperMedia. Hypertext, incidentally, is not a new idea: it has been hanging around for decades waiting for the commercial technology to catch up (which is what provokes the all too familiar yawns of boredom from computer buffs who cannot see what the fuss is about and consequently fail to see the enabling potential this form of referential linking has bestowed upon "word engineers" such as ourselves!). One of the earliest commercial packages for the IBM and Macintosh, OWL International's version of GUIDE, allowed people to not only link or replace words with picture graphics, but also to exploit the use of different fonts and text styles along with cursor symbols and icons. All this use of visual effects on top of plain text inevitably enhanced the concept of what Hypertext was about and one inevitably hears experts using the term Hypertext when they are really referring to all kinds of linguistic signs, symbols, icons, phonetics or graphic cues embedded within the layout of plain text.

Hypertext

I used to argue that the term Hypertext should be reserved merely for text in its two-dimensional book form, since the inclusion of graphical items projects the mind into a more three-dimensional world of perception and understanding. But this rather dogmatic stance is immediately hard to sustain when one considers the heavily illustrated texts now very familiar to us in children's literature, along with 3D pop-up books, and adventure novels which allow alternative reading paths. These are very much akin to the associative nature of Hypertext and its three-dimensional representation of knowledge, and it would be foolish of me to sustain this artificial separation of text and graphics - it is precisely this over-simplistic attitude to text that Hypertext is itself meant to help overcome through the new technique of referential browser learning. However, I do think it useful to think of Hypertext as having its main roots in text, if only to distinguish it in some meaningful way from the other terms of HyperMedia and MultiMedia.

Through HyperMedia to MultiMedia

If the term Hypertext is thus fraught with problems of clear definition, what can we say for HyperMedia? I would like to argue that HyperMedia is properly the term to be employed whenever more than one "medium" of communication (text, image, or sound) is combined with others in order to represent and coordinate knowledge. Again, the 'feel' of the term for me implies the interlinking or relating of not only text, but also graphics and sound in a manner over and above the traditional linear methods of learning, i.e. not just sequentially reading the lines of a text, watching a sequence of pictures or listening to a continuous tape of music or the spoken voice. It is essential to note that a combination of all three can be found in the subtitled foreign movie or cartoon, but this does not produce HyperMedia. The essential ingredient for providing its "hyperness" lies in the interconnection of the media in order to present knowledge in a non-linear way, i.e. the interlinking of information whether visual, audible or textual into some meaningful combination which can be accessed from different entry points and along different learning paths. Part of this ingredient is therefore expressed in that other buzzword of the new technology - "interactive".

Perhaps the interactive facility is what initially distinguished HyperMedia from MultiMedia: HyperMedia implied an interlinked and interactive form of information presentation, whereas MultiMedia simply implied the physical combination of multiple media for different presentation purposes. Unfortunately the distinction has now been blurred and people seem to use the terms interchangeably. This is especially so with the renewed emphasis on interactive video. Initially this just implied an ability to hitch up a VCR or videodisc to a computer for controlling a sequence of video frames in response to given requests from the user, but now the ability to overlay subtitles, the use of superimposed or interleaved graphics, and the interfacing of various computer applications (to provide a "front-end" to information accessed from peripherals such as videodiscs, CDs, videotapes and television) have all led to quite a different phenomenon.

MultiMedia

For my own part, MultiMedia has more the 'feel' of film and television: at present it harbours an emphasis on visual motivation and entertainment rather than interactive informativeness. To quote a cautionary paragraph from an article on MultiMedia by Tim Davis (Davis 1990):

> ... multimedia occupies the senses in a similar way to television. MultiMedia disregards the reader's ability to assimilate from books, charts and conversation, and teaches in the manner of an advertisement. The result is a devaluing of content in favour of style. I don't say television has no intellectual merit, but programmes aimed at mass audiences rely on entertainment value.

Note how the idea of informing through visual techniques leads the critic inevitably to lament the mass entertainment angle, because that is unfortunately where the commercial producers appear to see their market - indeed one manufacturer has already coined the term "edutainment" to describe this feature! We shall have to wait and hope that all MultiMedia does not take the mass media path.

HyperMedia versus MultiMedia

As an educator, my hopes lie much more firmly with HyperMedia than with MultiMedia, despite the latter's interactive promise. One of my main reasons for this is that the authoring tools for HyperMedia are at present far more productive, flexible, updatable and economical than those for MultiMedia. In addition, the people producing MultiMedia will have a far greater learning curve to contend with, having to master the same daunting techniques required of professional film and theatre directors to cope with a fully three-dimensional medium. Present HyperMedia on the other hand requires just a reasonable quota of artistic flair for handling the graphics, animation, layout and highlighting, together with an analytical approach to ordering one's information. Once you have your text data structured correctly, you can add on the sound and graphic elements quite easily. When HyperMedia takes on more of the features of MultiMedia then the structuring of visual elements will require just as much care, and the marrying of the two will become far more complicated.

One picture may be worth more than a thousand words, but it takes more than a thousand frames to produce just one minute of video. Besides which, interactive video is often merely "responsive" rather than fully "interactive", and is not thereby HyperMedia: note the distinction made by Phillip Robinson (Robinson, 1990) in his definition:

> MultiMedia uses the computer to integrate and control diverse electronic media such as computer screens, videodisk players, CD-ROM disks, and speech and audio synthesizers. If you make *logical* connections between

those elements and make the entire package interactive, then you're working with HyperMedia. (The emphasis on "logical" is mine.)
The point here is the logical or meaningful linking of media, not just their physical connection.

Cross-referencing, for example, is an accepted way of linking meaning in texts, but in pictures the result can all too easily be a loss of emphasis, texture or even meaning, as often happens in soap opera with its predilection for cutting from one scene to another and its repetition of themes and motifs Consequently, I feel interactive video can only produce reliable learning if it sticks more closely to tutor-directed learning methods or what, in HyperMedia terms, would come under the heading of guided tour techniques. It is not so well suited to the self-directed, free-browsing, cross-referencing methods more familiar to Hypertext and HyperMedia. Communication of knowledge through textual and graphical information lies somewhere between two- and three-dimensional planes in our minds, whereas video is much more fully a three-dimensional environment: in video one moves through space, rather than across, under or over it; one can freely move left, right, up, down, in or out of items of information in a Hypertext, but only dream sequences, surrealism and animated cartoons can perform these links meaningfully in the realm of video; it may be amusing to run a video backwards, but not normally educative or informative - unlike HyperMedia, the natural progression is forwards, with flash-backs or repeats being only a rhetorical or stylistic device.

Finally, and before we lose ourselves completely in the multi-dimensional, nebulous warps of HyperSpace, consider yet another view within all the fog of terms, this time from Ken Morse, regarding the meaning of the term "media" in MultiMedia:

> ...there is no one definition of what multimedia is. It is, however, possible to split multimedia into its component medias [sic] -- let's call them visual, audio and touch. Visual medias include text, graphics, animation, still images and full motion video. Audio medias encompass digital sound, music, Midi, voice recognition and voice synthesis. Finally, the touch medias cover the methods available for user interaction with the system, namely keyboard, mouse and touch screen, to name the most common.

Notice how the differentiation in MultiMedia is made more in terms of the physical hardware and emitted visual and sound signals, whereas HyperMedia distinguishes between the intellectual contents, i.e. the ways in which text, sound, graphics and moving images are integrated.

Towards a working definition of HyperMedia

Given all these hopelessly blurred concepts, let us leave the niceties of linguistics and concentrate on HyperMedia as the central phenomenon. I shall try to lay down a clear, working definition of what we might mean by it and thus progress to dealing with the practical realities faced in using HyperMedia for language learning.

Considering all the above, I would propose the following main features of HyperMedia:

- a main emphasis on the associative linking of data items, whether in the form of text, images or sound ("text" includes all symbols, characters, fonts, styles, etc; "images" includes all graphics, icons, scanned images and video images; "sound" includes all synthetic and digitized noises, music or spoken utterances).

- the linked data is presented on a single screen, though allowably in different windows or areas of that screen - i.e. an emphasis on a common interface or focus of attention.

- interacting with HyperMedia is normally therefore on a one-to-one, learner-machine basis.

- it exploits the "travelling" or "wandering" metaphor of three-dimensional space to encourage self-directed or 'browser' learning, with only a minimum of control or guiding constraint. In other words, the learner should be free to ask questions at any stage and thus go off and gather the answers. Conversely, guidance should preferably only be present in order to make sure the learner does not get "lost in HyperSpace", and to act as a landmark, or major point of reference, along the learning path.

- it is "interactive" in the sense that the user is generally in charge of not only the pace of his/her learning, but also the level of assistance given, and the order in which the data is accessed. (The emphasis is on the learner telling the computer what to do rather than being told to interact when prompted by the computer.)

As a simpler definition, therefore, one can say that HyperMedia is a way of interlinking data in any form to be accessed under the interactive control of the user.

Its power lies in the fact that the data elements are arranged, not sequentially as in written text, but in discrete "nodes" or independent blocks of information (a close analogy can be found in the clauses and sub-clauses of a contract which can be inserted, deleted, or rearranged and cross-referred). The single nodes can thus be linked in any manner of ways to any other nodes. In addition, not only is there the possibility of adding new links at any stage, but the same node should be capable of being accessed any number of times by any number of other nodes.

Some examples of HyperMedia applications
Authoring packages: GUIDE
As stated earlier, one of the first commercially available HyperMedia packages on both IBMs and MACs was GUIDE. It is based on the idea of windows of text and/or graphics, with authorable links from words or pictures to other words or pictures. The links form sensitive "buttons", so that when the mouse cursor passes over one of these sensitive areas the cursor changes shape and denotes the type of link in the button. By clicking the mouse over the button, the browser is immediately taken to the linked information. Several types of link were originally allowed: reference links from one window or area of text/image to another; replacement links that swapped one piece of text for another; note links that popped up related information in a note window; and an inquiry link that revealed further links; it could also launch into other applications such as databases and spreadsheets or control videodisks and CD-ROM, thus giving it MultiMedia possibilities. New enhanced versions are on the way.

The original version, however, belongs mainly in the area of Hypertext tools: its ability to "interact" is limited in that it cannot accept any input from the user and process it in any way. This is its major difference with HyperMedia toolkits such as HyperCard. It is first and foremost, therefore, an authoring package for reference systems or, as its name implies, "guided" learning modules, and it is probably still the best and most user-friendly application for producing this form of material.

GUIDE: its use in languages
One can see its potential in language learning immediately: as a means of annotating grammar or literary texts to supply helpful commentary or explanation on the individual elements, giving information in either text or visual form; as a translation tool, especially in older or idiomatic texts, where the replacement link can hide or reveal the relevant translation for any unknown term; as a reference help system for historical, cultural or literary materials, possibly linked to a wordprocessor for writing up a student essay on the subject; as a simple multiple choice quiz system on language or culture, through use of the nested reference buttons.

Fully programmable systems: the example of HyperCard
HyperCard, however, can be considered to be the first application to really provide a fully programmable system for producing individually designed HyperMedia materials. It was soon followed by SuperCard and PLUS on the

Macintosh and HyperPad on the IBM. The first two were enhanced colour versions of HyperCard and the last an attempt to mimic HyperCard on the IBM, but with limited graphics capabilities. The next arrivals on the IBM were LinkWay (which added better graphics and an interface to videodisc), and Matrix Layout which provided a structured authoring system and produced code in various procedural programming languages. Now with Windows 3 on the IBM we have colour Toolbook, a more equal rival to HyperCard.

Since Hypercard is probably the most widely distributed application and covers most of the features that programmable systems have introduced, I shall use it as my example.

The GUI screen age
HyperMedia is now fully dependent on what used to be called a WIMP (Windows, Icons, Mice and Pull-down menus) interface and has now grown to become a GUI (Graphics User Interface). The possibility of interaction with the screen through pointing with a mouse and clicking has in many instances relegated the keyboard to second place. The simple method of clicking on "buttons" in GUIDE is extended in HyperCard to making the buttons trigger all kinds of events and take the user to all kinds of places. They can be made sensitive to the mouse entering or leaving the location of the button, so popping up a message whenever the mouse passes over areas of text. They can also pop up pictures or play sounds and speech. "Button"-type objects can even be picked up and moved around the screen, or control other objects on screen such as a volume or speed control.

These are just a few examples of what makes HyperCard not really an authoring package, but a complete visual-programming toolkit for the Macintosh interface. It is wrong to take its name literally and view it as a card-based rolodex (contrasting it with GUIDE's scrolling text windows): it can in fact have all its data in hundreds of buttons, scrolling text fields or windows on just the one card. Whether one uses the term "card" in HyperCard, "page" in HyperPad and Toolbook or "window" in GUIDE, the key concept is that of a "screenful" of information which can be linked to other bits of information on the same screen or a different screen (cf. the "nodes" referred to earlier).

The programmable interface
The facilities therefore available under a programmable Hypertext are merely dependent on those of the interface: Hypercard can manipulate menus, dialogue boxes (for responses to questions or choices), windows, text fields, text buttons, icon buttons, picture buttons, sound buttons, desk accessories and launch in and out of other applications. Although many of these are authorable via the inbuilt menu system, HyperCard's full power comes in its background programming

language, HyperTalk. With this scripting language one can control virtually any function of the machine: for example it can simulate a mouseclick at any point on the screen without user action; Select and then Cut, Copy or Paste any object button, field, text or picture in and out of the Clipboard under programmed control; change the font, size and style of any text; select a word, go to another card stack, find that word, retrieve associated information, return and place it in another field, all at any preprogrammed time of day.

I hope the reader can now see the almost limitless potential of such a system and the importance of such a facility to education. Despite the teething problems they are bound to bring, these are the authoring tools most people previously merely dreamed about. The responsibility now lies with us to separate the bad design features from the good and build up the necessary "libraries" of successful techniques and applications. For, like it or not, true authoring packages for teachers will have to be built on top of these authoring systems in order to make them genuinely useful to education.

HyperMedia: a change in learning/teaching methods?
Language teachers are now quite familiar with the change in emphasis that our learning methods have undergone, especially away from so-called "grammar" towards communicative skills. The emphasis can therefore be seen to have moved away from passive learning towards interactive learning: students now are encouraged to not only receive prompts but to produce the prompts themselves, thus becoming active agents in the language process.

In a way, one may see HyperMedia filling a similar role as intermediary between the student and the language produced by the computer. We are not yet at a stage (thank goodness) of talking to our computers. But clicking on a button "TALK!" can substitute the function of the spoken word and the computer will understand it and produce digitized speech. Clicking the word "QUIET!" will similarly shut it up. Interaction and communication through a given form of language can thus be achieved and certain facts and knowledge be exchanged. The real problem lies in exploiting this capability in a way that promotes learning. The major problem of all Hypertext, HyperMedia or MultiMedia is in fact one of design: we now have so many facilities and means at our disposal that we ourselves have to learn how to use them before we can teach with them. This is the cause of the real hiatus at present facing the world of education regarding the use of these new technologies.

Non-linear ordering of information and the association of ideas
HyperMedia also requires another change in viewing the learning process. It deals with information in a totally different way from the normal textbook, sound tape or video: they are all basically linear (i.e. sequential) in the way that

they present their information. The world of HyperMedia is mostly non-linear and non-sequential in its presentation of information: its main focus is on the association of ideas and the relationship between one item of information and any other(s). We are thus faced, as it were, with an Einsteinian revolution where Relativity Rules OK! But we do live in such a referential world, and all linguists know that a word only acquires meaning relative to the context in which it is used. So teachers using HyperMedia will have to face up to the possible shift in methods or else leave well alone!

The other associated problem for those who do use it will again be dependent on design: loosely linked structures give the student freedom to enquire and also encourage exploratory learning, but too loose a structure will lead to eventual disorientation - the "lost in hyperspace" phenomenon!
There must therefore be a conscious effort made to design packages that afford as much "navigational" freedom as possible while at the same time maintaining an awareness of both direction and bearing (i.e. the student will be saying: "I want to learn something in this direction, but later on I shall want to know both where it is leading me and where it has got me so far"). Only with the integration of artificial intelligence techniques perhaps will this ever be fully achieved, but it must be maintained as a general goal right from the start.

Maps and guided tours
Developing educational HyperMedia systems will therefore always be a question of maintaining the fine balance between learner freedom and tutor control. The best known methods of achieving this are "maps" and "guided tours". Many techniques have been evolved for presenting the users with a map of their present position in the hierarchy using pop-up map windows, iconic indicators, ticks in hierarchical menus, marker buttons, etc. The idea behind the guided tour metaphor is to suggest to the user various preset routes through a hypersystem, thus encouraging learner choice while controlling the path taken. The latter is a good example of the need to compromise between CAI and CAL, i.e. between the need for instruction and the need to promote learning.

Theory into practice: what can HyperMedia offer us in the real world of language teaching and learning?
Too much space has perhaps been devoted here to the theory, definition and problems of HyperMedia. It would be wrong therefore to leave the reader with the same "negative", "woolly", "hyped up" impression I complained about at the start. For there are very positive, practical uses already being implemented.

What a basic HyperMedia system should provide
If one is to move into the production of HyperMedia materials, the most flexible package available must be sought or one which covers all the forms of

data manipulation envisaged. If possible it must permit at some later stage the transfer of that data to other platforms, i.e. other machines or other types of software package (for example, there is now a product, ConvertIt, which will translate HyperCard stacks on the Mac into Toolbook books on IBMs). Since we are still dogged in education by the constraints of cash, compatibility and commonality, it would also be sensible to use something which is modest and will run on as basic a machine as possible in order to reach the largest number of learners (one of my reasons at present for preferring HyperCard and Linkway, despite their limitations).

With multiple text fonts and styles available, colour is not really necessary unless a lot of graphical (especially video) data is being used. The following, however, are some of the features I have found desirable when authoring with HyperMedia.

Basic features
- inbuilt or easily accessible paint/draw tools or commands;
- inbuilt or easily accessible tools to edit cursors/icons/dialogs/etc.;
- inbuilt or easily accessible sound play/record tools or commands;
- an automatic inbuilt programming system via menu/keyboard commands;
- ASK and ANSWER-type commands which prompt for user input/choice which can then be processed under program control;
- a FIND or SEARCH command - capable of matching both part and whole strings (I still have not found a package that fully meets the needs of foreign languages in this respect!);
- a SORT command - capable of sorting in ascending or descending order, either by text, international (i.e. extended ASCII), numeric or date/time values;
- a command to GO to any program module's screen/card/page by name or ID number;
- an ability:-
  - to show/hide or add/delete menu facilities and set the level of those facilities available to a user;
  - to password protect any program/module;
  - to lock any program/module such that user interaction does not alter the data stored in it; likewise to 'unlock' it for alteration;
- basic string, logical, math functions/operators; numeric constants; control structures; functions/procedures;
- user-definable functions or procedures;
- identification of any object by its string name, ordinal number or unique ID number.

Secondary features
The ability:

- to program the actions and interactions of button, field, window, screen/card, or graphic objects;
- to report or control the movement, location and style of the mouse cursor;
- to report or control key-presses from the keyboard;
- to produce simple animation effects via graphics tools or sequenced frames/screens/cards/icons/etc.;
- to produce basic visual effects on screens/windows for user orientation purposes (e.g. zoom in/out, scroll left/right/up/down, dissolve, etc.); similarly to lock or freeze the screen while hidden events take place;
- to create fixed links between buttons and screen/card objects;
- to link any one object (button, field, window, screen/card, graphic) to any other by means of the package's program/script features without fixed linking (i.e. via a search facility);
- to click on or select any text in a field or window and process it using program functions, without the need for previous "tagging";
- to store or find text in containers (i.e. fields, windows, string variables, files) as characters, words, comma-delimited items or lines enabling the processing of such text according to either string or list processing rules;
- to enter program commands directly from the keyboard in real time;
- for a program/script to edit itself (metaprogramming) in response to user interaction;
- to enter and control the script/program of any other program/module so as to use the objects, functions, facilities and properties already found there without need for reprogramming (the basis of Object Programming);
- to log to a stored file all data selected, all object interactions and the properties, locations and times of such events;
- to access or control any menu, graphics tool or DA/TRS command from the programming level;
- to compile at least part, if not all, of any program/script;
- to report the date, hour, minute and second of any user action via keyboard or mouse (and save to a file if desired - for analysis);
- to set the volume/record level of sound devices;
- to set the properties of any button, field, window, screen/card, graphic object, in response to a fixed program/script, an event-driven user interaction or a predetermined lapse of time (this must include the ability to hide or reveal any object or set its visible style, location and size);
- to send messages between one object and its handler in another object, such that from any initial action it is possible to trigger off a series of

further actions (an example is a tutorial instruction session which, once started, mimics the actions of the instructor and performs key presses, mouse clicks, menu selection, text selection, entry into the area of a field, button, etc., all under program control);

■ to evaluate any string expression as a program command;

■ to print text data within fields, windows, etc. directly to a printer, as well as through a named word processor;

■ to exit directly to any another application and later return to where one initially started from;

■ to copy and paste text, graphic and sound data/resources from other such applications via a clipboard;

■ to read and write from data files on disc or network storage in real time;

■ to read/write from/to a serial communications port;

■ to communicate with external devices such as VCRs, videodisc, CD-ROM/optical drives, sound digitizers, scanners, etc.;

■ to index text and other forms of data such as videodisc frames;

■ to perform file-handling functions under program control.

Some examples of "visual programming"
The truth is that with this range of flexibility almost every kind of language teaching software could be readily adapted to a HyperMedia environment. I, personally, have already generated the following over 18 months: reference dictionaries, vocabulary and phrase lists, commercial term banks, automated verb tables, a number generator with written output and digitized speech; exercises based on multiple choice, keyboard input, gap-filling, matching up of words and split sentences, matching up of pictures with words and/or sounds, moving words on screen to their correct location in a text; interactive advice systems on the use of the subjunctive mood (primitive artificial intelligence is possible); tutorial modules on pronunciation and points of grammar, commented text for grammar or literary extracts, scanned image presentations on cultural aspects of the foreign country with music and textual commentary added. Apart from the sound and scanned images, all were produced and run on a basic Mac Plus with hard disc. Even if I were a highly proficient programmer in C or PASCAL (and I am not), I could not have been this productive. Present HyperMedia systems now give a very quick form of visual programming: the author merely draws, sizes and positions objects such as images, buttons and text fields directly on the screen and can immediately type data into the text fields or else import data straight from a text file; one can also copy images, text and sounds from another application and paste them into screen objects, all in a matter of seconds. What HyperMedia really adds to all the traditional forms of drill and grammar software is the facility for linking text in exercises

to other texts, explanations, images, sounds or on-line help systems such as dictionaries and verb tables.

Modularity or "macro-linking"
The added bonus of using HyperMedia resides in its scope for modularity. With a programmable system it is possible to link one window, "stack of cards" or "book of pages" to any other. One can also do this "invisibly", so the user never knows where the computer went to get its information: it locks the screen and then accesses say a verb table, retrieving the relevant tense form and when the screen is unlocked it is already displayed to the user. The implication of all this is that autonomous modules can have an individual function, such as for teaching vocabulary, but they can be "re-used" at any time in a plural function as on-line look-up facilities for other exercises. Similarly the verb tables can be used as a direct reference system for drilling purposes, but can also serve as an on-line verb help system to any other module.

HyperMedia systems in the future will only really take off in education when sufficient modules of this kind have been built, so increasing the productivity of teachers and giving them the necessary building blocks for their own teaching systems.

Adding sound, animated graphics, visual effects and other user aids
Apart from the obvious use of sound for speech in language teaching, these facilities should perhaps be kept to a necessary minimum and only employed when they add something to meaning or help understanding. They certainly have their uses: sounds can be used quite economically as prompts or explanations and can sometimes be far more effective than a distracting pop-up window; pictures can often illustrate a cultural point far more effectively than descriptive text; animation can show abstract ideas with supreme ease and can be used for illustrating syntax and language structures.

Since design is a major problem in producing good Hypertext, the need for judicious use of these aids to design can be appreciated. Anything that distracts the student's attention from the focus of attention, such as a picture in one corner, a large white space over part of the screen, a button flashing or moving at the wrong time, or a sudden loud beep - all will distract the learner from the main point of the exercise. Similarly HyperMedia brings a wealth of possibilities for help facilities in language learning, but they must be placed readily available in the background, away from the foreground activity.

Linda Hardman has produced several invaluable articles (Hardman, 1988, 1989) on guidelines for producing hypertext material and I would recommend anyone embarking on HyperMedia to read them attentively: it took me a long time to discover some of her suggestions for myself and I would have saved immense effort if I had had the opportunity to read them first.

CD-quality sound and full motion video
Applications such as HyperCard, Linkway and GUIDE already have the capability of controlling some or all of the new storage media for digital sound and images, such as video recorders, videodiscs and optical discs (CD-ROM, CD-DA, WORM, CD-I and CD-ROM/XA). It is still very expensive to put full motion colour images onto a computer screen and the best hope lies with what is known as DVI (Digital Video Interactive) which compresses and decompresses the images in real time, thus being able to produce the 30 images per second needed for true motion video.

The ability to access CD quality sound in huge quantities is an obvious advantage for communicative language purposes, but useful compact discs are yet to appear for foreign language use. The same remains true for foreign video material. Perhaps, through the proliferation of satellite broadcasting, projects will materialize which amass such resources for others to use, but the commercial and financial nature of things seems to dictate against this at present.

Conclusion
HyperMedia systems are certainly of enormous potential in the development of new computer tools for language teaching. They imply a certain shift in learning techniques if they are to be fully exploited for what they do best. They will inevitably be disappointing to some people, unacceptable to others and no doubt problem-ridden for all until the design aspects are fully appreciated and ironed out. But in the end it is not the technology itself that counts - it is what you put into it, the content. As Alan Kay says (Kay, 1990):
> People think there is content in technology. And there isn't content except in what it makes us into. And that's something we have to decide. That's what our value system has to decide. ... you can come in with a piano, you can come in with a computer, and you can amplify the hell out of it because technology is just an amplifier. If you've got junk, you're going to get junk amplified a millionfold.

In the case of HyperMedia we are dealing with extra dimensions and therefore we have to consider not only content but context - not only what we are presenting but where and how. To quote Mark Frisse (Frisse, 1988): "both content and context are important when creating true hypertext". My instinct is that the learning curve for good HyperMedia will certainly be shorter than for MultiMedia, but it will still be longer than people think.

Nevertheless, HyperMedia packages have definitely already gained a foothold in many educational quarters and development moves on apace, so that in the years to come they will no doubt become second nature to our computer-literate young, who will not be afraid to click on a computer screen and ask the time of the next train to Lisbon - in Portuguese!

Bibliography

Cameron, K. (ed.) (1989) *Computer Assisted Language Learning*, Intellect Books.

Conklin, J. (1987) Hypertext: an introduction and survey, *Computer*, 20,9.

Davis, T. (1990) Multimedia: in praise of the written word, *Personal Computer World*, **August**.

Dixon, G. (ed.) (1988) *Literary and Linguistic Computing*, Oxford University Press.

Fiderio, J. (1988) A grand vision, *Byte*, **October**.

Fox, J. *et al.* (eds.) (1990) *Educational Technology in Modern Language Learning in the secondary, tertiary and vocational sectors*, University of East Anglia and the Bell Educational Trust.

Frisse, M. (1988) From text to Hypertext, *Byte*, **October**.

Hardman, L. (1988) Hypertext tips: experiences in developing a Hypertext tutorial. In *People and Computers IV*, *op. cit.*

Hardman, L. & Sharratt, B. (1989) User-centred Hypertext design: the application of HCI design principles and guide-lines. To be published in the proceedings of the Hypertext II Conference, held at York 1989. (For a discussion of the problems of losing oneself in a hypertext see also: Edwards, D. M. & Hardman, L. 'Lost in Hyperspace': cognitive mapping and navigation in a Hypertext environment. In McAleese (1989).)

Jones, D. M. & Winder, R. (eds.) (1988) *People and Computers III & IV*, Cambridge University Press.

Kay, A. (1990) On computers in education, *Byte*, **September**.

Marx, G. (1987) *Welcome to our Non-linear Universe*, Vézprem.

McAleese, R. (ed.) (1989) *Hypertext: Theory into Practice*, Blackwell.

Robinson, P. (1990) The four multimedia gospels, *Byte*, **February**.

11 METHODOLOGY FOR CALL
beyond language teaching paradigms

Alida M. Z. Bedford

The need for methodology in CALL
In this chapter I shall argue that there is now an urgent need for a methodology for curriculum development in Modern Languages which includes the use of Information Technology and that the curriculum development methodology adopted should be capable of transcending the limitations of working solely from within a particular language teaching methodology. Only in this way can an understanding of where IT can be used within the domain of foreign language teaching be made accessible to all.

Currently 'methodology' within language teaching/learning tends to relate to a particular model for classroom practice, for example the Communicative Approach. A methodology for curriculum development, however, should be wider reaching and not be based on a particular model of language learning. Instead it must seek to identify which model, if any, is to be used, and how resources and practices might be developed for known groups of users within a given learning situation. It should also consider the constraints of any learning situation, since knowledge of these will help teachers to make more informed decisions about what resources could be used before impractcal plans are drafted about how resources are to be used.

The reasons for developing a methodology, and a possible way forward will be discussed later in this chapter. But first we need to look at the concept of methodology, and then discuss the implications of methodology for the particular problem of the introduction of new technologies into language teaching.

What is a methodology?

It is probably impossible to get two people to agree on a definition of methodology. For the purposes of this chapter, however, the following definition will be used:

> A methodology is a systematic way of combining techniques and methods to solve problems. It is always based on a philosophy, and needs to address the views and objectives of those using it to fulfil a purpose. The purpose may be known beforehand, or may be an emergent property of part(s) of the methodology being used, according to the underlying philosophy.

It needs to be understood that a methodology without a philosophy is merely a method. This is because the philosophy provides the identity of what the methodology is based on. Sometimes this is referred to as a model or a paradigm. Unless there is a basic model no reference pegs for a methodology can exist. These 'pegs' are essential to understand what a methodology seeks to address. For example, the Communicative Approach could be seen to be based on the philosophy that human beings need to be able to interact with one another in a meaningful way. To be able to do this, the individual needs to understand enough of the culturo-linguistic system s/he wishes to communicate within, and be able to produce utterances acceptable for a variety of social contexts.

Information systems and IT

It is essential to understand something about the nature and purpose of human communication, for this is central to any activity which involves people. Using language is fundamental to human activity. As language teachers we are all in the business of helping learners gain competence in another language.

Part of learning about another person's language involves assimilating:
- appropriate speech acts within particular social contexts;
- appropriate behaviour within those contexts;
- how to make effective communication within groups: i.e. what information systems are at work, and how to use them.

Learning another language is, therefore, not merely a matter of transferring what you know about your mother tongue to the new language, even when the two languages are very similar. This is because the cultural assumptions behind the two languages are not the same. At a more individual level, it is easier to function within a variety of social contexts, where the same mother tongue is used, if we have learnt how to switch quickly from one linguistic code to another. (We would not speak to our bank manager in the same way as we would to a close friend.)

In any society, whether it be the wider speech community of a political state or a particular working environment, there is always a need to pass and exchange messages. The means by which this is achieved represents a form of information system. An information system can be thought of as a network used to convey:

- new information;
- signals;
- existing information;
- the norms and values of a society;
- expectations that society has of an individual, group, or groups.

Because language is used and developed by people who are subject to changing environment(s), any information system is dependent on the people who use it. An information system is therefore very much a social network which uses a sophisticated form of coding, i.e. language.

Owing to environmental changes, language is a living organism constantly being adapted by those who use it. Learning a new language is therefore a complex activity, for it is as much about learning new information systems as about the way speech acts are constructed. It also involves keeping up with culturo-linguistic changes. Anyone who has been away from his or her mother tongue environment for more than a few months will tell you that coming back requires a period of adjustment in order to assimilate such changes.

Bringing computers into the working environment

When computers were introduced into work domains a misunderstanding arose about the nature of information systems. Computer systems themselves, rather than the people who use them, were seen as the focus of information systems. Computer programmers wrote software without much, if any, consultation with the people who would have to use it. This often resulted in the software not being used. There were a number of reasons for this:

- the software could not be used for what people really needed it to do;
- employees were not consulted sufficiently about the introduction of computer technology, and therefore became suspicious about why it was being used. This could result in their not using it, or even abusing it;
- there was insufficient training of staff to enable them to use the hardware and software;

■   the software could not be matched with the existing information systems in the workplace.

A computer on its own can never be an information system. It is only a tool which may be used as part of an information system, where appropriate.

In the language learning domain, if and when we decide to use the computer as part of language learning activity we need to be very aware that the computer is only a tool and, indeed, is likely to be only one of many tools. Once we become aware of the central focus of an information system - the people or community it serves - this affects our thinking about the use of computer technology in the language teaching classroom. The relevant question then becomes: how can we use the computer to serve an information system?

One way of answering this is to see how computers are already used in society. For example, we may see that word processing has effectively replaced the typewriter in the office and at home. Here, then, is a sensible use - people need to write as part of their everyday life. Being able to do this in the target language will be a skill worth developing, and most syllabuses in second language teaching should provide opportunities for practising this skill, using a computer.

However, we must be careful that just because we find a good use for the computer, we do not ignore other important skills, such as being able to write by hand. The emphasis should be on the continuous enhancement and development of a repertoire of skills. We do learners a dis-service if we deprive them of opportunities to develop less 'modern' skills through an over-emphasis on the use of particular forms of 'new' technology. People need to be empowered through education.

Once we begin to see the computer in its proper context we may become far more cautious about some of the types of software applications already available. Is it really of use to a group of learners to spend much time on games software without more communicative supporting materials? Indeed, would it not be wiser to look at existing materials and ask whether the computer truly adds anything worthwhile to what these materials already offer? If the answer is 'no', then we should either not use the computer at all, or find out what it might be useful for from others with more experience.

What do we understand by methodology in modern language teaching now?
At present there appears to be a clear understanding in foreign language teaching circles that methodology is related to classroom practice, and that this is based on a particular model. One example of this is the Communicative Approach which can be identified by its strong emphasis on communicative

activity between language learners. This falls within our earlier definition of a methodology as a systematic practice of methods and techniques for solving problems, based on a clear philosophical foundation.

Other widely known language teaching methodologies also conform to this model. There is no strong evidence, however, that these methodologies incorporate any strategies for integrating new forms of technology into language teaching or learning. By this I do not mean a particular form of technology, but any form of technology at all. A methodology is required which provides for the incorporation of all forms of technology (including personal computer, video, language laboratory, and so on). We would be ill-prepared for future developments if we ignored any forms of technology already available.

Another problem associated with current language teaching methodology is that each methodology in its 'pure' form is very paradigmatic, in that each identifies with its own model of language learning. But many teachers prefer to be eclectic and use various techniques from many methodologies that suit themselves, their learners, and the domain they find themselves working in.

Although training in a methodology provides focus for all and security for the new teacher, there comes a time when it is necessary to reach out beyond the safety of its framework. We need to be aware that this is the case for many teachers, either to satisfy a need for personal growth or because the teaching domain requires change and flexibility. Additionally, it is possible that some teachers have a need to use IT-based resources that are not limited to a particular way of seeing the world. Learners will certainly expect this once their knowledge of IT becomes more sophisticated.

It is possible to identify an historical development of classroom methodology in foreign language teaching (Richards & Rodgers, 1986). The reader should be aware, however, that this does not mean that all sectors of language teaching have followed the same path, and at the same time. Factors such as the delayed implementation of new syllabuses affect the speed at which teachers adopt new practices. Hence there are differences in classroom practice, with many 'old' practices still alive and well.

I have stated above that methodology in foreign language teaching is largely related to classroom practice. In the past this may have been a sufficient, though not necessarily effective, means of carrying out foreign language education. In recent years education has witnessed, and is still seeing, many changes. At the same time technology has developed rapidly. There is much more for teachers to cope with now than there was even ten years ago.

What I would like to propose, in an attempt to encourage learning and creativity in the current climate of change, is an extension of foreign language teaching methodology to include:

- a) analysis of the teaching domain, as a system affected by other systems;
- b) curriculum development which comes from an understanding of that domain;
- c) a cyclical approach to analysis and development, so that change can be monitored as part of pedagogic practice.

In particular, a cyclical approach would link up with the idea put forward in recent articles on language learning that learning does not take place as linear progression, but is an outward spiral, whereby the learner constantly moves forwards through action then backwards for reflection. The spiral effect comes from an overall pattern of forward progression.

Why do we need a wider methodology in modern languages?

I have already pointed out that in the world of computing the need for people-centred analysis has been recognised, and this has resulted in the development of socio-technical and participative approaches to systems analysis. These approaches have in particular been pioneered by Checkland (1988) and Mumford (1983).

Systems analysis became more people-centred in computing because this was necessary if business was to survive in an increasingly technology-oriented world. The introduction of computers into the working lives of so many people precipitated this change. To have offices full of computers that employees would not or could not use, was simply not cost effective.

In education, however, there seems to be a genuine lack of awareness that people-centred systems analysis could greatly contribute to this domain. Most teachers never study systems analysis, although they may participate in computer-based courses. This would actually be a very useful area to cover, especially if it could be linked to management in education. The reason for this is not too difficult to appreciate.

Education, particularly in the UK, is undergoing so much change that teachers have difficulty in keeping pace with developments. Although it may not be immediately apparent, changes within an education system affect individual teachers' abilities to cope with their job. Teachers are being expected to cope with too much change too quickly, and this is undermining the education system. In the eyes of practising teachers, the integration of IT may seem the area of least immediate concern. They may quite rightly decide that this area can wait. But they are still expected to incorporate the new technologies and the longer they ignore them the more difficult they will be to introduce. This is supported by the following observations:

- IT has been undergoing rapid development over the past few years;
- this has made it more accessible to society, but
- more difficult to understand in terms of where to start the learning process about IT, i.e. why is it important in language learning and where do we start? and furthermore
- what and how much needs to be learnt by individuals for professional and personal use;
- computer technology in particular has a sophistication that makes knowledge of it both quantitative and qualitative. In terms of classroom practice, it is not a simple tool to assimilate into learning activity, unlike less sophisticated technology such as the cassette recorder;
- in order to make decisions about fitting software to learner needs it is often necessary for the teacher to run through the whole software application at least once, and this must take place where there is a compatible computer with all the peripherals required for it to run. Although textbooks also require time in order for their effective use to be learned, they can be dipped into, used without machinery, and read easily in most situations. They do not additionally have set technical routines the user has to endure.

We can see from this that there are very many factors which impinge on the effectiveness of the use of IT in the language teaching classroom. Too many of those factors are overlooked or simply ignored when we analyze the problems facing us. The introduction of IT into the classroom is not 'simply' a matter of increasing the technical skills of the teacher; it affects and is affected by a much wider environment, over which the language teacher has less and less control.

What we see at present in education, then, is a system where the people who work within it have less and less control over how the system operates, whilst more control is being exerted by external forces. These forces have not initiated a control system to manage the changes they demand. A case of coercion without enablement. As a result, the system is constantly being overloaded. The people working inside it are expected to assimilate change without help. For change to be effective, the variety in the system must be met by equal variety in the organisation. Where a system is being overloaded with change, the variety in the system increases, but without the necessary control system to monitor the subsequent effects. In practical terms, the education system needs to have an organisational structure which helps teachers to work effectively to accommodate changes that have to be made. In-service training needs to be more effective, and more accessible. In addition, it must be related to current issues, whether these are macro-issues, such as government policy, or micro-issues, such as how to introduce new knowledge into the classroom.

Another prerequisite of an organisational structure is that it should contain an effective system for monitoring what is happening, and why: for example, establishing whether teachers are finding it possible to use IT. If the answer is negative, it could be that there is insufficient appropriate training. It is difficult to see such a control system at work in the foreign language teaching domain. But the time of 'making do' has passed: the time for confronting change in a systematic, organised way has arrived.

We have already discussed the idea of information systems using IT (as opposed to IT being an information system), and observed that the expansion of the use of computer technology in business necessitated a change in attitude. Leaving everything to the programmers alienated the people working with the systems they produced. It was acknowledged by several systems thinkers (Checkland, Mumford, Hirschheim) that people, and not the mechanical tools in the work place, are the centre of information systems. It took the Software Crisis in the 1970s to cause this change of attitude. The lesson which must be drawn in foreign language teaching is that people are also central in that system. How and why they are central needs to be both analyzed and understood in terms of the overall system. When this happens, it should be obvious that teaching methodology cannot exist apart from the system it operates in. Methodology, then, has to include everything that people do, or are likely to do.

Systems thinking - an overview

Throughout the first part of this chapter I have emphasised the point that a methodology for foreign language teaching needs to include the analysis of the teaching domain, and of the wider environment within which it operates.

From the time of the 'Enlightenment' to the earlier part of the twentieth century the philosophy of Reductionism was the dominant orthodoxy, and this was responsible for the view that everything in the universe could be understood if it was studied in small parts. The basis for this view was that most things are too complex to understand when taken as a complete unit.

The problem with Reductionism was that it failed to see how everything is in fact interconnected. It tended to take the view that by looking at one part of an organism, often in a deceased state, this would tell you how the rest of it worked. But one part of any system does not tell you how the rest of it works. Yet much knowledge seeking was carried out according to the Reductionist philosophy. Everything was reduced in order to explain it.

Systems thinking, sometimes referred to as the systems approach, recognises that relationships, processes, connections and inter-connectivity are what underlie the dynamics of any system. One system does not live/exist in isolation from other systems. A system viewed as a whole is always greater than the sum of its parts.

According to systems thinking the properties of systems cannot be reduced to smaller units. All systems are wholes whose structures emerge from the interaction and interdependence of their parts. This implies that the most important property of a system is not a rigid structure, but its organisation. If we now try to relate this to the concept of information systems, it is not difficult to see that these are systems organised by people for communication with one another.

We may be able to observe the different parts of a system, whether this be an information system or any other, but the nature of the whole will always be different from, and greater than, the mere sum of all its parts.

System lifecycle

An important idea that is used in systems thinking, and often used in the development of sophisticated software such as expert systems, is that of the system lifecycle. This recognises the fact that systems do not remain static within their environment, but need to adapt to survive. For example, the first computer used on a widespread basis in UK education was the BBC micro. Within a very few years of the BBC micro being adopted in schools, computer technology in the outside world had developed rapidly (although not necessarily in ways that could be or were predicted). At the same time the microcomputer had spread increasingly into the workplace and the home. The BBC is now old-fashioned and cannot match the sophistication and performance of more recent computers. The computer companies serving the needs of education have had to respond by updating hardware. However, it is not sufficient simply to keep replacing outdated hardware with more advanced technology. Much greater thought needs to be given to the purposes that the new hardware and software will serve; to the analysis of current and future needs; to the links with existing technologies; and to the potential for further development. This is the value of using a lifecycle, where planning, action and review (as the basis for further planning) form the basis of a continuing programme of development. We do this all the time when we learn, but most of us are not consciously aware of our own learning processes.

What needs to be done to plan a learning programme for others is to formalise a lifecycle. A lifecycle based on the integration of IT into modern languages could usefully include:

- analysis of the present system. This should also consider any outside influences that are likely to affect it, such as government policy, or any other constraints;

- what we would like to/have to do to improve/update the present system;

- very basic examination of the courseware that the institution already owns. This must precede the next two steps, and should include basic issues such as: how do you get the software to work? are there clear instructions? can the user get help from the software/manuals easily?

- examination of teaching approaches that existing staff have, and the beliefs on which these are based;

- examination of any syllabus requirements, plus learner needs. It may be a good idea to focus on a particular learner group at this point;

- the formal outlining of a 'plan of action', which includes design and task specification;

- the action itself, which will involve the production of a prototype;

- prototype testing. This needs to be carried out with the target group in their normal learning situation;

- adjustment, and usually some re-testing;

- implementation of the final product;

- some form of monitoring, so that change can be evaluated and acted upon, if necessary.

This lifecycle could be used as the foundation for developing a wider-reaching methodology in foreign/modern language teaching, with particular focus on integrating IT. It does not limit itself to any model of language learning, but rather seeks to understand the processes, relationships, interconnections and organisation of any language learning domain, and use this understanding to aid sound curriculum development.

The relevance of systems thinking to modern language learning programmes
Dispelling old myths

Foreign/modern language teaching underwent a rather difficult period following the introduction of the language laboratory. At the time of its introduction, it was based on the behaviourist model of learning and used as a teaching machine. Furthermore, it was often run by people unqualified and inexperienced in the art of language teaching. Language school administrators were seduced by the technology into believing that the language laboratory would revolutionise instruction by training students up to near-native fluency through absorption and drill. Subsequently a great deal of damage was done. Many learners became disenchanted with language learning, and it has taken a long time for interest to be re-awakened (McCoy & Weible, 1983, in Underwood, 1984, p. 34). As a result, some teachers are worried that the computer is a new incarnation of the teaching machine. Teachers need reassurance that the days of the teaching machine are over, and the human teacher can never be replaced. Any technology used with learners is only a tool, and must only be used as such. Language is not dependent on machinery for its transmission. It is dependent on people and the ways in which they choose to transmit language.

Systems thinking as a tool for curriculum development
Systems thinking has as its basic philosophy that the whole is greater than the sum of its parts. The simplicity of its philosophy enables it to be adopted by any discipline, individual or belief system as a way of understanding the universe and our place within it. It allows infinite possibilities for exploration. It is because of this that it is suitable for examining Modern Language learning programmes. It does not seek to impose a model of learning, language learning or classroom practice, but instead asks questions like: "What are your personal beliefs about learning? How do you understand language to be structured? And how does this relate to what you do in the classroom?" What it does is make one examine the relationship between one's beliefs and one's practice.

Co-operative curriculum development as policy
Education is currently undergoing great change, but only a small part of this change is really due to rapid technological development. (And our perception that this is rapid is based entirely on subjective experience.) Education is very much in need of co-operative management of human, more than material, resources. A large part of this management should be concerned with curriculum development. Effective management relies on knowing your resources - knowing your colleagues and what they already possess in terms of personal skills, knowledge and experience. If the whole is greater than the sum of all its parts, people who work together must have a greater potential for creativity than those who work apart. We cannot ever hope to have all the skills and insights we need as individual teachers. We would be unable to cope with reality if our senses could take in everything we were expected to know at a conscious level. To be able to cope with change we must learn to work on curriculum development together. Part of that development may involve computer technology.

Analyzing constraints to realise freedom
Part of the analysis of a system should be aimed at finding its constraints. There is little point in leaving out this stage if planning is to go forward into design. If an educational establishment has to use its present computer technology for the next five years then that is what has to be worked with.

In addition, all learners have needs that must be addressed now, and this means using resources that are to hand. It also means making sure there are sufficient staff who know how to exploit these resources. Knowing resources and expertise available now is a foundation for planning the future. It may not be possible to have a new computer, but it may be possible to send someone on a computer-related course so that effective use can be made of the BBC micros gathering dust in the stockroom. Once the limitations of a language teaching system are known, it becomes possible to direct creative energy into potential goals.

Conclusions

This chapter has introduced a particular perception which arose from the following influences:

- ■   a) a personal experience of teaching;
- ■   b) knowledge gained about the computer and information systems;
- ■   c) research which was based on the realisation that integrating IT into foreign language teaching is far from simple if the integration is to be effective and appropriate.

Taking on computer technology as an extension to one's professional development and classroom practice requires a lengthy process of personal evolution. The computer is a sophisticated technology whose future is far from predictable. Hence, to make the computer the focal point of a langauge teaching methodology would be to deny our pedagogic responsibilities. The technology has already pervaded the entire spectrum of human activity without our help, and this indicates that it cannot and should not be confined to a narrow (and thereby exclusive) model of the universe. We each construct our own universe (Novak, 1983), and in our work we should ideally seek to motivate others "... to more meaningfully enrich, refine and expand their perceptual worlds" (*ibid*, p. 320).

What we need now is a much broader overview of our domain so that we may effectively incorporate new technologies into language teaching and learning. We can do this by taking compatible ideas from systems thinking, since its underlying philosophy enables us to look at ourselves and what we do as educators within a wider perspective.

Bibliography

Checkland, P. (1988) *Systems Thinking, Systems Practice*, John Wiley & Sons.
Jones, S. (1988/9) Interaction of language and culture, *NIMLA* 20/1.
Mumford, E. (1983) *Designing Participatively*, Manchester Business School.
Novak, J. M. (1983) Personal construct theory and other perceptual pedagogies, in J. Adams-Webber & J. C. Mancuso (eds.) *Applications of Personal Construct Theory*, Academic Press.

Richards, J. C. & Rodgers, T.S. (1986) *Approaches and Methods in Language Teaching*, Cambridge University Press.

Schoderbek, P. P., Schoderbek, C. G., & Kefalas, A. G. (1985) *Management Systems*, Business Publications.

Underwood, J. H. (1984) *Linguistics, Computers and the Language Teacher*, Newbury House Publishers.